Lisa,
Keep in touch
- Mitch

THERE'S NO SUCH THING AS RIGHT AND WRONG

THERE'S NO SUCH THING AS RIGHT AND WRONG

Matthew D. Anderson

Foreword by Dr. Ronald F Cichy, O.M.

HOLON
PUBLISHING

Copyright © 2022 Matthew D. Anderson
All rights reserved. No part of this publication may be reproduced, distributed, or transmitted in any form or by any means, including photocopying, recording, or other electronic or mechanical methods, without the prior written permission of the author, except in the case of brief quotations embodied in critical reviews and certain other noncommercial uses permitted by copyright law. For permission requests, contact the publisher at:

www.Holon.co

ISBN#: 978-1-955342-18-6 (Hardback)
ISBN#: 978-1-955342-17-9 (Paperback)
ISBN#: 978-1-955342-36-0 (eBook)

Published by:

Holon Publishing & Collective Press
A Storytelling Company
www.Holon.co

To Kristy:
Nothing I do is possible without you.

To Bree, Bryce, and Brooks:
When I'm done with my job on this world, it'll be better for you than it was when you found it. Everything I do is for you.

Words will never do justice in expressing
the love I have for each of you.

Contents

Supporters	ix
Author	xiii
Art	xv
Foreword	xvii
Prologue	1
Introduction	7
Killing	15
Drugs	47
Abortion	67
Sex	81
Media	93
Racism	111
Politics	139
COVID	185
Results	225
Metaethics	247
Understanding	261
Collaboration	279
Epilogue	303
References	305

★ ★ ★

Supporters

———————————
———————————

Thank you to all of the incredible individuals who have supported this book. Each person listed below contributed time, energy, financial resources, or personal counsel that positively contributed to making this book a reality. Some are included in honor of another person who made those contributions. Each person played a key role in making this finished product what it is. Without these individuals, you simply would not be holding this book right now.

To each Supporter:
You have my deep and heartfelt appreciation
for the role you play in my life.

Influencers
Jeff & Jenny Anderson
Megan & Kyle Ankerson
Eric & Katie Beth Dragicevic
Charlie & Susie Green
Ryan Kiernicki
Alan & Nancy Leszczynski
Chris, Kelly, Hazel, & Sienna Lonergan
Kirby Buchanan & Stephanie Peck-Buchanan
Dale & Lisa Peterson
Wendee & TJ Richardson
An Anonymous Friend

Advocates
Dr. Ryan Cunningham
Britt & Megan DeRoos
Ariel Dixon
Sadie Green
Will Green
Bryan & Lori Heckman
Bob & Diane Jackson
Emily, Mike, Joshua, Matthew, & Mary Klingbeil
Nicole Moyer
Maureen Nagy
The Reneski Family
Mike Schiffer
Daniel & Kristin Slocum
Karen Swan
Dr. Katrina Weirauch & John Engle

Changemakers
Thomas Ackerson
Dr. Kimberly M. Castle
Billy Downs
Rev. Dr. David Dressel
Mark Eddy
Kelli Ellsworth Etchison
Michelle Lantz
Christopher Laus
Missy Lilje
Ken, Jaime, & Emma Jackson
Mitchell Kennedy
Dr. Shalom Charles Malka
Rich Martinson
Jessica Medrano
Dan & Erica Nye

Aaron Osler
Christian Peck
Zander Peck-Buchanan
Jessica Penner
Doug Prizer
Rich & Judy Rau
Garrett Ritterhaus
Kimberly Schafer
David Smith
Katie Smith
Rebekah Spivey
Jessica Starks
Amy Venema
Bret & Kelsey Wamhoff
Scott Watkins

Special Thanks to
Dr Ronald F Cichy, O.M.
Phil Hickey
Chris Holman
Governor Rick Snyder
April Vassau

&

Jeremy Gotwals

Author

Matthew D. Anderson is the Chief Executive Officer of Leadership Coaching for Results, a virtual coaching company focused on helping individuals all over North America to become the Leader that they need and want to be.

Anderson has been recognized by Dale Carnegie & Associates as the #1 Corporate Trainer in the World; holds an MS in Conflict Management, an MBA, and a BA in Hospitality Business; is a member of Mensa, the international high IQ society; and is the author or collaborating author of numerous nationally published works.

His second book is currently in pre-production, and will continue this book's theme of overcoming conflict by seeking to understand, respect, and collaborate with The Other. It will focus on diversity, equity, and inclusion, exploring the intricacies and intersectionality of those with diverse backgrounds, and will advocate for ways in which we can each choose to demonstrate greater empathy and respect for one and other.

Anderson resides in East Lansing, Michigan with his wife, Kristy; three children, Bree, Bryce, and Brooks; and Great Dane, Odin.

★ ★ ★

Art

The cover art for *There's No Such Thing as Right and Wrong* is a painting by the author, titled, *The Flag*. Anderson's artwork has been featured in exhibits, installations, residencies, and public art all over the country. He was honored in 2020 as "Best in Show" for a national Under 40 juried exhibit for a painting titled, *Politics*. His art is intended to be big, bold, and fun. Often drawing inspiration from the challenges and strife of the world, he seeks to illuminate the emotional outcomes of conflict. Working primarily in an abstract environment, his goal is to evoke an emotional response in the viewer.

The description of the cover art follows:

> *The Flag* is a rugged representation of the American Flag. Featuring various applications of spray paint on particle board, the lack of uniformity of the wood and natural chaos of the paint symbolize the challenges our nation has faced in the past, the blood spilled in its defense of freedom, and the racial and political turmoil we face today. The piece is imbued with the conflicting emotions of hope

and despair, and was created with the belief that America is better and stronger when we show love, compassion, and respect for one another, and when we come together as *One People* in spite of our differences.

If you are interested in acquiring a replica or original reproduction of *The Flag*, or if you would like to see images of other art referenced throughout the book, visit www.MatthewDAnderson.com

Foreword

Picture a monk. The word monk stems from the Greek *monachos* and the Latin monachus. A monk withdraws from the world to seek silence and solitude, sometimes in community with other monks; sometimes as a solitary alone as a hermit.

A monk who lives alone is one of the few who does not experience conflict with others. That is not to say that the solitary monk does not have conflict within the self. These inner conflicts are based on the monk's values and beliefs, essentially who they are at their core, and **why** that is so.

Those who believe in and value growth, personally and in relationships with others, view conflict as based on an essential understanding of self and others. Fundamental to that understanding is an exploration of **why** you believe what you do, and **why** others believe what they do. In other words, **why** values are valued. It is this understanding of **why** that leads one to challenge and accept their own beliefs and values, as well as the values and beliefs of others.

With his view of conflict as natural and neutral, neither right nor wrong, Author Matthew D. Anderson opens the reader to the possibilities of seeing the world, and daily encounters with conflict, differently. By presenting a wide range of topics and associated conflicts, Author Anderson invites his readers to explore their own beliefs and values, contemplate their own experiences, draw their own conclusions, and answer **why**.

Author Anderson offers a thought-provoking approach to conflict. He provides insights into the power of choosing. He exposes a better way to live with conflict within one's self and with others. The result of Author Anderson's approach is there is no such thing as right and wrong. Rather, there is a better today and a belief that there will be a better tomorrow.

Dr Ronald F Cichy, O.M.
professor emeritus
Michigan State University

Prologue

Prologue

The word "conflict," carries with it overwhelmingly negative connotations, particularly in Western society, and specifically in America. The term is used to describe international affairs involving the military, while reading the news about our state and federal politicians, and as a key component of the dissolution of interpersonal relationships. Rarely is the word "conflict" used in a positive or neutral sense. This reality diminishes the impact conflict can have to move conversations, relationships, and negotiations in a positive direction with all parties feeling as though their needs are met, and likely even enhanced.

Conflict is inherent in life. The biological differences between men and women are the most basic example of the natural conflict that occurs as a function of life. Our bodies themselves are under constant conflict in order to maintain the successful respiration necessary to keep oxygen flowing through the body. Your muscles and bones are in a battle with air pressure and gravity in this very moment. Your body continues to win the conflict over and over with each breath you take, until you take your last. Siblings raised in the same home, at the same point in history, while cared for by the same parents, still manage to not agree on many things, from the trivial, like favorite foods, to the monumental, like lifestyle choices. As they reach adulthood, these individuals often become increasingly divergent from one and other, still maintaining many of the core elements from how they were raised, but also increasing in the underlying and natural conflict generated by their unique lives.

The function of conflict is neither good or bad – It simply *is*. What people do in conflict, how they react to their own emotions as well as those of the other person, and how they behave after the conflict, are all places where good or bad things can result. Conflict itself is neutral, the people involved are the variables that influence the outcomes. Here's an example: Two children both want to play with the same toy. If you have kids, a sibling, or have been a caretaker for children, you already know what normally occurs next – Conflict. Depending on the demeanor of the children, how rested they are, if they are hungry or not, and limitless other variables, the conflict will play out in a variety of different ways. The most likely and obvious outcome for this scenario is that one child yells or hits, the other may scream or cry, and both will end up unhappy. Another entirely realistic outcome may be that the first child simply asks to play with the toy, or offers another toy in exchange for the toy that they want – A moment that would make most parents beam with pride. In either of these outcomes, there was first conflict. The actions of one party and subsequent reactions of The Other are what lead to the positive or negative experiences associated with conflict.

With conflict itself being neither good or bad, it gives us the power to choose how we view it, respond to it, and behave in order to fulfill our needs and desires.

There was a time where I was teaching a short 90-minute seminar, and a colleague happened to be in the room watching the presentation. Based on a question asked of me by a participant, I took a detour in the content and shared my views on conflict. I explained how we have the ability to view conflict in any way we'd like, and that I view conflict as a positive force that moves conversations and actions towards further positive outcomes. This colleague, whom I deeply respected and viewed as a source of great wisdom, was stunned by my comments. The man who had been in the industry longer than I had been alive pulled me aside after the presentation and said, "In my whole life, I always viewed conflict as negative and something to avoid. You have entirely changed my perspective on the topic! This will be huge! I can't thank you enough!" This change in perspective truly was monumental in his life. He went on to have the best sales years in his career, developing lucrative new accounts until his retirement, all because he no longer feared the conflict of sales.

I was once coaching a young woman who was struggling in her new marriage. She was growing concerned that the relationship might fail, and sought my counsel on how to "get things back to the way they were." I asked her a series of questions, then asked, "What are you really afraid of?" Her response was that she didn't want to argue with her husband to work through their issues, and thought it might be easier just to leave him. After hearing about his behavior, this outcome may have been appropriate in the eyes of many. I replied, "Great! You already know the answer to your problem – You just need to divorce your husband." She physically turned away from this idea and started to cry. She shared that even though she wasn't happy at that period of time, she really did love her husband, and didn't want to leave him. I then asked a series of more challenging questions, and finally asked, "Do you really want to stay with him?" She did. "Then you're going to have to work hard to solve this issue, because you can't change him, you can only change you."

Her real fear was not in trying to fix the relationship with her husband – She was afraid of the conflict it would take to fix it. By removing that variable and suggesting she just avoid that conflict altogether by getting divorced, she was able to think more clearly. There is abundant conflict in divorce, but where she was in that moment, the concept was far enough away and so new in her mind that the psychological fear of conflict induced by divorce was not yet a variable. With the fear of conflict brought on by arguing out of the picture, she could see what she actually wanted, which was not to avoid the conflict, but to grow together with her partner past the conflict. By changing her perspective, she was able to change her own behavior, which was necessary. By changing her behavior, she was able to more easily appreciate the positive things her husband did, and more easily ignore or forgive the negative things he did. Her behavior was ultimately reciprocated, and years later the two are happier than ever.

We have a choice when it comes to conflict. We can fear it and continue to reap the same outcomes we've reaped for our entire lives, or we can choose to view it as an opportunity to have positive growth. By choosing the latter, we remain in control of our behavior and maintain the capacity to benefit from scenarios that most people would run away from. We have the power to choose. *You* have the power to choose. I'll show you how.

★ ★ ★
Introduction

Think about the different conflicts you've experienced in your life: Being a child, attending school, making friends, the relationship with your parents and other family members, doing homework, taking tests, getting your first job, dating, the choice to pursue post-secondary education or not, having roommates and neighbors, deciding to change jobs, entering into a long-term relationship, ending a long-term relationship, death, birth, health, who you spend time with, how you spend your time, boredom...

You have experienced minor and major conflict innumerable times. How many of those conflicts do you regret? How many people have you hurt unnecessarily? How many people have hurt *you*? How many relationships have ended in your life? What if you could have different outcomes? What if relationships didn't have to end, but instead both parties could feel heard and respected? What would happen if you took control of situations and had the outcomes you wanted instead of letting life happen *to* you? What if you could put your own ego on the shelf long enough to accept that those you disagree with feel right, justified, and entitled to their beliefs, *just like you*? What if you discovered from time to time that other people have figured out better courses of action than you have, and if you listen to them, your life will be better, too? What if, instead of fearing or avoiding conflict, conflict makes you feel excited for new possibilities? What if you could live a life of peace, happiness, and fulfillment, free from frustration, pain, and regret? What if?

Imagine feeling heard and respected by your family, friends, neighbors, and colleagues, even when you disagree. Imagine enjoying the holidays without the conflict of differing ideals. Imagine people holding each other up for what they passionately believe, even when they have opposing views. Imagine the work that could be done for the good of our nation if our political representatives in Washington D.C. could work harmoniously instead of antagonistically. That's the vision this book was created to inspire. Conflict is natural. Collaboration is optional. We can *choose* to work together and to respect each other. Some of us don't know how. Some of us don't try hard enough. Some of us just need to be inspired to behave as a Leader to those around them.

Our beliefs, values, and opinions are based on our individual experiences and worldview. In this book, we will explore the moral and ethical implications of our perceptions, exploring a series of topics that tend to have "camps." In the end, we will discover that none of these topics truly have a universal moral hard line, that hard lines are moveable over time, and what this means for society if everything we believe to be true is only true for ourselves, or that collective "truth" may only be true for a fleeting moment in history.

The intention of this book is not to suggest that all behavior is permissible, that you should change your opinions, or that we should all conform to the beliefs of others to avoid conflict and live in harmony. In fact, this book does not advocate for any of those things. Rather, the intention is to challenge the notion of "right" and "wrong," and to challenge you, the reader, to think about your own beliefs and behaviors. Whether we have ever rationalized it in our own minds or not, we live in a world where "right" and "wrong" are not universally absolute. Our upbringings, experiences, socio-economic status, nation of origin, gender, faith, current station in life, current external forces, among countless other variables, all impact our behaviors and our perception of what is "right" and what is "wrong" in any given moment.

In this book, I have attempted to frame a thought experiment that can make your life easier and more pleasant. I have been fortunate to work with and coach thousands of individuals to live the life they need and want to live. Listening to their stories, and working to help them navigate the conflicts in their lives has enlightened me to the fact that if more people were open enough to simply listen to the experiences of others, the world would be a dramatically nicer place to live in than it currently is.

I've avoided sharing my opinion on most of these topics, as my opinion is not the point of this book. I do take a few moments of writer's privilege, though, to share my personal take when I feel it's helpful to illustrate a point. You may also glean hints of, or interpret through your worldview, my own biases from time to time. As a straight, White, Christian, cisgender, midwestern American, Millennial, pre-Trump conservative, I have my own beliefs that may bleed through into the narrative. Take it for what it's worth, and choose to agree or disagree. I make no claim that I, myself, am in fact "right" at any point in this book. What is "right" and what is "wrong" is up to you to decide. That's the whole point.

★ ★ ★

The main argument of this book is framed in regard to the morality of the average person, with the assumption that people are inherently good and strive to live happy and fulfilling lives. Instances of mental illness and other outlier situations, like insanity, that cause a person to intentionally seek to harm another person, are not addressed within this scope. We also will not tackle topics that have broadly accepted universal truths like, "the sky is blue," or "there are 24 hours in the day." Some could argue that the sky only *appears* blue because of the way light is scattered by molecules in the air, or that time is a social construct, but the reality is, as a global society, we broadly and generally accept these things to be true. Instead, we will focus on issues of ethics and morality, in which there are not broadly and generally accepted truths, particularly when the issue is perpetually topical and dyadic.

This book is filled with first- and third-party research, anecdotes, and real-life examples. It is the culmination of nearly a decade of professional training, research, real-world application, and graduate studies. The original draft served as the master's thesis which earned my MS in Conflict Management in 2019. I also share a number of personal stories that are intended to help illustrate the points being made. These stories are the place where my personal opinion is the most likely to bleed through, though again, that isn't the purpose of sharing the stories.

Given the moral and ethical contexts we are exploring, there are numerous stories and examples that, depending of a reader's worldview, could be deemed as insensitive. These examples are intentionally utilized to set strong grounding points for the differing perspectives individuals have. These examples are not utilized for the sake of shocking or insulting. If you feel that you have a strong reaction to an example, I encourage you to explore your own thoughts, feelings, and emotions about the topic and your reaction. Asking yourself, "why did I react so strongly to this example? How could someone think so differently about this than I do? What if there is more than one way to look at this scenario? What if, even though I disagree, from the other person's unique perspective they believe their opinions or behavior are appropriate?"

Topics of conflict like abortion and immigration are great examples of deeply entrenched beliefs held by two separate sides, with no real action ever taking place. All politicians talk about these topics and play to their base, but rarely, if ever, do they actually do anything to move the needle. As a result, at the end of the book I will suggest a series of "middle ground" solutions to the conflicts we explore in the chapter titled Collaboration. The intention behind this is to illuminate a potential path forward that seeks to keep in-tact the core priorities of each opposing side, therefore maximizing the benefit for all concerned. Once again, this is a place where my biases may become apparent, but I state that with a caveat: I do not personally agree with all of the things that I believe are in the best interest of the greater good. We'll explore that internal conflict, too, particularly in the chapter titled Metaethics.

The conclusion of this book, titled Understanding, will teach you tools to use as an alternative to destructive interpersonal conflict, and instead work towards finding solutions that serve all parties maximally. We will also explore how using these tools can lead to greater understanding of conflicting opinions, increased respect and appreciation for *why* people think differently than you, and collaboration in spite of differences. The outcomes we will explore are applicable at the individual level, the organizational level, in communities, and can be more broadly applied to national and international conflicts.

My hope for you when you are done reading this book is that you will be more open to opposing viewpoints, that you will have a greater respect for what other people believe even when you disagree, and that you will have ability and desire to successfully navigate the countless conflicts you will inevitably encounter for the remainder of your life. If that doesn't happen, either I failed you, or you weren't ready for this book. You'll decide, and in either case, you'll be right.

★ ★ ★
Killing
_____
_____

There's No Such Thing as Right and Wrong

Think for a moment: Have you ever believed in something so deeply that you would be willing to die for it?

In 1999, Dylan Klebold and Eric Harris, students at Columbine High School, sought to murder hundreds of students during the lunch period. The plan was to shoot and stab their way through the school, before ultimately blowing up the cafeteria filled with over 400 kids. They were successful in taking the lives of many, but were fortunately unsuccessful in achieving their vision. Their makeshift propane bombs did not explode, and hundreds of lives were spared.[1] During their 49-minute reign of terror, the boys made a stop in the library where they found Cassie Bernall. The killers asked if she believed in God. As a strong young Christian woman, she was not willing to deny her faith, and replied, "Yes." She believed in her faith so deeply that she was willing to die for it, and was murdered as a result. This story was heavily publicized for its bravery, and became the basis for books, songs, and a movie that all advocate for standing up for one's faith. As time has passed, questions have arisen in regard to the actual details of the account[2] but the impact remains, and holds as a symbol for those facing persecution for their faith. Bernall believed in her faith so strongly that she was willing to die for it.

Now think for a moment: Have you ever loved something so deeply that you would be willing kill for it?

I remember shortly after our first child, Bree, was born. We took her to church for the first time, and introduced her to our long-time friend and counsel, Pastor Dave. He was my mentor all through undergrad, and became a close confidant as I moved forward in life. He asked, "You feel you'd do anything for her, don't you?" I replied, "Oh, I'd kill for her." He paused and said, "You mean you'd die for her." To which I reinforced, "No. I'd kill for her. I have no intention of dying and leaving her to live a life without me." I meant it then and I mean it even more now – If necessary, I would absolutely kill in order to protect my children. As a parent, I am not unique in holding this belief, though I may be more assertive in my declaration of it. The reality remains: As parents, we all would do whatever is necessary to protect the precious lives that we bring into this world.

★ ★ ★

Members of our military willingly and gladly put their lives on the line every day in the name of Freedom. Abandoning the comfort of home; subjecting themselves and their families to the pain of absence for months or years at a time; missing birthdays and holidays; and knowing fully that at any moment they may be forced to make the ultimate sacrifice in defense of their country. PTSD, drug and alcohol abuse, lost or damaged relationships, homelessness, ridicule and judgment from civilians, and a dramatically increased incidence of suicide are all potential outcomes for those who choose to serve our nation. These are individuals who love their country so deeply that they are willing to sacrifice their lives for it, and to kill in its defense.

In 2014, President Barack Obama awarded the Medal of Honor to Staff Sgt. Clinton Romesha. The Medal of Honor is the nation's highest award for valor. Of the approximately 2.5 million individuals who served in Afghanistan and Iraq fighting the War on Terror, only 16 individuals have received this highest honor, with seven of them being recognized posthumously.[3]

A common sentiment among service members who are recognized for their actions is that their brothers and sisters at arms were equally heroic, though only a small fraction of our nation's warfighters are acknowledged in this way. SSGT Romesha was being recognized for what President Obama called one of the most intense battles of the entire war.[4] On the morning of the fight, 53 US troops were ambushed by over 300 Taliban fighters. The small military outpost in Afghanistan was surrounded. SSGT Romesha said of the overwhelming odds, "we weren't going to be beat that day."

With the Taliban successful in penetrating the perimeter, SSGT Romesha was inspirational in keeping the troops focused on defending the base. With wounds to his neck, shoulders, and arms, the Medal of Honor recipient was successful in taking out an insurgent machine-gun position, called in an airstrike that eliminated 10% of the attackers, and survived an RPG strike that blasted his cover. His actions in protecting the surviving 45 US troops and America's interests were heroic. To provide context, for every US solider lost that day, our troops killed an average of 38 enemies.

Few civilians can comprehend what it's like to have a job that includes the regular extinguishing of another person's life. Historically, conversations around mental health for veterans came second to national defense, making the stories that keep our veterans up at night off limits to share even with counselors. The University of Southern California released a study in 2016 in collaboration with the San Francisco Veterans Affairs Medical Center which determined that killing in war leaves veterans with psychological and emotional scars that can last for decades.[5]

One of the study's authors, Natalie Purcell, PhD, had this to say, "Many veterans feared that, if they talked about killing, they would be judged or mischaracterized by other people's notions of what it means to be a combat veteran." She added, "Being asked about killing left many veterans feeling anxious, isolated and even angry because most felt that someone who did not serve in war could not possibly understand what it was like to kill."

Of killing the enemy, Lieutenant Colonel Tim Collins of the British Army had this to say to his men in 2003 before an assault in Iraq, "It is a big step to take another human life. It is not to be done lightly. I know of men who have taken life needlessly in other conflicts. I can assure you they live with the mark of Cain upon them. If someone surrenders to you then remember they have that right in international law and ensure that one day they go home to their family. The ones who wish to fight, well, we aim to please."[6]

A Texas A&M Professor, Marian Eide, PhD, interviewed 30 former military service members as she researched their experiences for her book, *After Combat: True War Stories from Iraq and Afghanistan*, co-authored with retired Army Col. Michael Gibler. Of the interviews, Eide shared this story in a reflective article that was released in the lead-up to the 20th anniversary of 9/11:

> One soldier shot back from his guard post when under fire from a nearby house. His unit entered the house to find a dead man with a warm rifle. But the guard was discomfited when congratulated on this kill by fellow soldiers. To his comrades, he had acted in self-defense and protected others from the shooter. But even in

this situation of militarily justified killing, he felt he had crossed a line by taking a life.[7]

For our service members, killing is a part of the job. But the psychological toll killing another person takes on our military veterans results in as many as 50% experiencing significant difficulty re-acclimating to civilian life, with 33% experiencing mental health diagnoses that include PTSD, depression, and anxiety.[8] The US Department of Veterans Affairs released a report that stated, as of 2018, 17.6 veteran lives are lost to suicide each day.[9]

★ ★ ★

In the Bible, God commanded Joshua and the Israelites to kill the entire people of Canaan – Men, women, and children alike.[10] They then assumed by force the control of Jericho before working to overthrow the city of Gibeon. In these battles, the Bible says that God assisted by attacking those who opposed the Israelites by raining down hailstones. These killings were considered appropriate, necessary, and legitimized by God.

Dying for your faith. Killing to protect your children. Killing in defense of your country. Killing to follow your deity's will. These examples demonstrate that there are instances where circumstances dictate that we consciously cross a moral hard line – Killing another human. There is another example of people willing to die and kill for what they believed in – To protect their children, in defense of their nation, and in the following their deity's will: 9/11.

★ ★ ★

As Americans, we remember September 11th, 2001 vividly. It was the first time since Pearl Harbor that our nation was so blatantly violated. Never before had we been attacked and provoked in such a way. It is the deadliest act of terror in world history, with 2,996 lives lost between the attacks in New York, Washington D.C., and Flight 93 in Pennsylvania. Nearly 6,000 people were injured. Fires at the World Trade Center site burned for 100 days.[11] The costs associated with rescue, repair, rebuilding, federal economic support, stock market crash, and the War on Terror, total at approximately $8 trillion dollars. Some 900,000 individuals have died from all over the world as a result of the war efforts that took place over the following 20 years.[12] And virtually every single American who was old enough to remember that day carries a permanent psychological scar of knowing *exactly* where they were when they heard about the first plane crashing into the North Tower. What those terrorists did was wrong – In our eyes. But why did they do it?

★ ★ ★

In 1944, President Franklin D. Roosevelt signed an accord with the British government called The Anglo-American Petroleum Agreement, and said, "Persian oil... is yours. We share the oil of Iraq and Kuwait. As for Saudi Arabian oil, it's ours."[13]

In 1948, President Harry S. Truman was an active supporter of the creation and formation of a state of Israel. America was the first country to recognize Israel,[14] and continues to be one of its strongest allies nearly 75 years later. No Middle Eastern nations supported or recognized Israel at the time.

In 1953, under the new administration of President Dwight Eisenhower, the United States and Britain assisted in overthrowing the Prime Minister of Iran, Mohammed Mosaddeq.[15]

In 1967, Israel captured the West Bank and other territories in a Six-Day War with Egypt, Syria, and Jordan.[16] The United States, under President Lyndon D. Johnson, backed Israel with weapons and financial support.

In 1977, President Jimmy Carter mediated peace accords between Egyptian President Anwar Sadat and Israeli Prime Minister Menachem Begin. For this action, Sadat was assassinated in 1981 by Islamic militants who opposed the agreement.[17]

In 1979, the US placed economic sanctions on Iran,[18] after supporting the Iranian Revolution that started a year earlier. In retaliation, 52 Americans were held hostage by Iranian militarized college students for 444 days.[19]

In 1984, the United States, under President Ronald Reagan, began supporting Iraq in the Iraq-Iran War, after a falling out between Saddam Hussein and the Soviet Union. In turn, a Soviet-Iranian Alliance was formed, and the United States provided chemical and biological weapons technology, as well as other forms of intelligence and technology, to Iraq.[20]

In 1990, under President George H.W. Bush, the United States led a coalition of nations in the Gulf War against Iraq due to its invasion of Kuwait. Once the coalition won the war, thousands of military forces were left in the region. This indefinite presence was perceived by Muslims as a violation of religious tradition that prevented non-Muslims from residing in the Arabian Peninsula. This single action was considered to be the most significant violation of Muslim practices, and is attributed as a defining moment in the formation of the terror campaign against America.[21]

In 1998, under President Bill Clinton, the US launched a four-day campaign against Iraq for refusing to cooperate with the UN Security Council searching for weapons of mass destruction. The Clinton Administration claimed it was not an attack, but rather to "degrade" Iraq's ability to manufacture and produce WMDs.[22] Three years later, on September 11th, Osama Bin Laden and his followers were successful in retaliating against the United States for violations that they could no longer abide.

For nearly 60 years, the United States directly, indirectly, and intentionally disregarded the sovereignty of individuals on the other side of the world. Most Americans were completely oblivious to the way these actions were perceived by the Muslims who lived in countries with names that they could barely pronounce. And yet, the most significant terror attack ever was occurring here on American soil. It was hard to comprehend in the moment, but looking objectively at the order of world events, we would be wise to ask ourselves if 9/11 was more justified in the eyes of our attackers than we've been led to believe.

★ ★ ★

And here is our first conundrum in the debate over "right" and "wrong": I just equated terrorists as being sympathetic characters equal to Champions of God and American military heroes.

Did a bunch of murderers spend years planning to hijack a few planes because they were insane, or did our decades of disregard for their practices lead directly to this retaliation? When the US perceives a threat to have occurred or be imminent, we attack to protect ourselves. Since the 1940's, American foreign policy *did* directly violate the religious laws and edicts of those who live in the Middle East. The reality of the attacks on 9/11 is that those who we have labeled as "terrorists," were, in their own minds, "heroes" based on their world-view, upbringing, and faith. Just like our military troops, the terrorists were willing to die to protect the land they loved, to protect their families, and in the name of their god.

Taking this one step further, why is it acceptable for the Christian God to direct followers to kill the men, women, and children who do not subscribe to that faith, but we struggle to comprehend the logic behind Allah commanding his followers to kill nonbelievers? Faith is simply that: Faith. We don't *actually* know that God or Allah even exist. But we do know that both deities have commanded their followers to kill non-followers. Which religion is "right," if the deity for each faith is calling for similarly reprehensible action? Which nation is "right," if both are acting in their own defense? When is killing justified and when is it a violation of humanity? Who is really the hero and who is really the villain in this story? Are there any heroes and villains at all, or just a bunch of people killing each other in poorly handled conflict?

Regardless of how we personally feel about any of these examples, this is what we should be asking ourselves: Why would a nation or religious followers feel the need to kill those who are "The Other?" Is there a nonviolent way to engage with one another? Is there an opportunity to hold respectful dialog? Is there an opportunity to learn about one another, and seek to understand our differences? Is there a way for both parties to peacefully coexist without infringing on the happiness and fulfillment of those who are different? Is there a way that we can actually all be better off by collaborating with those who are different than us, rather than fighting and killing?

★ ★ ★

As Americans, we remember the morning of September 11th, 2001 as an abhorrent act of violence, a violation of humanity, and the first real demonstration that our nation is not impenetrable. Some may take umbrage with my suggesting that mass murder was justified in the eyes of terrorists as a direct result of the role of the US in the Middle East. This would be particularly true if you were to have a personal investment in the terror attacks or subsequent War on Terror, like the loss of a loved one. And yet, the context with which a person lives is what defines their perception of moral issues, which is why the terrorists felt justified in the fact that they were acting on behalf of their god and their people. If we can remove our emotions and deeply held beliefs from the equation for a moment, and look at the issue in black and white, we can objectively look at the facts and see where *both* parties could have been better. For example, if the US had engaged with local leadership in the various countries that we were perceived to be occupying, we could have sought to find a resolution and create a sense of stability that did not violate the tradition that prevented non-Muslims from residing in the Arabian Peninsula. This type of outcome requires asking questions, listening, seeking to understand The Other, respecting the differences that we do not necessarily agree with, and working together toward a collaborative solution that both parties can agree creates an outcome that maximally serves those concerned.

For the purposes of this book, who is "right" and who is "wrong" doesn't actually matter. We know that the event has occurred. We know that tremendous fallout took place after the fact. We know that countless lives have ended in the name of this fight. Arguing over who's right does nothing to change any of that. This is true for any conflict you will ever experience – The outcome is actually more important than the conflict itself. In the case of 9/11, nothing positive came out of the conflict between America and those who felt violated by the actions of the United States in the Middle East for decades – Only death. What you and I have the opportunity to do, is to learn from this lesson, and seek to make our lives and our world a better place by behaving in a way that leads to positive outcomes instead of negative ones.

★ ★ ★

If I have one regret in my life, it's that I didn't serve in our military. I have tremendous respect for those who have made that choice. It is still my hope to be of service to our country, though, and it has been since I was young.

When I was 5 years old, my kindergarten teacher taught us that we could become anything we wanted to be when we grow up. I remember this day vividly, because we also made macaroni necklaces, and our teacher took my picture in class. I got home and was excited to show my Mom the necklace. She asked what I had learned, and subsequently asked if I knew what I wanted to be when I grew up. I shared, "I might be an astronaut... Or a dinosaur bone digger... Or maybe I could dig up dinosaur bones on the moon!" My Mom smiled and sent me to hang my new craft up on the bulletin board in my room while she made me a snack.

As I stood in my room looking at my bulletin board, I remember thinking, "if I can become anything I want when I grow up, I could even become the President of the United States." That became my dream job and focus for the next 28 years.

When I was 15, I had a conversation with myself as I planned my future after high school. It was around this time that my passion for serving our country grew from simply a childhood fantasy into an actual goal. I knew that politicians often needed to have money of their own to inject into a campaign, so I pragmatically decided that I would work towards becoming a business owner. Thinking about the type of business I'd someday like to own, I thought about all sorts of industries, like starting an automotive company (and quickly decided that it didn't seem practical) or a movie theater (which also seemed to be capital-intensive). As I was thinking and working through everything in my head, I thought about my love for dining out, and how special restaurants can be in people's lives. I also knew that if a restaurant was successful it could be replicated, and that success would likely provide the financial resources necessary to run for office. Within 15 minutes of self-reflection and contemplation on a weekend afternoon, I decided my path post-high school would be to study business with the goal of becoming a restaurateur. A few years later I was officially studying Hospitality Business at Michigan State University, which is consistently ranked as one of the best hospitality schools in the country, and is occasionally even ranked as the best in the world, like it was during my time as a student.

I spent 10 years in the service industry, which helped me to learn about emotional intelligence, because at this point, I had virtually none to speak of when it came to work. Instead,

I earned the nickname, "The Hammer," because I was a complete and total jerk to the people who worked for me. I wasn't intentionally a bully, not by a longshot, but I also had no regard for the feelings, emotions, or personal issues that my employees faced. I was very much on a mission to achieve results, and I succeeded on every objective. The challenge with that was that I saw all of my people as a means to an end, not as the most valuable asset they really were.

This attitude helped cause a vicious cycle of reinforcing my aggressive attitude and the staff fearing me, and I ended up becoming our restaurant's chief disciplinarian. My colleagues did not enjoy writing people up or firing them, as they felt bad and lost sleep over it. I didn't specifically enjoy it, but I also didn't lose sleep over it, so they asked me to fulfill that function for them. I was good at it, and even got so good that a guy once thanked me and asked if he could hug me after I fired him. This didn't change the fact, though, that I had the old school attitude of "check your baggage at the door." It wasn't until I left the restaurant industry that I learned how to change my behavior.

In college I had been the vice president of my church. The president and I spent an exorbitant amount of time together and became friends. His name is Rich. After college, Rich and I would get together for lunch every year when I came back to visit for MSU's Homecoming. One day he asked me, in quite a few more words, if I would like to join his company. He wanted to grow the business for about 5 more years, then broker the sale with someone he trusted – Me. I knew absolutely nothing about the professional trades or heating and cooling, but I knew that I wanted to be a business owner so that I could eventually run for office, and I knew that selling anything is basically like selling anything else. After talking with my wife about moving back home and starting a new role, I eagerly agreed.

I rebranded his 70+ year-old company and grew the sales revenue by 19% every year I was there. It was an incredible learning experience. The best learning experience, though, came when I was forced to figure out how to work with someone that I would have previously written up and fired without a second thought. The problem was, this guy who worked for me sold half of the annual sales for the company, so I couldn't realistically replace his productivity. He was untouchable for his performance, even though his attitude was toxic, disrespectful, and explosive. I was also acutely aware of the difficulty he would likely have in finding a new job if I were to fire him, as his stark white hair, beard, and deep wrinkles made him appear even older than he was, and agism can be very real for individuals late in their career. At the risk of sounding dramatic, it did seem like firing him would be a death sentence, at least to the life he had grown accustomed to.

One night, I bumped into an online ad for the Dale Carnegie Course. I had heard of the program in the past, but was basically unaware of what it would do. I saw "leadership" as one of the focuses, and it stuck out to me. I knew that I had been a Leader in college, and I could tell that I wasn't behaving like one in my professional work. I had hoped that I would learn how to work with the guy that I wanted to fire, and I did. I also had an intense moment of epiphany when I realized during the class that I made my mother cry, and my wife, and my brother, and virtually every person who had ever worked for me. I realized that I was a jerk. I realized that I didn't need to focus on being a leader, but that I needed to change how I communicated with others. I realized the need and importance of pouring myself into the study of emotional intelligence. I realized that I needed to treat people like people instead of like human cogs.

I shifted my behavior, and immediately had new outcomes. People started coming to me for counsel! I liked how it felt to be perceived by others as a Leader. I also knew that to achieve mastery of any subject, a person needs to be able to teach it to others. With that, I decided to become a Dale Carnegie Trainer, and in 2019 the franchisor, Dale Carnegie & Associates, recognized me out of over 3,000 global trainers as their #1 Corporate Trainer in the World.

★ ★ ★

In 2014 Matthew McConaughey was recognized with the Oscar for Best Actor. During his acceptance speech, he shared about how, as a teenager, a person he admired asked him who his hero was. After much thought, he shared, "Myself in 10 years." A decade later the same person asked him, "Are you your hero yet?" He laughed, and said that his hero is him 10 years from that point, and so on. His message was to live up to that hero.

It never occurred to me until I was expanding my original thesis into this book, but the one person who has been driving me all of these years, pushing me to do things that other people can't or wouldn't choose to endure, the person who holds me accountable to making choices that I won't cringe at or regret, and the person who inspires me to give everything I have to those I serve, is the vision of myself in the future as the President of the United States of America.

I don't know if I'll ever achieve that ambition, or if I'll even end up being worthy of having folks vote for me to be of service to them and our incredible country. Maybe they'll elect me to a lower office and leave me there, or they'll decide that I'm not cut out for politics and will never vote for me at all. To be honest, none of that really matters, because by God, I have made every important decision in my life based on that hero, and I'm not going to let him down now.

The purpose of this autobiographical detour is to provide insight into my mindset for what comes next, and to demonstrate how important service is to me. Between my childhood dream, education, career choices, and real-world accolades, being of service is a foundational behavior in my life, and will inform much of the rest of this book.

Now, let's get back to talking about people killing each other.

★ ★ ★

The typical knee-jerk response to killing is that it is a disgusting crime. The victim's life is extinguished unnecessarily and prematurely. Their loved ones are left with tremendous loss, pain, questions, anger, and a desire for justice. The perpetrator's life is changed dramatically, as well. Either living with a dark secret or facing the criminal justice system. Those who are incarcerated and later released often struggle to secure employment, making them disproportionately more likely to re-offend and be incarcerated for a subsequent crime. The act of being imprisoned is a permanently life-altering experience. While many former inmates are fully reformed and positively contributing members of society, the overwhelming majority end up in a continually downward spiral of poor choices that negatively affect themselves and those unfortunate enough to be caught in the crossfire.

My father has spent the entirety of his career working for the State of Michigan, with nearly 40 years of service to the Department of Corrections (MDOC). In the 1980's he was one of four individuals in the country who had the capacity to statistically project a state's prison population based on a variety of criterion, like public policy changes. Throughout his career, he would regularly testify before the Michigan State Legislature regarding the policies they were contemplating signing into law. He ultimately became the State's equivalent of the MDOC's Chief Information Officer.

For much of my youth we had one car, and would drive my Dad to and from work in downtown Lansing each day. In my young age I always enjoyed the view of the State Capitol Building, and still do, just a block away from the MDOC Central Office. I would often say as we were driving near it, "Someday that's where I'm going to live." As a child I aspired to become the Governor of Michigan on my journey to serving our country as the President, but didn't realize at that time that the building does not include a residence.

At the end of the day, my Dad would often bring us gumballs from the incredibly popular gumball machine on his desk, and we'd casually listen to him talk about his day with my Mom on the ride back home. He was most often focused on the high-level issues that determined the need to build or close prisons throughout the state, and was rarely engaged in the specifics of individual inmates. He toured facilities out of necessity, not as a normal function of his work. This all informed the way he talked about his work, and the way I came to understand the prison population system as a teenager.

I once asked my Dad how much it cost to keep a prisoner incarcerated for a year. His answer, from sometime in the mid-to-late 90's, was approximately $34,000. I asked who pays the equivalent of a person's annual salary just to keep a criminal behind bars, hoping that the answer would be, "They pay it back when they're released." I expected that if a college student makes the conscious decision to incur debt in hopes to better themselves, so should the conscious decisions of those who commit crimes be treated as debt. That wasn't the answer I got – Tax dollars are used to keep criminals behind bars.

I was disgusted and annoyed by this answer. If the hard-earned money of law-abiding citizens was used to pay to keep incarcerated individuals held indefinitely, that seemed like an extreme waste of money, particularly for those who were serving life sentences. My solution was blunt and easy: "Why don't we just kill them?" Bless my Dad and his patience. He spent an exorbitant amount of time explaining to me that occasionally the person convicted of a crime is actually innocent, and killing them, while a pragmatic solution, would unnecessarily end the lives of individuals who could eventually be proven innocent and released. I was still unsatisfied. His explanation essentially meant that taxpayers necessarily supported all prisoners for the sake of the exceedingly small percentage of the prison population that was truly innocent. What was one wrongly convicted person's life worth? Literally millions of dollars? I couldn't rationalize that in my mind, and for years believed that the broad-scale application of capital punishment was a better social solution than life sentences. But what about the times that someone actually *is* innocent? That's a human being who was in the wrong place at the wrong time. Is it appropriate to end their life simply because you and I could have slightly lower taxes?

The Death Penalty Information Center was created in 1990, and exists for a variety of national policy-based functions. One of the tools they have created is an Innocence Database.[23] It features a series of individuals who were convicted, sentenced to death, and later exonerated. Dating back to 1973, 185 individuals throughout the country have been found to be innocent after sentencing. 185 lives. Is that a lot or a few? It's less than 4 per year throughout the country – Does that framing change anything? Does supporting the killing of someone who kills someone else make us just as bad as the killer? Does eliminating the death penalty embolden individuals to act more drastically? Does instituting the death penalty for all life sentences similarly embolden criminals to be even more brazen if they have no hope once convicted? Is killing within this context "right" or "wrong?"

★ ★ ★

What about suicide? Is killing yourself "wrong?" A devout Catholic could quickly say that, "suicide is a mortal sin that immediately sends a person to Hell." Pope John Paul II modified that harsh language in the early 1990's to accommodate for mental health crises, though the extreme aversion to suicide by Christians persists.[24]

In Western society, we place a high value on life, and hold an open yet unspoken belief that a person should not kill themself. Our attitude is that a variety of alternative solutions exist that are not terminal. We suggest counseling, medication, the removal of one's self from harmful environments, pain mitigation, rehab, and a litany of other options. When someone says, "I'm depressed," the normal reaction is not, "Are you thinking about killing yourself?" Ironically, research states that this is exactly the question one should ask a suicidal person in the midst of a mental health crisis.[25]

★ ★ ★

I was incredibly suicidal as a 19-year-old. The details would only paint another person in a negative light, which isn't necessary. And admittedly, I had a role to play in the relationship, too. Specifics simply don't add anything of value to this story. The bottom line was that I felt absolutely trapped in a toxic and manipulative relationship. To be honest, I'm not sure the other person truly understood how I felt, but I was miserable and didn't know how to end my misery without ending my life.

I almost took my life twice during that period of time. When you're in that headspace, the allure and comfort of nothingness is so much more pleasant than the thought of continuing to suffer. My experience was that I could "see" into the abyss. It seemed welcoming and like it had a personality of its own, and in that moment, that thought wasn't scary to me at all. I later learned that I was clinically depressed, and should have been hospitalized to protect me from myself. It's actually a miracle that I'm alive. Ending my life would have been very easy. If it weren't for the fact that I was concerned about the emotional impact my actions would have on others, there is no doubt in my mind that you wouldn't be reading this book right now. The only reason why I didn't follow through on my plan the second time was because I knew very clearly that it would have been my mother who found me. I knew how much she loves me, and I wasn't willing to devastate her like that. Seeking to protect her from the pain I would cause is why I chose to endure through that darkest moment.

Not long after that critical episode, the negative relationship mercifully came to a close. I immediately felt healthier and less depressed, but I was still unpacking a lot of mental baggage. My mother encouraged me to go to a counselor to talk through what I was processing. He was the perfect person for me in that moment. Not because he held my hand, or told me that everything would be okay, or because he became my ally and damned the other person for their behavior. Instead, he asked questions. He listened. He shared pain he had endured that was similar. And he told me stories that helped me to see parts of myself that I couldn't see without that context.

Life is really fucking hard. It sucks. It's painful. I've wanted to call it quits so many times and just go live a life doing something that I perceive to be easier than the paths I've selected – Or easier yet, just stop living. Then I realized one day, as I reflected on the opportunities I've had to work with and coach thousands of people: No one's life is easy. Not a single person. That's also part of the beauty of life.

Think of a time where everything just fell in line and everyone held you up for the success. It feels great to have a really easy and impactful win, but it also feels completely empty. As humans, particularly in Western society, we place a high value on hard work and earning our wins. When things just fall in our lap, we don't value them, and we don't appreciate them. Without challenges, we'd feel empty, aimless, and lost. With challenges, we have the opportunity to focus on a goal, drive towards its completion, and feel fulfilled with accomplishing the objective. Much of our happiness and fulfillment does not occur at the culmination of a goal, but in the overcoming of the obstacles in our way to achieving the goal.

I share these stories because what that counselor did for me shows how easy it can be to be emotionally intelligent. All you have to do is step outside of yourself and your priorities for a moment, humble yourself, and be human with another human; ask hard questions, but with care; share parts of yourself, and stories that you've learned along the way; and honor the other person for the good things they have done, can do, and will do.

I'm not ashamed to talk about my personal struggles with mental health because I know that it helps to normalize it for others, and it lets them know that they aren't alone. And because of my struggles, I live a life where I very intentionally refuse to live with regrets. This has made my life rich, full, and exciting. It also makes me appreciate my incredibly supportive wife, Kristy, and our three beautiful children so much more than I may have otherwise appreciated them. They're each a blessing in my life, and I know it.

★ ★ ★

A fantastic example of emotional intelligence and mental health is Simone Biles at the 2020 Olympics. Biles knew that she could perform virtually anything she wanted to when it came to gymnastics. Through intensive training, she understands her body and mind in a way that most people will never experience. Part of knowing your body and mind is knowing their limits. Stress, health, diet, environment, and countless other variables can impact those limits. Biles understood that, and while she very much wanted to compete, she simply couldn't perform at the level she knew she needed to. Had she attempted to ignore those limits, she may have caused herself and her teammates undue harm.

Evaluating her physical and mental state, and saying, "no," when everyone else expected her to say "yes," was a demonstration of emotional intelligence focused toward herself. Choosing to stay in the arenas and cheer on her teammates was a demonstration of emotional intelligence focused on others. Even though she knew she couldn't do what she had spent years working towards, there was nothing stopping her from encouraging and holding up those she served as the Leader of Team USA.

We are all humans. We don't become superhumans or robots when we start working and go back to being regular humans when we stop working. We're humans all of the time. Humans have limits. Everything breaks when too much pressure is applied – Even us. Understanding and honoring our limits is the most compassionate thing we can do for ourselves and our mental health. In that regard, Ms. Biles should be a role model for all of us.

★ ★ ★

In 2018 I had the opportunity to secure a project on behalf of a mental health nonprofit that I was representing. My colleagues had been trying to close the deal for 10 years. They kept getting close to having a contract signed, but just couldn't seem to get it done. I was given the opportunity as a Hail Mary. They said, "We think this is the last shot before this thing is toast. We haven't been able to get it done, and you've made some big deals happen in the past. Would you like to give it a go?" One meeting later, I secured a 5-year contract to deliver an in-seat proactive mental health program to high school students.

The program was designed to increase a young person's mental resilience; build bonds between diverse populations; show them how to advocate for themselves; and provide a venue for processing experiences that had been harmful. In the first year of delivery, I embedded myself as one of the facilitators so I could see for myself first-hand how well the program was going, and identify ways to improve the outcomes for the young people we were serving. This meant working in the high school 5 days a week, 4 hours a day, working with two groups of 9th graders that totaled to 44 students. It was an incredible experience unlike any coaching I had done to that point. As a Dale Carnegie trainer, I was used to working with white collar professionals in Fortune 400 companies, helping them overcome themselves so they could get promoted. This was so different. The kids were energetic, disengaged, and hormonal. I couldn't work with them the way I worked with adults, but at the same time, they were virtually identical to adults – They all just wanted to feel heard and respected.

While running the program, I quickly identified eight of these 44 14-15-year-olds were self-harming, mentally retreating, and were casually exploring thoughts of suicide. What surprised me was not that there were kids who were struggling, but that there were so many of them. Nearly 20% of these children had resorted to behaviors that were causing them further pain and difficulty. Then one day I was stunned by a 9th.

As the class ended for the day, one of the boys came up to me and asked if I could talk for a minute. This young man was one of the quarterbacks of the football team, had good grades, was tall and attractive, and had virtually everything going for him. He looked at me and said, "I think about suicide every day of my life."

Of all of the kids in the two classes, he was the last one I would have expected to say something like this. I was truly taken aback for a moment. I also knew that I had a responsibility to him to behave in such a way. I prayed, "Help me to help him," then I "heard" the response, "Trust yourself."

I didn't let my shock show through – I instead started asking questions. I could quickly tell that this was a true crisis situation, and that the way the conversation went would directly inform the decisions the boy made later that day. I also knew that he trusted me, and that I could leverage his trust to positively influence him. After asking enough questions to understand the context I said, "You know me, and you know that I care about you. Do not misunderstand what I am about to ask you. You're telling me that you're in pain, and that you have a solution to end your pain which you think about every day, and for some reason you haven't done it. Why haven't you killed yourself yet?"

The boy started to sob in my arms and said, "I just couldn't do that to my mom." And with that, I knew how to help him.

My question may seem cold and crass, and realistically, that's a fair assessment. It's also the appropriate way to confront someone who tells you that they are suicidal. The reason why is because of the mental state a person experiences during a mental health crisis. When asked about a plan to kill themselves, they don't lie. At that lowest of the low points, they feel as though they have nothing left to lose, and are incredibly honest about their plans. That's why asking questions like, "Do you plan to kill yourself? How do you plan to end your life? When do you plan to take your life?" and the like, are all questions that give you the playbook to help prevent them from being successful. With that information, you can secure the support of emergency services or a mental health practitioner before they make an attempt on their life. And in this specific situation, this question showed me how to prevent him from acting out at all – It was the same thing that saved my life – Point to his mother.

As the boy cried in my arms, I held him and reminded him that he was loved and cared about. At the point when we could continue the conversation, I set a new context for him by saying, "What I'm hearing is you have pain; you have a solution to end your pain; and you would rather endure *more* pain than cause pain for someone else. Man... That's strength. That's Leadership. That's the kind of person *I* want to follow." And with that, he started to sob again.

What I knew about this boy was that he desperately wanted to feel seen as a Leader – Capitalized for representing a person who motivates, inspires, and empowers those they serve. By rights, he was lowercase leader – The individual who leads the pack. He was an alpha amongst his friends, he was a bigshot in any sport he played, and he was admired by many. He didn't feel like a Leader, though, and that was destroying him. By framing his strength in a way that spoke to his deepest desire – by showing him that he was seen the way he wanted to be – he was immediately released of the source of his pain. It may seem trivial or stupid to you, or you may completely understand where he was coming from, either way it was the first key to ending his pain and depression. By knowing that his mother was the lynchpin to keeping him alive, I was able to give him what he wanted so badly: I showed him that he was seen as a Leader – And coming from someone that he respected made it even more powerful. With additional supports immediately in place, he never thought about suicide again. On the last day of the program, he hugged me and said, "I love you. Thank you. You saved my life."

★ ★ ★

Some 15 months later, Dale Carnegie & Associates, the global franchisor for Dale Carnegie Training, recognized me as their #1 Corporate Trainer in the World. The award was completely unrelated to working with that boy, but it was related in that I was being recognized for my efficacy in coaching others. Dale Carnegie measured the success of their trainers with two client-generated metrics, Net Promoter Score (NPS), and Voice of Customer (VOC). Both metrics are cross-industry standards for measuring satisfaction, used by companies like Amazon, Coca-Cola, American Express, Google, Walmart, Apple, Ford, Boeing, and others. A good score is 30 out of 100, with 50 being considered excellent, and 80 being considered world class. My score was over 96. I personally knew that my outcomes from coaching were unusually strong, but it was completely out of my control that my scores were the highest in the world in 2019, out of about 3,000 trainers. It was a huge honor, and something that I appreciated tremendously. What was really cool, though, was when the President / CEO, Joe Hart, handed me the crystal award in front of some 800 of my peers at the North American Convention, I saw the face of that boy. That is what that honor represents to me – The lives I've had the opportunity to touch, and the people that are living their best life because I had the opportunity to serve them for a brief moment in their journey.

I've been blessed to play a critical role in the lives of many, including numerous individuals who have battled with suicidal ideation. Even with those experiences to guide me, never had I played such a direct role in keeping someone alive. Knowing that I was able to be what that boy needed when he needed it is a gift that I cherish. I also know that what I did for him isn't the right thing for all people.

★ ★ ★

Jack Kevorkian was a Michigan native, and his name became synonymous with "assisted suicide," in the late 1990's. He had been tried three times before finally being sent to prison in 1999, having claimed to have assisted at least 130 people with ending their lives.[26] When I was in college, I spent a year working for the Michigan Department of Corrections as a student assistant in the records maintenance department. I worked in the same building as my father, though in a completely different function. It was my opportunity to test if the 9-5 office world was a lifestyle I enjoyed – It wasn't, but the experience was valuable. I was responsible for adding paper documentation to the files of Michigan inmates, and for occasionally transporting records throughout the building for a variety of reasons. Most files were no more than a few dozen pages, with the really bad guys having files that were 1-4" thick. In 2005, as Kevorkian was attempting parole, I had the opportunity to transport his banker box of a file – The largest I had ever seen.

The crux of the case against Kevorkian revolved around two primary variables: If he was helping people to die or if he was murdering them; and if choosing to die in a "compassionate way" was or was not socially acceptable. During the period of 1994-1999 when he was in and out of court, the social debate was noticeably divided. People either thought he was a perverse murderer who preyed on the weak, or a saving grace who helped to end the suffering of the terminally ill. Because of good behavior, Kevorkian was released from prison in 2007, after serving 8 years. He was given orders not to medically serve senior citizens or attempt to assist in ending anyone else's life. He attempted to run for congress in 2008 and lost. Quite unwell with liver cancer, kidney issues, and pneumonia, "Doctor Death" died in 2011.

In the time since Kevorkian's work was the focus of nightly news and HBO specials, attitudes toward "compassionate end to life" have continued to soften, though real movement on the topic has been nominal. Talking about consciously choosing to die is still quite taboo. While America was founded on the notion of religious freedom, we are an overwhelmingly Christian-oriented nation, and have adopted behaviors, attitudes, and laws that stem directly from Christianity. With suicide once being considered a one-way ticket to Hell, how could ending your life earlier than God's timeline ever be appropriate? But what if you aren't a Christian? What if you're definitely going to imminently die a painful death? What if you'd rather end your life with dignity, saving your family time, energy, and resources, and preventing them from having to remember your less pleasant end-of-life experiences? What if we could choose the date, time, location, and environment of our final moments? What if we treated adults like adults, and let them decide what's best for them, even if we don't think it's the best decision for us (at this moment)? What if Jack Kevorkian was actually a societal influencer – Someone who sacrificed his freedom in the name of everyone else's right to choose to die, as his tombstone proudly declares?

★ ★ ★

Killing for the sake of killing is wrong. It also violates one of our unalienable rights – Life. When killing for personal protection, national defense, in the name of a deity, as a form of punishment, due to individual pain and suffering, or as a way to end life with dignity, there is no moral hardline. The situation, context, and individuals all play a critical role in whether or not killing is, in that moment and for that individual, "right" or "wrong."

We may reflexively feel that "killing is wrong," but the reality is, sometimes it isn't.

★ ★ ★

Drugs
_____
_____

Two fine dining managers, Harrison and Declan, had been in a conflict that ended poorly. Harrison was a tall and broad Indigenous American in his late 30's who was very proud of the career he'd built for himself. He was stern but also warm and funny. He was also unrelenting when he thought he was right. Declan was a mid-30's, larger than life good ol' Southern gentleman. He was always the best dressed in any room, and completely full of himself in a way that you couldn't help but find strangely charming. Both men were fantastic in their professions, and both acted like it. After shouting at one and other, Declan threatened to hit his colleague before Harrison suggested that they both needed to take a break from the argument. After furiously burning through three cigarettes, Declan went to talk to the general manager, George, a wise and thoughtful veteran of the industry. In a large private dining room lined with rich wood paneling and ornate fixtures, Declan huffed and snarled through the blow-by-blow, frustrated with how the argument concluded. George listened calmly with his hands in his lap, intentionally not reacting or interrupting. As Declan slowly lost steam and waited for a response, George finally said, "Perception is reality."

"You see," he went on, "each of you believes what you believe based on the sum of your life experiences. From your upbringing, to early education, to formative events, to higher education, to experiences with others throughout your life and in previous organizations. Neither of you are right or wrong in this situation. Each simply believes what you believe as a result of what you have seen, done, learned, felt, and experienced. Those experiences inform your perspectives on life, and become the lens through which you each view your respective realities. Each of you is looking at this situation from a uniquely personal perspective, backed with real-world evidence."

"But," Declan argued, "how can neither of us be right? We're not arguing about what is and isn't legal. This argument is about a moral issue. There *has* to be some hard line that civilized people work from to find a solution!"

"Excellent," George replied, "you bring up a valid point. Let's walk through this together. You are responsible for controlling our liquor costs and have proven over the years to be quite good at it, haven't you?"

"Well, yes."

"So let's take an example from your context and responsibilities to decide where a moral hard line should be. We have guests who are staunchly against consuming alcohol, yet we actively choose to sell it. Which side is right?"

"I mean..." Declan fumbled, "We're definitely not wrong. It's legal to sell alcohol, and we have guests who want to drink."

"Exactly. Now, think of a time that we served someone who we felt was legally competent to drive away. If they were to get in an accident, who's at fault?"

"It should just be them, but with the Dram Shop Law,[27] we could be sued, too," Declan said with a frown.

"That's correct. We have a legal obligation to ensure that our guests are not over-served alcoholic beverages in our establishment, and share that responsibility with any other establishment that a guest may visit in a given evening. That said, is it our *moral obligation* to prevent a guest from drinking or getting drunk?"

"Hmm..." Declan paused to reflect.

After a moment, the General Manager continued, "One hundred years ago, some American politicians saw, from their perspective, an epidemic of alcoholism. Their solution to solve the moral problem was to institute Prohibition.[28] Times changed, and today you are responsible for making sure this restaurant realizes profitability on the sale of that same product. Which is the correct moral hard line?"

Declan shrugged, realizing that this scenario didn't necessarily have one right answer.

"You see," George expanded, "in issues of morality, there is no hard line. No one is specifically 'right' or 'wrong.' Even when there *is* a broadly accepted hard line, time itself can move or change it. So, instead of criticizing or arguing, we need to work to understand those with different perspectives. We must seek to understand why they believe what they believe. A saying that helps me in these types of situations is, 'The opposite of criticism is understanding.' When we understand the other person, we may still not agree with them, but it is difficult to criticize them when we understand them. In fact, when we understand why they believe what they believe, we often have greater respect for them, even though we disagree. This respect allows us to then choose to collaborate with the other party toward a solution that makes both feel satisfied."

"So, what should I do now?" Declan asked.

"If it were me, I'd ask Harrison to sit down for a drink or a meal and ask him questions about why he believes what he believes. In the end, you will likely find that his stance makes more sense to you than it does now. You may also find that you simply have differing perspectives on the topic. After an adult discussion, you should both be able to leave with a mutual understanding and respect for one and other. You may even find that your unique views make you both stronger together."

★ ★ ★

This story never happened as I've framed it, and the names have been changed, but the characters, incidents, and outcomes did all take place during my time working alongside three incredible gentlemen in a fine dining restaurant. The general manager in particular was inspiring in his capacity to demonstrate emotional intelligence. What this parable says about conflict is valuable for our thought experiment, and what it says about alcohol prohibition can be directly applied to the conversation around drugs in America.

In 2017, the average lifespan of an American continued an annual decline, from 78.9 in 2014 down to 78.6, as a direct result of the opioid epidemic.[29] There are two primary camps in regard to how to combat this issue that has ravaged the nation: Prohibit all drugs, jailing those that use and deal illicit products for recreational or medicinal purposes; or begin the process of state-level and federal decriminalization and legalization.

The attitude that drugs are destructive and ruin lives, families, and communities has been pervasive since the War on Drugs began. Contrast that with the fact that one of Coca-Cola's original ingredients was cocaine, which was completely eliminated by 1929, during Prohibition, making Coke a "soft" drink alternative to hard liquor.[30] In more recent history the viewpoint that adults should be able to make decisions for themselves, and that they should be able to acquire and consume drugs if they feel that usage is appropriate in their lives, is beginning to gain momentum. American culture is shifting, and the timing of the conversation is shifting favor toward those who believe the War on Drugs has been a failure.[31]

As of 2021, 36 states have legalized medical marijuana, and 18 states have legalized recreational use for adults.[32] It's hard not to imagine a world 100 years from now where the same parable could be true with the word "alcohol" replaced with "drugs." Thinking back to the Prohibition Era, a period that lasted from 1920-1933, it's simultaneously foreign and topical. Alcohol is abundantly available in grocery stores, bottle shops, and gas stations. It is the only drug available on the planet that a person who doesn't use it is asked to explain themselves to others for not using. Compare that with marijuana, which is increasingly available recreationally to adults, even though it's still illegal federally.

I'm always fascinated by the idea of individual's attitudes toward alcohol in the early 1920's – Were they excited to be able to drink? Did they think drinking was morally or socially wrong? Did people look down on others for drinking? Was it considered slightly taboo or inappropriate to discuss drinking openly? Because all of these things are currently true about marijuana in America. And yet, nearly every networking event or celebratory party you've ever attended has had alcohol available in abundance. In how many decades will it be normalized that cannabis edibles or joints are offered to the guests of weddings and business functions? This thought may seem impossible, but this casual relationship with alcohol likely would have seemed unreal to the citizens of a century ago.

Recreational cannabis is legal in my state of Michigan, so I know from experience that both substances, alcohol and marijuana, result in similar side effects, with variations for each based on type and volume consumed, as well as gender, weight, amount of prior experience, environment, mindset, and others. Compared side by side, alcohol and marijuana are remarkably similar. Arguably, alcohol may actually be worse, as it's been proven to be addictive and a leading contributor to liver disease and other ailments.[33] Marijuana use has no such long-term negative physical effects.[34] Further the ability to overdose on alcohol is tragically common, while there have been no known overdoses of marijuana ever.

And yet, in America we demonize marijuana, and a litany of other "controlled substances," while our doctors prescribe painkillers like Tic Tacs. I was in a serious car accident when I was 19 years old that caused persistent and intolerable lower back pain for 16 years. I had seen four physical therapists before I found one that I connected with who was able to help me manage my pain – Saige. She has been a blessing in my life for nearly two decades. After she fixed me up and taught me how to care for my body, I was dramatically better. Then I would inevitably do something that I knew wasn't wise for my injury, like help a friend move, and I would reactivate the pain. In those instances, I was occasionally able to recover by taking a muscle relaxer or pain killer and resting my back for a day or two. They always made me sleep harder than I preferred, but they worked pretty well. While I never abused my drugs, my primary care physician and I both knew that I was using them on an "as needed" basis. This was helpful, because

I didn't have to ask for 2 pills every time I threw my kids in the air or carried a heavy box. It also meant that I didn't really have any rules to follow – At least in my own mind.

★ ★ ★

There was an incident in 2016, when I was 31, where my back was on a rapid and significant decline that I knew would result in needing to go back to physical therapy. This type of incident typically occurred every 12-24 months, and required 6-8 weeks of PT. This one was really serious, and I couldn't endure the pain as I waited the day or two to clear my schedule and get in to see Saige. I had taken a muscle relaxer the night before and it didn't do anything to help. The pain killers weren't helping much, either. I decided that I'd take two muscle relaxers that night, and cross my fingers that I'd wake up in moderate pain instead of excruciating pain. As I was getting ready for bed, I decided to text my children's godmother, Katrina.

Katerina and her husband, John, have been great friends to Kristy and I since we were in undergrad. She is now an ER doctor, and has only ever known me with my injury. I texted her and asked, "Can I take two of these?" She quickly explained to me that I was already on a maximum dose, and if I were to take two, my body would likely relax to the point of not being able to maintain respiration. Essentially, if it weren't for her response, I would have accidentally overdosed, suffocated in my drug-induced heavy sleep, and died. So answer your texts – You might unintentionally save someone's life, like Katrina did for me.

This incident, which would have been considered an opioid-related death, was my wake-up call to the dangers of prescription drugs. That year over 42,000 people overdosed on opioids – 66% of all drug-related overdoses that year.[35] I didn't begrudge my doctor for prescribing me the pills – I appreciated it. I didn't feel like an idiot or a pill popper for being so cavalier – I wanted to control my pain. It was this event, though, that caused me start to think twice about prescription opioids, and when I became more curious about marijuana.

At this point in time, I was actively involved in the Lansing Regional Chamber of Commerce, and was serving in an advisory capacity as a member of the Small Business Association of Michigan's (SBAM) Leadership Council. Both policy-influencing entities were actively monitoring the assumed-to-be impending legalization of recreational marijuana in the state. Each group held special events, roundtables, and invited featured speakers and policy experts from all over the country to help provide information to small business owners and operators. The goal of each lobbying firm was to capture their members' opinions about the topic and effectively advocate on behalf of them. By this time, I was curious about the state policy, workplace safety, sociological, and the criminal justice implications of legalization. I was also increasingly thinking about how this may be a more natural solution to helping resolve my chronic back pain than a pill that I could accidentally take twice in my forgetfulness, or drop on the floor and have one of my small children tragically discover.

At around this time, one of my closest friends opened up about his past and current use of medical marijuana. Medicinal use had been previously legalized nearly a decade earlier in Michigan, in 2008. This friend is a veteran of US Marines. During his multiple tours in forward operations and active combat, he twice broke his neck. The first time was while his base came under attack in the middle of the night. He jumped into a vehicle to engage the enemy. The driver had the headlights off to avoid telegraphing their position, and didn't know that a sandstorm had blown in and covered a series of crates. The sand created a ramp that they hit in the dark, flipping the vehicle upside-down, breaking my friend's neck.

The second time was even more harrowing, as he and a group of other warfighters flew a mission in a helicopter. This Marine had previously executed multiple fast rope descents, which is basically a controlled fall from a hovering helicopter. The way it works is a soldier is clipped to a rappel rope while wearing special high-temp gloves that melt from friction as they control their speed. This type of entrance allows soldiers to land on the ground in seconds, ready to fight. The highest descent my friend did was 800'. On this day, insurgents were nearby and successfully fired an RPG at the helicopter. It crashed belly-first from 400', breaking his neck a second time.

I met my friend after he had returned to civilian life. He'd been out of the service for almost a decade, and lived with chronic and intense neck and shoulder pain. The VA alternated between being sporadically helpful and frustrating. He had multiple surgeries, nerve blockers, and countless other attempts to alleviate his pain. While I was getting pain killers and muscle relaxers for my back by the dozen, he was getting them mailed to him by the hundreds.

One New Year's Eve, we were celebrating the holiday with two families that became an extension of our family, including the Marine's family. Our kids were all the same age, we lived mere houses apart, we were all in a similar place in life, and we all had a blast being with each other. We would spend time together almost daily, vacation together, and celebrate everything as one big friend family, or "framily." That evening we had amazing steaks, crab legs, and lots of alcohol. The Marine mentioned his neck pain, and how he discovered a strain of cannabis that made his body feel numb, but didn't impact his ability to think clearly and be present with his children, should they require him past bedtime. I was intrigued.

★ ★ ★

When I was 6-years old, Bill Clinton was running for President of the United States, and was lampooned for his answer to a question in an MTV interview that was attempting to make him look hip and appeal to young voters. He was asked if he had every tried pot, and responded, "I experimented with marijuana a time or two, and I didn't like it. And I didn't inhale. And never tried it again."[36]

I remember seeing that all over the news, thinking, "This guy looks like an idiot. If I ever want to run for office, I don't want to look like an idiot like this, so I will not smoke pot or do anything illegal, unless it becomes legal." That was truly my train of thought when I was 6 years old. That was how I reacted to that interview. I never drank under age (except for one time with my parents when I graduated high school), I didn't try other drugs or cigarettes, and I never smoked pot.

At the point of the New Year's Eve party, Michigan had not yet voted to legalize recreational use, but based on all of the information I had from the Chamber and SBAM, it was obvious that there was no question that it would pass. As a reaction, different cities started to legalize or decriminalize the use and possession of pot. One such municipality was our capital city, Lansing, which is where I worked, played, and spent the majority of my time. While we lived outside of Lansing, the process of impending legalization, combined with a new social attitude, in addition to the fact that I was a 31-year-old adult with an incredible wife, a great job, a house, and two kids... I decided trying it wasn't going to derail my whole life if I smoked.

And I felt nothing. I remember asking, "Is this even working?" Apparently that was exactly the point – You weren't supposed to feel it in your head, and your pain was supposed to disappear. It actually did work really well, and I was impressed. I wasn't comfortable buying an unknown product from an unknown dealer, and I didn't like the idea of having to be put into some system for a medical card when the federal government still was in opposition, so until the recreational dispensaries opened in our state, I didn't use it very much. But now I have a new option to manage my pain, and I don't have to worry about accidentally overdosing.

★ ★ ★

You have some response to this right now. You likely are feeling one of the following: Ambivalent to my being so open with my marijuana usage, or you now have a degraded opinion of me.

This example is intentionally included as a real-world, real-time opportunity for you to contemplate your opinions, and accept or reject the choices of another person. You can think that I'm logical, cool, or a stoner. You can understand my thought-process, agree with it, or disagree and be of the belief that I should continue to manage pain through prescriptions. The reality is, your opinions don't affect my choices at all, but they do affect your perspective of me, and that impacts your willingness to accept the rest of what is shared in this book.

If you agree with or respect my choices (notice those are not the same), that's great. If you don't agree with or respect my choices, I pose to you another way of thinking about this: When was a time that you faced a problem, investigated and attempted multiple solutions, found one that you were comfortable with, resolved your problem, and had someone you like or respect belittle your decision? How did you feel? What did you wish they knew?

You've experienced criticism for your choices throughout your whole life. From the clothes you wear, to the food you eat, to the places you visit, to the individuals you spend time with, and on, and on, and on. The reality is, no one likes being criticized for their choices. So instead of damning others, we can seek to understand the *why* behind the choices others make. Just like we learned in the parable of the restaurant managers, when we work to understand The Other, we inherently respect them, whether we agree with them or not.

I'm not trying to influence you to agree with me – Not at all. I *am* trying to influence you to respect my choices, and therefore expand this respect to the choices of everyone else you'll ever interact with. We don't have to agree in order to respect each other. And we don't need to change our own opinions in order to respect the opinions of those we disagree with. We just need to understand the other party, choose not to damn them, and then work from there.

If you are an individual who holds anti-drug opinions and disagrees with my choices, that's your right and prerogative. If you are that same type of individual, and you respect the choices I've made even though you disagree with them – Congratulations! You've passed the first test. You're well on your way to behaving the way this book advocates.

★ ★ ★

There's a story about a group of boys who accidentally burned down a historic wooden bridge in their town.[37] The boys were caught, arrested, and tried for their actions. Interestingly, the judge gave them an option – They could face jail time (retributive justice) or face their community (restorative justice). Each boy sat in a room with a group of people and listened as the community rallied around them to share how the incident impacted them personally. The outcome was that the boys had the opportunity to understand the magnitude of their mistake and apologize in a meaningful way; the community was far more tolerant and understanding of the mistake; and the boys did not begin the often-vicious cycle of being caught in the criminal justice system. Imagine if a convicted drug user was forced to sit in a room with their loved ones, the community members they impacted, and those that they respect…

When we discuss drugs, a natural point of conflict that we can explore is our prison system and the balance of retributive justice as opposed to restorative justice. An example of this is the long-gestating debate over punishment for victimless crimes like drug use and sales. A conservative viewpoint on this topic might be that the drug is a cancerous product that not only claims the life of the user, but spreads its influence to those around the user as well and should therefore be punished to discourage others from repeating the behavior. A liberal viewpoint might be that the user must have an undiagnosed illness and is subconsciously medicating with drugs to compensate for their challenge, and therefore we should provide mental and physical health supports to ensure that the individual is cared for appropriately. A Libertarian viewpoint might advocate that if a person wants to introduce poison into their body, as long as they don't hurt anyone else, they are free to do so, whether the poison is an illicit drug, legally purchased alcohol, de-worming medicine for horses, or anything else. None of these viewpoints are explicitly wrong, though some provide more freedom for individual rights, and some create additional inherent risk.

We could also look at public opinion on the topic of drugs. A 2021 Pew Research Center study found that 91% of Americans believe that marijuana should be legal for adult consumption, with 60% in favor of recreational usage.[38] A separate study released within a week of the first, this one by the Drug Policy Alliance and ACLU, found that 66% of Americans support decriminalization of all drugs by, "eliminating criminal penalties for drug possession and reinvesting drug enforcement resources into treatment and addiction services."[39] It's important to pay attention to who is doing the research so we can glean inherent biases that may be baked into the results. It's obvious to even the casual observer that the ACLU has traditional left-leaning priorities, and it's clear through their name alone that the Drug Policy Alliance would have skin in the game to see drug policy changes. Pew Research Center, though, has been independently evaluated by over 3,800 community-based individuals, and through their assessment, the organization is ranked as being centrist in their media bias.[40] This helps us to see that the data reported is likely very honest, and reinforces the data shared by the Drug Policy Alliance and ACLU. Add to this the fact that on the 50th anniversary of the War on Drugs, 83% of Americans believe it to be a failure,[41] and we know clearly where the country stands on the topic of drugs. With this, we can reasonably assume future courses of action that would be preferable to the majority of Americans.

For the sake of a balanced argument, let's assume for a moment that the continuation of War on Drugs is the right path forward – As some 17% of Americans believe. In 2020, 1,155,610 individuals were arrested for drug violations. Of those, 150,229 were for sales and 1,001,913 were for possession. Over 2.3 million individuals are currently incarcerated for drug related offenses.[42] With this many people violating the law, the question becomes, should the punishment be incarceration, or could we be equally (or more) successful at rehabilitating the criminal user by introducing restorative justice practices, like the boys and the bridge? Does having a drug user sit in a cell for an indefinite period of time have an impact on the accessibility of the prescription pills that fueled the opioid epidemic? Does that indefinite amount of time in a cell, and the stigma attached to the individual as they seek new employment or re-engagement with their community, have a net positive or net negative impact on their life? Do we *know* that incarceration is the most effective way to make sure that they "learn their lesson?" What possible alternative paths of rehabilitation could we explore that ensure someone who chooses to consume illicit products has a new desire within them to not return to usage? Could we make a drug user face their family, friends, coworkers, and community members in a circle, and have each person share the way they are impacted by the user's choices?

★ ★ ★

As I've shared this argument with various individuals over the years, one point of confusion tends to be in the definition of "restorative justice." It is important to note that when

I reference restorative justice, I am not in any way referencing "defund the police," and other social movements that are topical in the late 2010's and early 2020's. I am also not advocating for the ignoring of upholding established laws, as some activist district attorneys around the country have unilaterally chosen to do – That's dereliction of duty at best, and criminal in itself at worst. The messaging of "defund the police" and its actual intent – to have less Black deaths at the hands of police officers – are in dramatic misalignment, which is why so many 2021 ballot initiatives to defund police departments around the country failed, including in cities like Minneapolis, where the movement started as a result of the murder of George Floyd. I'll openly share my opinion here: Arguing to defund the police is stupid and serves only to cause more problems. If the goal is less Black deaths by police, we should actually invest *more* money into our police departments to ensure that a variety of issues are identified and resolved, not the other way around.

With that said, what I am advocating for when referencing restorative justice is that we adopt the centuries-old practice of identifying crimes that are victimless or nominal, and use community engagement and support as an alternative to incarceration. There is a time and a place for both forms of corrective action – It's not an either / or proposition.

If the War on Drugs were to be continued, the restorative justice approach could be a significantly more effective means of rehabilitating drug users, and victimless criminals in general. If we were to deal with these actions in a restorative justice model, as opposed to a retributive justice model, we would have the opportunity to more rapidly rehabilitate our friends and neighbors. This concept is supported be the belief that we should treat each individual as an equal human, rather than treat individuals differently based to those who have made "better" decisions in life, and those who have not. Restorative justice is also endlessly less costly, and the strain on our criminal justice system would immediately begin to decrease. Further, the offenders would likely have an easier time gaining lawful employment without having to deal with a criminal record while applying for jobs, which will further assist in the true rehabilitation of the offender. Restorative justice certainly isn't the solution for all crime, but it is an excellent solution for some.

★ ★ ★

In the article, *A Path to Peace in the U.S. Drug War: Why California Should Implement the Portuguese Model for Drug Decriminalization*, the author, Mallory Whitelaw, argues that the criminalization of drug usage leads to greater negative outcomes than decriminalization would. Interestingly, she advocates for the decriminalization of possession of not just marijuana, but all drugs.[43]

Whitelaw outlines many of the commonly repeated themes of those who advocate for the legalization of drugs: The burden on public safety officers, overpopulation of prisons, the preying on vulnerable population groups and people of color, and then moves to the argument in support of Portugal's shift toward drug policy in 2000. She notes the attitudinal change in the minds of politicians, doctors, and citizens, away from a criminal activity and towards a public health issue. It's important to note that Portugal did not legalize drugs, they rather decriminalized them. It is still illegal to obtain drugs, but instances of discipline result in "administrative offenses," as opposed to criminal offenses. Decriminalization led to decreased instances of drug usage, and reduced overdose deaths, outcomes similar to those found in the states in America that have legalized marijuana.[44]

This article is effective in stating it's case, and helpful in demonstrating how one path to reducing drug-related conflict could be to intentionally decide not to engage in conflict at all. We could choose, instead of disciplining a drug user, to shift the paradigm and help those who are self-harming. Instead of taking a side, we can collaborate and take up a cause.

★ ★ ★

The examples and data in this chapter prove that our opinions of moral hardlines ebb and flow throughout history, and that time itself is a variable that influences our perspectives of what is "right," and what is "wrong."

In 1971, President Richard Nixon declared the War on Drugs saying, "America's Public Enemy #1 is drug abuse. In order to fight and defeat this enemy, it is necessary to wage a new all-out offensive."[45] 50 years later, the majority of Americans oppose this course of action.

Whether we personally support the War on Drugs or not, the results speak for themselves – The war will be lost. If that weren't true, it would have been won by now. By accepting this reality, we can save taxpayers untold sums of money; serve our communities in new ways that prioritize health over retribution; and afford responsible adults with the opportunity to make decisions for themselves, which is the essentially the definition of one of our three unalienable rights – Liberty.

★ ★ ★
Abortion
_____
_____

"**F**uck you. We're done."

In college I had the opportunity to work in an incredible restaurant. It was actually a train wreck from an HR perspective, but if feeling each other up, downing unlimited booze, and laughing about friends breaking the seat off of a toilet during rowdy party sex at your boss' house is your vibe, it was incredible. I had been working there for only a few days when the manager walked behind me while I was talking to a table, and he casually stuck his finger up my butt. Without flinching, I kept taking their lunch order. When the guests were done ordering, I walked over to the oyster bar he was leaning against and asked, "What the hell was that?" He smiled and said, "You passed. You didn't react when I checked your oil. You'll make it here."

A few weeks later, one of the girls who trained me walked up and grabbed my ass while I was filling a soda. "Hey," I asserted, thinking of how Kristy, then my girlfriend, would react if she knew what had just taken place, "that's my butt."

"It's my butt now..." she taunted, with a suggestive smirk.

Some time later, a guest was offended by seeing a male staff member grope the breasts of a female server from behind. The guest asked to speak to the manager to complain. Little did they know, it was the manager that they had just seen perpetrating the "playful" act. After that incident, the new rule was that we could only grope each other in the kitchen, away from the eyes of guests.

When we wanted to drink, we'd go to the bartender wearing a lobster bib. It was a (very not) discrete code for asking for a shot.

When we were hungry, we'd just order food and then claim we screwed up ringing it in. When we wanted to party, it involved giant inflatable children's slides with little-to-no clothing and handles of vodka, or enormous bowls of Jungle Juice that contained God-knows-what other substances. We lived in the Wild West of the restaurant industry, and it was a blast.

Over the next four years, I would go on to become a very strong server, in addition to serving as a trainer, administrative assistant, intern, and shift supervisor. I never fit into the drug scene, as I was still adamant that if I should end up running for political office at some point, I wasn't interested in trying anything and looking like an idiot like Bill Clinton did during his MTV interview.[46] In a committed relationship with Kristy, I also never fit into the casual sex scene, much the chagrin of a number of my colleagues, male and female alike, who all thought it was funny to see if they could be the one to persuade me to cheat on her. I did fit into the work, though, and I was good at what I did. On Saturday nights, after working all open hours since midday Thursday, I'd offer to close the restaurant for the friend who wanted to leave early for a party. Bright and early on Sunday mornings, I'd bring in bagels while everyone else tried to push through their hangovers. I covered for both the dining room manager and bar manager when their respective, and coincidental, maternity and paternity leaves overlapped for a few weeks. It was hard, exhausting, and back-breaking work, but I loved my job.

One night, a friend and I were sitting at the bar relaxing after a long night of serving. Three drinks in, the conversation suddenly switched from causal to heavy. We were talking about the future, and she shared that she was concerned she would never be able to have kids. I asked why she thought that and learned that she had aborted three pregnancies, and that her now mid-20's reproductive system was no longer functioning normally. She eventually said, "I totally used abortion as a birth control, and now I regret it."

Years later, I became acquaintances with a fiercely conservative and devout Catholic. He shared with me a story about his wife's pregnancy. At a regular OB appointment, the doctor alerted the couple to the fact that something was critically wrong with the baby. He informed them that the baby had a less than 10% chance of surviving, and if the mother attempted to deliver the baby, her odds of survival were about 50%. They learned this at 9 months – Days before they were expecting to meet their child. The couple was faced with a decision to attempt the birth and likely lose the lives of both mother and child, or terminate the late-term pregnancy, which went against everything they stood for earlier that morning. His wife lived.

In 2013, my church called a new associate pastor. Having spent a decade in the restaurant industry, combined with a reputation for having planned and successfully executed nearly 800 events during my career, I was asked to coordinate the party to celebrate the important day for our congregation. The day of installing Pastor Curt was Father's Day.

I woke early and was surprised to walk into the kitchen to find that Kristy had made pancakes for breakfast. We sat together and enjoyed a quiet moment before she slid an envelope across the table. I opened a card that said, "Happy Father's Day." I was confused, as we had no children. I then opened the card and found a pregnancy test inside. I was absolutely thrilled.

A few weeks later, Kristy and I traveled 12 hours North with her parents to Copper Harbor, a remote town in the Upper Peninsula of Michigan, for the 4th of July holiday to gather with her extended family for a reunion. They were reliving various experiences she had as a child, and reminisced about the peak of the annual reunion a decade earlier when there were over 70 family members in attendance. Kristy's sister, Kelly, and her Australian husband, Chris, were visiting from overseas, as well. It was an opportunity to hang out with my brother-in-law and watch our wives relive great memories from their youth.

At some point we stopped at a large still pond that was covered in gold pollen. The scene was otherworldly, and it felt in that moment that we were the only ones in the UP. Chris and I skipped rocks while the girls walked around with their mother, looking at stones and taking pictures. As two couples, the four of us posed for a portrait near the shoreline. It was a really cute shot that for years I couldn't stand to look at because of what happened immediately after.

Kristy said she needed to use the restroom and walked to the nearby outhouse. When she came back, I could tell something wasn't right. She wasn't sure exactly what was wrong, nor could she see much in the dark environment, but she knew that she had started to bleed. I wanted to throw up, but I also knew that it was important to stay calm and not cause her any additional stress. I also didn't want to stir anything up and have her parents get unnecessarily nervous. We made up some bullshit excuse and got everyone to head back to the lodge that we were staying in together.

The bleeding didn't stop, and my unease continued to grow. Denial wasn't changing anything, and neither was prayer. I started to beg God to make everything be okay, while trying to keep a smiling face at a family dinner full of people who were strangers to me. We went as a group to watch fireworks, but all I could think of was the fact that my 8-week pregnant wife was now spotting to the point of needing to use a maxi pad. I was in my head the whole night, praying, begging, and pleading to God to make the baby be okay. Later that night, it was clear that the pregnancy had ended.

"Fuck you. We're done."

There have been a handful of incredibly dark points in my life, but this was the darkest. I couldn't move. I couldn't eat. I could barely talk. I wanted to die. I wanted to end my life to be with the baby. I dared God to kill me so I could be with the child that we wanted so badly. "Fuck you. We're done." I repeated that statement in silent dialog more times than I can count, hoping that if I said it enough, God would finally send a lightning bolt through the roof of the lodge and kill me. Then at least I'd be with the baby.

Lightning never came, and that pissed me off, too.

The next 12 hours were just pain, tears, and anger. I was distraught and inconsolable. My wife, the one who physically experienced the life and death of our first child, was the strong one throughout this trauma. I couldn't talk to anyone, and didn't want to hear the tragic apologies that could never come close to bringing peace. Kristy's poor father was distraught, and wanted nothing more than to take the pain away from us. I wasn't ready and couldn't deal with it. Chris, the visitor from the other side of the world who was here to be on vacation, didn't seem to have any idea of what to do. No one really did. Especially us. Feeling like vomiting and sobbing were the only things I could comprehend.

We left for the nearest hospital, something like an hour away. We called Pastor Dave on the way. He pained for us, knowing that we were both so ready to be parents. I'm sure he tried to console us, but there was little he could do other than pray. I wasn't going to in that moment, still trying to tempt God to kill me, so I was glad to have someone else do it on our behalf.

There are some moments in life that we remember vividly every single detail. The hospital visit was one of those for me. Pulling up to the mostly empty building, staring at an ultrasound that clearly had no fetus in the image, waiting for*ever* for the results... "Spontaneous abortion," is what the anxious, obviously brand-new, Doogie Houser-looking doctor called it. The physically small young man's nervous tell was a smile, which was massively inappropriate in the context of the moment, almost making it appear as if he thought the situation was funny. His emotional intelligence was approximately zero. It physically took everything in my power to keep myself seated and not stand up to strangle the little prick against the wall for using such a cold medical term to describe our loss. I pictured his feet kicking and then dangling against the pale-yellow cinder block wall more times than is appropriate. Kristy was cleared as healthy, but the pregnancy was officially over.

★ ★ ★

We often hear politicians attempt to stoke their base to support or damn the topic of abortion by using examples of a woman who uses the procedure as a form of birth control, or of instances where a person would desire to terminate a baby late into the third trimester. I happen to personally know individuals who have experienced both extreme outlier scenarios, and I can share that neither were happy.

Some years later, I had the opportunity to train a group of Fortune 400 managers about opinions. This was actually the point that I realized I would eventually need to leave being a Dale Carnegie trainer, as I was so firmly engrained in my mindset toward conflict that I accidentally taught the exercise incorrectly. I basically taught an early version of this book instead of the lesson I was meant to. It was also the first time that I completely and unintentionally realized that I am pro-choice.

As a Christian, the go-to attitude towards abortion is that it is wrong.[47] Having all three of these stories to inform me, I shared that my opinion on the topic of abortion is not that is it either "right" or "wrong," but rather a deeply personal, and often tragic, decision for those who have to make it. Something I learned from my own experiences and from the countless individuals who have confided in me about their abortions over the years, is that no one *wants* to have an abortion. Some individuals would benefit from pre-operation counseling that may inform their decision such that they choose not to have the operation. Others have no choice. I shared with this group of managers that it was my personal opinion that the decision to abort a child is not only tragic, but incredibly disrespectful to those who wish to have a child and are unable to. This was my opinion, formed by my experiences. I then shared that I had come to the conclusion that, even though I don't personally support the act, this topic is too personal and emotionally-bound for any group of elected officials to determine whether it is "right" or "wrong," and that each individual should have the right and responsibility to make that determination for themselves. In that moment, having backed the opinion with evidence, even the staunchest anti-abortionists in the room, of which there were many, felt compassion and gained a sense of understanding for those who face this heartbreaking decision in their life. They later shared that this series of stories helped them to realize that the issue of abortion is not as black and white as it is painted to be. Through this understanding, they all came to respect that the choices of one individual are based on the unique experiences of that individual.

I want to make an important note of distinction here: While I personally believe that every pregnant person should have the right to choose, I do not personally believe that abortion is the right choice in my life. Kristy and I were very happy with two children before we were surprised to discover that she was pregnant with a third. After the shock subsided, we both asked if we wanted to have the third child, and both decided that terminating the unplanned pregnancy was not the right choice for us. We're blessed to have Brooks in our lives, and we would not change our decision to bring him into this world. The purpose of calling out this distinction is that even though I don't agree with making the choice to terminate a pregnancy in my life, that doesn't mean that I don't support other people having access to that option if they believe that it is the most appropriate path forward for them.

I have deep respect for those who are advocates of the cause to protect the lives of unborn children. There appears, at least to me, to be an increasingly vocal opposition to advocating for a person to birth a child, even if they do not intend to raise it. This suggests that being pro-life is becoming socially more difficult with time. I do believe personally that the cause is important and valuable, particularly when done with care and compassion for The Other. I am not pro-choice because I am opposed to the protection of innocents. I am pro-choice because I do not believe that others should be subjected to my definition of "right."

We are not obligated to agree with ourselves, nor are we obligated to say, "what's true for me must also be true for you." Such blanket approaches aren't realistic or possible in acknowledging the uniqueness of each person's life. We'll explore this more in the chapter on Metaethics, which serves as the philosophical core of our thought experiment.

★ ★ ★

A few months after Kristy's miscarriage, we lost a second child. The doctor advised that we pause our attempts at pregnancy for at least five months to let her body recover from the trauma it had twice experienced that summer. That second time we were just numb. I was further angry with God, but at this point I was completely apathetic toward God and my faith. We sheepishly arrived for another OB appointment a month later after we were surprised to discover that Kristy was pregnant for the third time. The doctor scolded us more than he expressed joy, but it was out of concern for our mental wellbeing, as we now had a track record to consider. I felt like I held my breath for 9 months, and my unease completely robbed me of the joy of the pregnancy, but fortunately, Bree was born happy and healthy a little more than a year after our first tragic experience.

The first time I told the story about our miscarriage, it took me 45 minutes of crying with a friend before I could even get out the first words. It took years before I could say the word "miscarriage," and years longer until the word stopped causing me physical pain whenever I saw or read it. I was deeply impacted by this experience.

My relationship with God was critically damaged during this whole process. Even with that being the case, I could sense the presence of a Higher Power, just like when I was a suicidal 19-year-old. For the next couple of years, our relationship felt more like a phone call from an old friend who you are no longer close with – Nice, but not necessary or valuable. I never lost my faith, but it took me a long time to feel reverent again. This bothered me, but it didn't change my faith-based behaviors or habits – They just felt empty. It took a few more years, but eventually my anger subsided, and I came to the understanding that if it weren't for those first two experiences, we would not have Bree in our lives. Further, the cadence of our lives may have been altered in such a way that none of our children would be born, and instead we may potentially have completely different kids in our lives. I cannot say that I'm happy with the experiences Kristy and I had, but I can say that I would not change them now, as our children are an absolute blessing in our lives. And while this is not intended to be a book about religion, for those who now question my perspective on faith as it pertains to this book, or who are concerned for my personal faith journey, my relationship with God continues to improve with time.

★ ★ ★

As a person who for the majority of their life has felt the unyielding responsibility to run for political office with the goal of truly serving the people, I expect that this chapter will be used against me by the Right to Life and others who would seek to disparage my character and make this into an example as to why I would be a poor elected official. As a conservative, I have consciously included my pro-choice beliefs to share with you as an example. For better or worse, and political leverage be damned, I believe that being compassionate towards others and trusting that each individual is the best person to make the decisions in their own life, makes for a Leader who is more fully equipped to represent *all* people as opposed to the few. If I do run for office someday, and the people choose not to elect me for being honest about my beliefs, it will be clear that they aren't ready for me to serve them anyway.

I committed to you at the beginning of this book that I would seek to avoid sharing my own personal opinion on these various topics in attempt not to discredit myself in your eyes or to sway your own personal beliefs about any given topic. Up until this point, my opinion has been shared as a challenge for you to reflect on your reaction. You have invested time and money to learn from my experiences and those of others – I respect that too much to violate your trust. This example was intentionally included to demonstrate to you how deeply intimate the decision-making process is for those around you. You may be the most pro-life person on this planet, and now have a less positive view of me. That again is your right and prerogative. I support and honor your commitment to the sanctity of life, particularly if you demonstrate care and compassion toward those who behave differently than you would hope.

And, people live their lives for themselves, not for you.

★ ★ ★

Sex

As a child, I remember getting into consistent arguments with my mother. I'm the first-born, for my first 20 years had the tendency to believe that I was infallible, and am still pretty immovable when I am convicted about something. My mother had similar tendencies. This led to a number of fights that dragged on for hours, climaxed in tears, and resulted in each of us realizing that we were both trying to accomplish the same goal all along, just using different means. After each battle, our relationship grew stronger, as we had an ever-increasing respect for one another once the realization phase had completed. This interesting and repetitive experience led me to seriously entertain becoming a lawyer, as I found the practice of debate to be both mentally and emotionally exhilarating. Until I was nearly 30, I believed that the best way to deal with conflict was head-on, with the goal of breaking everything down to its constituent parts and then ultimately building it all back up, renewed once both parties were on the same page.

One recurring conflict I realized that I had experienced throughout my career, and which most certainly was subliminally inspired by my interactions with my mother, had boggled me for years. In virtually every organization I had worked for, and in which I had a female supervisor, I had found myself in some iteration of conflict with the individual. While there were certainly disagreements with my male supervisors, and a number of substantial conflicts, the outcomes with my female supervisors seemed more stinging and detrimental to the integrity of our relationship.

In my first couple of jobs, I discounted the conflicts as The Other being negative or disagreeable. I thought, "I'm not the only person to have challenges with her, so it must be her."

As I moved to my third and fourth jobs, at that point beginning my actual career, I found that the issue persisted. Again, I wasn't the only person to have conflict with these women, but I was now moving into peer-level relationships as a leader within the organizations, and the conflicts continued.

Throughout this time, I would occasionally reflect, and at one point even asked myself, "Do I have a problem with authority, or do I have a problem with having a female supervisor?" I struggled with this thought, because I tend to befriend more women than men, and I have high regard for all of them. "They aren't your superior, though," I would think to myself. Then one day I finally figured it out.

There was a situation where my female supervisor and I found ourselves in a long-simmering conflict for at least the third time in so many years. The tension continued for about three months before I finally decided to tackle the issue. She was truly my boss, but our relationship was originally intended to be such where we worked collaboratively and equally. As such, I treated her as a peer rather than a supervisor, though I openly acknowledged that she ultimately had the final say.

I had spent my education and career focused on business, while she had spent her education and career focused on education. Our partnership was logical for an education consulting firm, and we mutually needed the other for the organization's success. I was in the beginning of the middle portion of my career, while she had been in that phase of her career for about a decade. My career had been spent in an environment of intensely emotional workplaces, casual swearing, open sexual relationships, abundant access to drugs, and extreme abuse of alcohol. Her career had been spent in an environment of protocol and behaviors that were far more "sterile" than I preferred to behave. As I was reflecting on the months of tension, I realized that I couldn't keep making the same excuses I had made in the past, and that it was time to step up to being the Leader I needed to be, even if that meant swallowing my pride. I decided to sit down with her and hash out our conflict.

I shared my perception of our conflict, and my reflection on other times we had been in conflict. The common denominator seemed to be that she became frustrated with me when I reacted to a notable situation in a way that she felt was flippant or too casual. She agreed. I shared that in my decade of restaurant management, in a crisis we moved fast, swore more, and acted rapidly to find a solution. Having been the responsible party to navigate through situations as serious as attempted robberies, physical altercations, life-threatening substance abuses, and a woman experiencing a heart attack and dying in my restaurant, I learned to react swiftly, and not worry about crossing T's and dotting I's until after the immediate crisis had subsided. This individual was much more measured, minded her words carefully, and wanted to ensure all instances of liability were covered before acting. Both of our mindsets had served the organization well in varying scenarios, and had led to our mutual success, though they were diametrically opposite to one another. This specific instance of conflict we were facing was not the result of me not taking things seriously, as she admitted to believing privately for months, but rather I had dealt with a crisis in the way that was not in alignment with how she preferred that I operate.

I shared with her that my behavior was a result of my experiences, and given the context of the environment we were in, it was not her responsibility to conform to me, but rather that I needed to conform to my environment. This realization and acknowledgment that different people have different experiences, and that those experiences directly impact their behavior, is important. It's important because we all believe what we believe based on those experiences. Neither she nor I were "wrong" in this situation. Conversely, neither of us were "right." I was operating under my context, and she was operating under hers. Both of us wanted the same positive outcomes, we were just achieving them differently, just as my mother and I regularly experienced in our conflicts. There *was* a more appropriate standard of actions and behaviors, though. There was a better way to be more productive in dealing with the situation, given the environment we were in. When I realized that I could change my behavior – and chose to – it changed our relationship, and made both of us more successful.

I went on to engage in more private reflection and realized that I didn't have a problem with female authority, but rather I had a problem with owning my role in conflict. I was also able to determine that it had been merely a coincidence that this had occurred in my life more with women than men. When I changed *my* behavior, it reduced the conflict in all of my interactions, including those with my mother. In the years since, I've been fortunate to continue to learn from my mother, and she has similarly learned from me. I truly believe that my interest and passion for conflict management stemmed from my relationship with her. And now we've both had the opportunity to help and serve one another to be better than we previously were.

There's No Such Thing as Right and Wrong

★ ★ ★

I was homeschooled and in high school in the early 2000's, and by that point I was very homophobic. The attitude wasn't instilled in me by my parents, it was just a matter of falling in line with the viewpoints of my Christian faith combined with the overwhelming egocentrism that I believed that all gay men wanted to have sex with me, even though that clearly wasn't true of all women. I'm embarrassed by my behavior now, but back then I used slurs, made derogatory statements, and believed things like, "they'll all burn in Hell." I also didn't know a single gay person.

A short while later, as a freshman in college, I started working in the restaurant industry and was surrounded by a bunch of individuals from the LGBTQIA+ community. It was early 2004, and the conversation around homosexuality being a choice or a trait at birth was being hotly debated. Having no first-person knowledge about homosexuality, aside from the fact that I was still uncomfortable around those who were gay, I decided to ask questions of the person who was the most tolerant of my naïvety. I had become relatively close with a gentleman, and asked him one evening as we were closing the restaurant, "I know you won't judge me for asking this, and I genuinely am curious: Were you born gay, or do you choose to be?" He responded with an answer that transformed my way of thinking.

He said, "I felt like I was different as far back as being a toddler in diapers. I believe I was born this way. I also know that I'm happier being in a relationship with another man. I don't *actually* know if I was born gay or not, but I know that I'm happier this way. If that means that I'm choosing to be gay, I don't care. I'm choosing to be happy."

Choosing to be happy. Who doesn't want to be happy? That statement was like an earthquake in my mind. I suddenly realized that people are living their lives for themselves, not to appease the beliefs of those around them. You – YOU – are living your life for yourself. Not for me, or anyone else. You make choices every single day that point you in the direction of living a happier life. Who gives a shit about the choices someone else makes in order to live a happy life?

Like a light switch, I immediately stopped being homophobic, because I understood The Other wanted to be happy, just like me. That meant that they weren't different than me at all – They were *just like me*. My new understanding left me no choice but to respect those that I had once condemned. With this newfound respect, I made countless friends in the LGBTQIA+ community, including one of my very best friends, Britt, who was the first person I asked to join me in serving others at my company, Leadership Coaching for Results. I've had the opportunity to learn from her, be counseled by her, attend her beautiful wedding, share endless laughs with her, and work with her to serve people so they can live the life they need and want to live. She is my friend, and nothing in our relationship would have been possible if I weren't willing to seek to understand The Other so many years earlier.

★ ★ ★

If I could control one outcome from this book, it would be that every reader, including you, is more inclined to understand The Other. I do not believe that anyone should change their beliefs or opinions unless they feel that they want to – Changing our opinions should occur organically in order to be authentic. With that said, I do believe, based on experience and research, that we'd all be better off if we intentionally sought to understand those who think and act differently than us. When we do this, we can't help but to show the other person respect. And with respect, we can choose to collaborate with The Other instead of perpetuating the divisiveness that has become so prevalent in our society.

You see, we do not have to personally agree with the choices The Other makes in order for us to respect them. We also do not need to change our deeply-held opinions and beliefs that have been informed by our decades of lived experiences. However, we do have a choice to respect those that we consider to be different from us. Those people who are different from you have lived a different life than you – It's completely natural that what is right for you and what is right for them will not always be the same thing. The cool part is, regardless of the choices we each make, we're all making choices that point us to the same goal: Happiness.

In the heat of the gay marriage debate, I shared with conservative Christian friends that gay marriage has nothing to do with our faith, and everything to do with their happiness. They argued that such behavior is not Christian, and therefore shouldn't be allowed. I then challenged them back, as a conservative Christian who was *just like them*, and said, "then we should prevent Muslims, atheists, Buddhists, and any other non-Christian from getting married, too. If we are to prevent a portion of the community from participating in the activity of marriage because it violates our Christian faith, other portions of the population should be excluded, too. Or, we can accept that there are two forms of marriage – Legal marriage and faith-based marriage. As Christians, we just so happened to have both occur simultaneously. Churches should remain free to refuse to marry anyone who does not subscribe to their beliefs, just as the Catholic Church denies me communion as a Lutheran. And all individuals should have the legal right to be married in a court of law."

My objective was not to "win" an argument, but rather to exercise weighing the facts in real-time with someone who held an opposing view, and help them to put their own personal biases aside long enough to come to a conclusion that serves the greatest number of people. In all cases, it worked.

You have this power, too. If you can't see it yet, you will by the time we're done together.

★ ★ ★

In the fine dining restaurant I managed in Minneapolis, I had many gay employees, as we were located in the third most populous LGBTQIA+ community in the country, based on per capita. One evening a group of four guys came in for dinner after finishing a day of golf. At the door they were cracking jokes and harassing each other like four guys are wont to do. While escorting them at their table, I heard a joke about "fags." Knowing that the server of the table I was seating them at was gay, I immediately had a young attractive female server take the table, thinking this would be an easy win for her, and would avoid subjecting my employee to harassment. Ironically, the male server was offended that I would "protect" him when he felt confident in his ability to fend for himself, and the female server was mad afterward because the four guys didn't tip her as well as they should have.

While both servers understood my actions were intended to be helpful and positive, neither were satisfied with what I

There's No Such Thing as Right and Wrong

did or the outcome. They felt that I had treated each of them unjustly. Given the scenario, I was not at that time willing to change my mind, as I had no intention of potentially subjecting one of my employees to harassment by a guest, and no amount of tip money for a server was more important than protecting my team. As a result of my actions, I inadvertently became the focus of a sexual harassment case study within the largest restaurant company in the world. This unique situation was analyzed and added to management training, and used as an example of what not to do in regard to diversity and sensitivity. Ironically, a senior manager told me that she respected my actions, and would have done the exact same thing in my situation, but instead of switching the servers and explaining why, she would have "accidentally" sat the group at a different table.

The lesson I learned was not, "don't protect your team," nor was it, "do allow your team to fend for themselves in the face of likely discrimination," but rather, "do what you think is right, even if it costs you." I'm proud of the way this story played out, because I know I did what I believed was right, even though it caused me unnecessary headaches afterward. I share it here with you to inspire you to do what you think is right, even if others disagree. This may seem counterintuitive to the whole premise of the book, but that's the purpose of sharing this example: Even though there is not a universal "right" and "wrong" for all things, we each hold our own beliefs and we *should* act on them, particularly if the intention is to help, serve, and protect others from having their happiness or fulfillment infringed upon.

★ ★ ★

There is inherent conflict in the gender differences of individuals. Behavioral styles, social interactions, preferences, and a whole slew of variables are naturally different between men and women and those on the broader spectrum of gender identity.[48] To support this notion, when training folks in a group-setting I will often ask those in attendance to raise their hand if they have a sibling. More often than not, most people raise their hand. I then follow that up by asking if anyone has a twin. Typically, there is at least one person for every 20 or so that have a twin. I then specifically ask one of the individuals with a twin about the preferences they have, and if those match up with their sibling. Every single time, the answer is that the preferences are different. I then challenge everyone to think about this: "Two people who were in the same womb at the same time, raised in the same home with the same parents, somehow," and with a bit of sarcasm, "mysteriously, don't magically agree on everything! If that's the case, how the hell could you ever expect anyone else you come into contact with to agree with you on even a majority of topics?"

The silver bullet to conflict isn't to try to agree with everyone, or to try and force everyone to agree with you, but rather to understand the other party, work through our differences, and allow those differences to make our collaborative efforts stronger and more robust. When we choose to do this, being the bigger person in the conflict if you will, a wonderful outcome naturally occurs – Our lives are enriched by engaging with those who are different than us.

★ ★ ★

Media

In the era of 24/7 news coverage, there has been a notable shift from investigative journalism backed with confirmed sources to talking heads pontificating based on speculation, "anonymous sources," and spewing ad revenue-generating inflammatory monologues by nationally syndicated mouthpieces. Content is king, and the reality is that in a 24-hour news cycle, there isn't enough objective content to keep the wheels turning without the transition to opinion-based "reporting." Media personalities like MSNBC's Rachel Maddow, CNN's Don Lemon, and Fox News' Tucker Carlson are prime examples of prominent opinion media personalities posing as journalists. While they truly are addressing current news stories, they morph the commentary based on their individual worldview and those of their employing network. These individuals have resorted to name-calling and deceitful sharing of information in order to continue to keep their viewers captivated. They are not behaving as the revered journalists they likely dreamed to become as children, but rather they are selling themselves as entertainment for the masses under the guise of reporting "facts." These folks that we get our information from are not journalists – They're prostitutes.

Research into the impact that the media has on the public got really interesting when an analytical review was used to determine the degree at which, if any, the reporting of terror attacks leads to more terror attacks.[49] Using significant statistical analysis, the idea that news coverage of a tragedy would in fact inspire more acts of terrorism may seem unlikely on the face, but proved to be more real than was initially anticipated.

The stated research problem was to determine, "that there exists a feedback loop between the share of media capacity devoted to terrorism and terrorist activity." The study produced an exhaustive statistical model utilizing data from the Global Terrorism Database (GTD) and existing work from other authors in regard to the perceptions of media coverage and their implications. Ultimately and unfortunately, the hypothesis was proven to be true. The caveat was that in the short run, media coverage does not increase the instance of terrorist attacks, though there is evidence to suggest the media increases the severity of previously planned attacks that are scheduled to take place in the short run of two months. In the medium run, of up to 10 months, there was also evidence to suggest that media coverage does in fact inspire additional attacks, therefore proving the hypothesis of the feedback loop.

This proves that not only does the media have the power to inform the public, but they also have the ability to sway public opinion and to influence behaviors and outcomes that can lead to tragedy. This being true, it is logical that countless individuals believed the assertions made by President Donald Trump, that the media is the enemy of the people. Such an argument from one of the world's most powerful elected officials, and perceived by many as a leader, certainly has the ability to impact the perception of the way people think about any large institution. With the advent of opinion reporting and the competition for ratings that lead directly to advertising dollars, it is easy to realize that the original intention of journalism and the current realities of the industry are not in alignment. That isn't to say that all news stations, reporters, or stories are wrong, manipulative, or subversive. Your local news reporters may very well be clean of bias, and certainly there are those at the national level who operate with integrity, though they are increasingly in the minority. With that said, in this 24-hour news cycle era, you and I now have the responsibility to be wary of the degree to which we allow any "journalist" to directly inform our opinions.

There's No Such Thing as Right and Wrong

★ ★ ★

Two incidents with popular media personalities occurred in one week in 2017. In both instances the liberal antagonist apologized, but the victim(s) damned them further after the apology – And rightfully, because they both immediately revealed that their apologies were actually bullshit.

Kathy Griffin posed for a photo with a bloodied, decapitated head of President Trump, and Bill Maher called himself a racial slur on HBO. Both of these individuals abused their power of public positions to make statements that added value to no one, and offended many. Griffin apologized, then within hours of being fired from CNN tried to blame Trump, saying, "He broke me... I don't think I have a career after this."[50]

Maher, in an interview with Sen. Ben Sasse, said, "I've got to get to Nebraska more," to which the Senator replied, "You're welcome. We'd love to have you work in the fields with us." Maher retorted, "Work the fields? Senator, I'm a house nigger." While he was quick to claim it was a joke, the offense is plain, and it opens up questions as to why that response was what immediately came to mind. While he apologized the next day, he positioned the offense as if it caused him to suffer unduly by saying, "Friday nights [the night of recording] are always my worst night of sleep... Last night was a particularly long night."[51]

Apologizing and then further antagonizing or playing the victim isn't truthful, honest, or sincere. It's clear, based on their behavior, that neither individual truly felt sorry for their actions, but rather were apologizing because it was the socially appropriate step to avoid further consequences. While Griffin did lose her job over the incident, Maher did not.

Contrasting the public reaction of these two with a popular comedian like Dave Chappelle is also interesting. In late 2021, Chappelle released his sixth of six contracted projects with Netflix. Titled *The Closer*, the stand-up special drew massive controversy over the handling of a series of jokes and comments about the transgender community. In watching the special, which is overwhelmingly off-color, it's clear that two things took place: first, Chappelle does in fact use terms that are offensive to the transgender community, while ironically striving to appeal to them; and second, the articles and damnation pointed at the comedian almost all seemed to miss the overall apologetic intent of the segment, which demonstrates that those who were the loudest and angriest about the bit likely didn't actually watch the special in order to understand the proper context for themselves, but instead fell victim to groupthink.

In the conclusion of the special, Chappelle shares a sprawling story of a friend from the transgender community, and how that individual's experience with cancel culture ended in tragedy. The entire point of the story, while littered with offensive terminology, was to make the case for being more open, accepting, and more tolerant of those whom we disagree with or do not understand, as Chappelle himself learned. It's a strange and politically incorrect apology to the community he offended in the past, and a plea for unity moving forward. It's clear that many completely missed the point, distracted instead by the terms he either didn't understand were rude, which he admits during the special, or were used intentionally as a part of the jokes that were interspersed.

To Chappelle's credit, in the immediate fallout of the special's release, which generated extreme controversy that some suggested Netflix desired for the sake of publicity (Which worked

– We're discussing it here), he continued to stand behind what he said, even going so far as to say that he would turn the special into a tour if it were removed from the streaming service. The sketch was itself an apology, so to apologize for the apology, however distasteful some may have felt it was, would be disingenuous. An apology would be similar to saying, "those people ruined my career," like Griffin did.

I have no skin in the game when it comes to Chappelle, and I'm not seeking to defend someone who has the right and responsibility to do that for themself. I personally felt that some of his jokes crossed the line, but I also knew what I was getting into by watching his comedy. The purpose of pointing out this story in particular is to highlight how emotionally-charged some conflict becomes, which proves to override people's ability to think critically about said conflict. If the LGBTQIA+ community or others want to cancel Chappelle over this special, they are entitled to do so by voting with their dollars, viewership, and Likes. Ironically, cancellation of an individual who came to his defense is what led a person to committing suicide, and serves as a cautionary tale that is the entire point of the bit. There is no denying that words are powerful, and that they can permanently impact a person either positively or negatively. We may not agree with Chappelle's choice of words, but there is a lot more to unpack and understand from his jokes and agenda for the special than *just* the words he used.

★ ★ ★

All individuals are the product of the sum of their cumulative lived experiences and circumstances. While mediating conflict, I often use the line from the restaurant manager parable: "We believe what we believe based on the sum of our life experiences." This means that individuals are inherently incapable of being truly neutral in regard to their own cognitive bias. As a result, even the most seasoned conflict practitioner invariably encounters situations where there is a very minor, though overall significant, bias toward or against a party in conflict. With this being true of trained professionals, it's understandable why the average person would struggle to listen, view, or engage in conflict feeling free of angst or frustration. The challenge, though, is that if we avoid conflict entirely, we remove our opportunity to hear contrasting viewpoints, learn new perspectives, and become more well-rounded in our understanding of those we care about. This is the danger of cancel culture, in that starting social movements to cancel things that make us uncomfortable actually cause more societal silos and echo chambers which serve to exacerbate the problems that the cancellation sought to resolve.

Let me be clear, I am not advocating for the permissibility of sexual predators and those who abuse their power, like Harvey Weinstein. Those criminals deserve every bad thing that comes to them, because they infringed on the happiness and fulfillment of others by using coercion and intimidation to violate innocent people. Those villains deserve to be cancelled. What we're discussing here are the opinions and statements that a mob jury on social media find offense and start hashtags to end careers.

If Kathy Griffin were truly cancelled for the photograph glamorizing the execution of the president, and she hasn't had much work since her termination from CNN, the question is what message we missed, like those who missed the point and criticized Chappelle. I personally can't think of something valuable that was missed in Griffin's cancellation, but that doesn't mean that my own biases have clouded my ability to see it. The point is, cancelling people comes with a cost. In some cases, it's careers. In others, it's lives. In all, it's the removal of a contrasting viewpoint that we have the opportunity to learn from, even if the lesson is that we become further entrenched in our own opinions.

★ ★ ★

When I was a teenager I was really into Eminem. Growing up in a conservative homeschooling family, Eminem was a refreshing change of pace to me, and a source of toxicity in the eyes of my father. I remember my Dad saying one time, "People vote with their dollars. Whatever we spend money on shows them what they can or cannot do. If we don't spend money on them, they change or go away." I spent lots of money on Eminem over the years because I enjoy his music. But there were times where I felt he crossed a line or was out of sync with what I personally believed, and so I wouldn't listen to those songs or would choose to buy the songs I did like individually online. Lots of people voted with their dollars to support Eminem, and he's still around 25 years later because of it. Compare that with bands who are one-hit wonders. Not enough people voted with their dollars, and they disappeared forever. Even established brands like Piers Morgan can be eliminated when the public no longer stands behind the things they say or do. We vote every day with our dollars, viewership, Likes, and actions. We vote for the world we have by supporting these folks, and we can vote for the world we want by demanding better.

★ ★ ★

While I have just outlined the dangers of cancel culture, the activity is actually a social phenomenon that supports exactly what I'm advocating for in this chapter. It is used to influence our culture in a way that removes problematic individuals from prominent roles. Starting with the #MeToo movement to remove those in Hollywood who grossly misused their power over the future opportunities and careers of actors, these sexual predators lost their careers, like Kevin Spacey, and some even faced criminal charges, like Weinstein. There were others who got caught in the crossfire with actions that are not appropriate, but also maybe not worth ending careers, like Johnny Depp. Holding actors and film producers accountable to the misdeeds against individuals is appropriate, but what would happen if we pointed this social weapon at politicians and blatantly biased media talking heads? Those who abuse their power to accrue more power, and whose misdeeds negatively impact the cultural fabric of our American society through inciting unnecessary division and conflict would be fantastic candidates for cancellation. How do individuals like Senators Ted Cruz, Rand Paul, Dianne Feinstein, and Bernie Sanders become multi-millionaires on federal salaries of $174,000? By misusing and abusing their power, and by sowing the seeds of division that help them to get re-elected every six years. They pay lip service to the base that forgives and forgets their less savory behaviors, and then more than 90% of the time, they get re-elected simply because they are the incumbent on the ballot.[52]

The problem with allowing these individuals to continue their poor performance and behavior without being cancelled is that it makes hypocrites out of all of us, as we continue to prop up bigger hypocrites who continue to slowly wedge us further apart from one and other. By turning a blind eye to the misdeeds of the candidate that is representing our party of choice (specifically not the people, but the party) and by tuning in to negative opinion reporting from media prostitutes, we are unintentionally supporting and sustaining the system that has so effectively learned how to divide us. Then we start arguing with one and other about topics without actually investigating the content itself for the potential merits they may provide. Or we falsely claim to have "done our research" on the topic because we watched a "journalist" report only the details that support their network's ad revenue agenda, watched a 5-minute social media video by some 40-year-old conspiracy theorist who lives in the basement with his parents, or read an article published by an anonymous author on some no-name website. That is not research.

Let me say it again: That is not research. Research is studying the content itself and the content behind the content by reading selections from the citations; reading journal articles about the subject and other topics from the same authors to start to understand their inherent biases; and taking part in the real-world study of a subject by interviewing experts who have invested their education and careers into a topic. Almost nobody you or I know *actually* "does their research" on a topic that became hot in the media 24 hours earlier. They instead are influenced and manipulated by the social media algorithms, media talking heads, and politicians that are trying to get them to follow blindly along so they can all continue to make more money, all while we continue to have greater division between our neighbors and family members. And they get away with it because they know the majority of us won't do real research. In this story, the American people are the losers.

What we could choose to do instead is hold our politicians and "journalists" accountable to the standard that we hold their opponents. If we would say, "Can you believe that moron did XYZ?!" then we should have a similar amount of outrage when the person we prefer to listen to makes the same type of foolish mistake. When we do this, we regain control of the narrative in our own minds, and then over time, we can be the source of powerful change that disallows for these people to manipulate and use us. Their jobs are to serve us. Their jobs are 100% solely and entire designed to SERVE US. If you're sick and tired of being sick and tired, you are the only one who has the power to stand up and say, "enough is enough." And when we all do, their game, with all of us as their pawns, will start to crumble beneath their feet. Then it will be our responsibility to either stand up and serve, or hold up those around us who will do a more effective job of serving, regardless of their political party.

★ ★ ★

When you choose to follow the path I'm recommending, you become part of the positively-oriented cultural change this book is advocating for. As a result, you play a role in the transformation of the very nature of conflict resolution that has already begun. Just because I was formally trained to do this doesn't mean that you can't – In fact, you can. It is no longer necessary that a trained "neutral mediator" arbitrate an argument, simply for the fact that restorative justice exists. In this situation, where the mediator may very well be a participant in the offended party, anyone with an intentionally calm demeanor and desire to understand The Other can mediate conflict between two parties. In the Understanding chapter, I'll show you a series of tools to do just this.

The interesting outcome of a restorative justice mediator potentially being a participant in the community that was offended by the perpetrator is that, as humans, we are all emotional creatures that are subject to the biological influences of the hypothalamus, and our natural "fight or flight" mechanism. This being the case, there is inherently an opportunity for the practitioner to overtly or inadvertently shift the progression of the mediation, if triggered. This possible outcome may be able to be prevented, though, if the mediator (you) also happens to have been the type of child that would have successfully completed the "marshmallow dilemma," and would therefore be more inclined to calmly wait through a scenario in order to earn a larger reward, rather than impulsively taking a smaller reward.[53]

Further, there are instances where individuals, are so committed to the greater good that they are willing to work against their own self-interests in order to ensure that the community at large is not unduly harmed. We typically call these types of individuals Whistleblowers. I prefer to call two of them by their names: Edward Snowden and Julian Assange.

★ ★ ★

In Edward Snowden's memoir, *Permanent Record*, he details his early life, career, and the actions that led to his name being associated with the media in this book. While his book is occasionally self-indulgent in exploring aspects of his life that seem to have little to do with the core of the story, something I suppose someone could potentially accuse me of here, his memoir is quite fascinating to read. Rather than re-trace the story he's already told, I'll share the cliff notes:

Snowden came from a family of military and federal workers. He joined the military in 2004, and was quickly discharged for an injury. He ended up working in security for the University of Maryland, involved in a project supported by the National Security Agency (NSA). This work, which required a high-level security clearance, led to his eventual hiring at the Central Intelligence Agency (CIA) in 2007. He was stationed in Geneva, Switzerland and was highly regarded for his abilities. In 2009 he joined Dell, the computer company, as a contractor assigned to work at an NSA facility in Japan, and in 2011 returned to the States to work for Dell on a CIA contract. In 2012, he was sent to Hawaii to work again with the NSA. In 2013, after ostensibly witnessing the Director of National Intelligence, James Clapper, "directly lie under oath to Congress," he quit working with Dell and started working for a consulting firm doing much of the same work with the NSA.

While each of these events was happening, Snowden became increasingly privy to a series of concerning programs and initiatives that violated the privacy of Americans and citizens all over the world. Some of his discoveries were the result of his work, and some were obtained inappropriately. In all cases, he attempted repeatedly to warn supervisors and officials of the inevitable implications of such tools, and the outcome of violating the privacy of US citizens. After numerous failed attempts to be heard through formal channels, and having his growing concerns for the privacy of the people ignored, Snowden took the matter into his own hands, and released the information to the world through actual investigative journalists.

This is the fast and detail-less version of the story. What ultimately transpired, though, was that Snowden discovered that the US Government was clearly spying on its citizens in the name of keeping us safe. To prove it, he stole some 1.7 million files that exposed programs like PRISM, which collects internet activity from companies including Microsoft, Google, Yahoo, AOL, YouTube, Facebook, Skype, Apple, and more; and MUSCULAR which collects global data, some 181 million records per month at the time, by tapping undersea internet cables.[54,55] It was also revealed that the NSA collected the online sexual activity of those they deemed a threat with the sole purpose of having the information available to discredit the individual in question, should it be deemed necessary, in a program called SEXINT.[56] Of the release, Snowden said, "I understand that I will be made to suffer for my actions, and that the return of this information to the public marks my end."[57]

Numerous individuals, up to and including then-citizen Donald Trump, called for Snowden's execution.[58] Addressing these concerns at approximately the time of release, Snowden said, "All I can say right now is the US Government is not going to be able to cover this up by jailing or murdering me. Truth is coming, and it cannot be stopped."[59] In 2020, a US federal court ruled that the mass surveillance program Snowden exposed was in fact illegal and possibly even unconstitutional.[60]

While Snowden has been somewhat vindicated through the ruling by the federal court, he still faces 3 felony charges that could result in up to 30 years in prison, not to mention the very real threat to his life for his actions. He continues to live in exile in Russia, as he has since 2013. Meanwhile, the US continues its mass surveillance of innocent individuals like you and I, utilizing many of the same programs he exposed.

★ ★ ★

Julian Assange is the Editor-in-Chief of WikiLeaks. He became a household name with the releasing of documents obtained by US Army intelligence analyst, Chelsea Manning, in 2010. The leaks, which included the Afghan War Diary, a series of over 91,000 documents that released sensitive details about the war in Afghanistan, and was called, "one of the biggest leaks in US military history;"[61] the Iraq War Logs, which included nearly 400,000 field reports from 2004 to 2009, detailing the number of civilians the US and Coalition forces had killed in warfighting, actually becoming the biggest leak in US military history; and a number of other sensitive items, like a video of US forces mistaking civilians for insurgents as they were gunned down by helicopter.

Then-Vice President Joe Biden and others called Assange a "terrorist."[62] Former US Presidential Candidate, Mike Huckabee, among other predominately conservative voices, called for Assange to be executed.[63] In 2014, there were documents released as a part of Snowden's whistleblowing that showed the US had added Assange to its "Manhunting Timeline," which is a list of efforts to capture or kill terrorists and threats to the country.[64] Support for Assange came from individuals both foreign and domestic, including the presidents of Brazil,[65] Ecuador,[66] and Russia,[67] as well as notable names like Noam Chomsky and Michael Moore.[68]

Interestingly, while Assange has generally enjoyed being viewed in more favorable light from liberals than he has from conservatives, WikiLeaks played a direct role in the negative casting of Hillary Clinton in the 2016 Presidential Election. The organization released documents that demonstrated favoritism by the Democratic National Committee (DNC) to prop up Secretary Clinton over her then-rival, Senator Bernie Sanders,[69] which some have argued played a role in her ultimate loss to Donald Trump. In 2019, under the Trump Administration, Assange was charged with 17 violations of the Espionage Act of 1917, which, if convicted, would equate to a 170-year sentence.[70]

So why am I highlighting Julian Assange instead of Chelsea Manning? Because after researching both individuals, their actions, and their stated motives, it is clear to me that Manning was not seeking to help protect Americans, but rather was seeking to indiscriminately air the US military's dirty laundry.

Now, someone could argue that Assange is the one who released the documents making him equally responsible for the fallout, and there's truth to that line of thinking. The difference is, WikiLeaks is a vehicle for reporting misdeeds, which Manning provided. Assange didn't have a motive behind the release of the documents, he was doing his job as a journalist. Manning did have a motive, and it was grounded in animosity and revenge for being bullied while serving our military. The theft and release of the documents added no value to anyone. The world was not better off for the release of these documents; citizens are not now aware that their government is actively spying on them; and her actions were not reporting. In fact, in many cases, the national defense of the United States was worse off because of Manning's attempt to embarrass the military, and as a result of her actions, innocent lives were lost.

Manning had no moral or career obligation to steal those documents. Assange did have the obligation to report the news, whether it was flattering or not. The moral implications of the content and the means by which it was discovered are not the concern of a journalist like Assange. He did his job as a reporter and paid for it. He was subsequently charged with sexual assault and molestation. If the charges prove to be true, that is hideous behavior, though there is far more reason to believe that the charges were made up in attempt by the US Government to have the man extradited to the country. And with the discovery of SEXINT, it's not unreasonable to assume that the charges are fake in attempt to discredit Assange in the eyes of the public.

In 2021, Assange continues to be held in a maximum-security prison in London, where he has been imprisoned since 2019.

★ ★ ★

When we contrast Edward Snowden and Julian Assange with the likes of Sean Hannity, Laura Ingraham, Joe Scarborough, and other "journalists" with multi-million-dollar contracts, it's clear that the mainstream media we rely on to stay abreast of national and world affairs is reporting the news, but they are not journalists. Chomsky once said, "He who controls the media controls the minds of the public." The media is not the enemy of the people, but they are definitely not our allies. It shouldn't have to be this way, but it's up to you and I to vote with our dollars, viewership, and Likes to cancel those who actively work to divide us – Politicians and media talking heads alike.

Racism

Racism in America is still very real. Diversity, Equity, and Inclusion is one of the ways to combat racism, though the topic itself has become a lightning rod. In the wake of the murder of George Floyd in 2020, and the many violent riots that followed, virtually all organizations jumped on the performative bandwagon of adopting DEI Statements and hiring DEI executives. While this happened at breakneck speed in corporations and governmental appointments, public attitudes ranged from skepticism to relief to angst. But here's the reality: It doesn't matter if any one person is supportive of, or in opposition to, the movement to create a more equitable and inclusive world – It's happening.

Let's get this out of the way: The term "white fragility" is derogatory. While there are lots of legitimate reasons why the term exists, using it shuts down the very people who we most need to enroll in the conversation – White folk. Further, diversity, equity, and inclusion means including *everyone*, which includes White people – Even those who don't yet value DEI initiatives. In this book, no one will assert that you are racist for the color of your skin. You show the world your character through your actions, not your appearance.

★ ★ ★

While our elected officials have been claiming to attempt to re-unite Americans for the past decades, the reality is that they really haven't been. Our elected officials actively play to their bases, rather than strive to serve the people in a meaningful and helpful way that creates an environment for unity to prevail. Using a term like "intractability" to describe this scenario seems too extreme, though it is true that Americans, a people with multiple ethnic and political cultures, haven't truly been united since the high level of nationalism and groupthink that the country experienced in the immediate aftermath of 9/11. With a national motto like, "United We Stand," the divisive path that we are currently on will only lead to negative outcomes for our country.

The division in America has always been a factor, dating back to the conflicts that led to the Civil War, women's rights, civil rights, race riots, LGBTQIA+ rights, and more. Division particularly increased under the presidencies of Barack Obama and Donald Trump. The first viable Black presidential candidate created a stir as the citizenry was faced with a proxy racial litmus test by having the opportunity to create history or maintain the status quo by voting for another WASP candidate in 2008. During Obama's tenure, racial tensions that could have ended instead increased, with a series of young Black men being killed by police throughout the country and his handling of those issues. Truly the media is at least partly to blame for over-publicizing crime-related deaths that have always taken place, unevenly reporting to play to the fears of their ad revenue-generating viewers, and opining instead of reporting. In any case, Obama was the president of our nation at the time that saw the creation of Black Lives Matter (BLM), a decentralized organization of folks who have advocated for equality while simultaneously advocating for the death of police officers in the name of preventing further Black deaths.

During the campaign and presidency of Donald Trump, racial tensions increased further, as he consistently taunted those he disagreed with, resorted to name-calling, and was slow to damn racially-charged acts of violence. All of this has led to a scenario where the underlying constructive conflict resolution values, including reciprocity, equality, community, fallibility and nonviolence between the citizenry has been violated, bastardized, and abused. Both Obama and Trump have consistently refused to admit fallibility. Obama's definition of equality often stripped rights from others, specifically in regard to religious positions on contraceptives under the Affordable Care Act and to business owners choosing who they have the right to refuse service while negotiating LGBTQIA+ rights; while Trump encouraged violence directly and indirectly by both what he said and what he strategically omitted; all of which adds to the division we see today in America.

While all of this was taking place, the Occupy Wall Street (OWS) coalition was also formed. The two viewpoints on OWS were that they were a group of educated individuals who had been taken advantage of, and were the representatives of the 99% of the population that "serves" the 1%; or that these people who camped out in city centers for weeks were simply out of work protestors who had nothing better to do than to complain about an invisible force of rich people. These two competing sides of OWS, which echo the same two competing sides of BLM in regard to one side feeling repressed by another, is still playing into the grander escalation of division between Americans. This division and conflict has been overwhelmingly negative and destructive to communities and to the mentality of individuals outside of those communities. The one potential positive that comes out of this destructive behavior is that all of these individuals simply want to be heard, feel secure, and have a semblance of their definition of equity. Assuming those things to be true, we can work towards constructive and collaborative outcomes that satisfy all.

With specific outcomes outlined, collaborative negotiations could take place, rather than protestors on one side of the street and militarized police officers on the other. It's clear in this sense that communication plays a tremendously critical role. BLM protestors could say, "We are communicating – We're saying 'Hands up, don't shoot,'" but the reality is that it isn't actually communication – It's a one-way chant that, intentionally or not, implies all police officers on the other side of the street are incapable of understanding a base responsibility of their job duties. This causes frustration, angst, and an emotional desire to defend one's self – It is not two-way communication, and instead creates an environment where one side does not want to communicate with the other at all, further exacerbating the problem.

★ ★ ★

It is not a stretch to think through all of the potential outcomes that occur by staying on the path of division that America is currently on. The divided nature of our national culture could lead to incredibly negative and violent outcomes, like increased racially-charged attacks, attempts to "roll back the clock" on issues like women's and civil rights, secession of certain states, and ultimately another Civil War. We have an infinite ability to segregate ourselves into smaller and smaller sub-categories of people who think, act, and behave in a homogenous way, or we can choose to open our ears, learn from our differences, respect human beings as human beings, and choose to work together in spite of our differences. The truth is, we will not always agree, and that's okay. This doesn't mean that if someone behaves out of line, retributive justice is always the best solution. We can, and should, consider alternative paths of working with each other to ensure that the needs of the community are met, that individuals are not causing harm to one and other, and that in the end, we are all learning from our respective differences.

As I said at the beginning, conflict itself is not a negative activity. Conflict can be highly productive and help move issues forward if those on either side are willing to work with one and other. Restorative justice principles do not need to be relegated to the fringes of society and disregarded as a second-class, Indigenous people's way of dealing with conflict. As individuals, we can work together to de-escalate conflicts by utilizing these modern, and in some ways ancient, modes of conflict resolution.

As I watch our elected officials, I constantly think about how I would handle a situation if I were in their shoes. How would I deal with North Korea testing nuclear bombs, or with ISIS killing innocents around the world, or with groups like Black Lives Matter calling for the death of police officers, or with hate groups like the KKK who engage in acts of domestic terrorism, or protests due to the straight-up murdering of individuals like George Floyd... There is no easy answer or none of these issues would continue to be affecting Americans. The thing I keep coming back to, though, is probably the most valuable lesson that I've learned from working with and coaching so many people for so many years: If we treat each other like humans, and work through challenges together, the results will be dramatically more valuable than if we just say, "screw you," and act impulsively, aggressively, and without thought. When we listen, give respect, and work together, we will get different results than by doing the same thing we've done for decades before. With new behaviors, we can start to influence a culture of collaboration.

★ ★ ★

Culture is an intangible experience and behavior of a group of individuals. Culture at the macro level can be viewed from nationality, ethnicity, socio-economic class, etc. Culture at a micro level could be how employees behave in a company, how families interact, or how church members help or ignore their community. Culture is not a thing that can be held – It's a sense, a feeling, and a way people, think, dress, eat, and act with others. Because culture is intangible, it makes sense that the concept of quantifying Cultural Intelligence, an analog of Emotional Intelligence, would be foreign and "new wave," like restorative justice is to some. The understanding of culture is a high-level order of thinking, which automatically implies that a small percentage of the population will pause to think about it intentionally.

When Kristy and I were finishing college, we had the opportunity to study abroad in Australia together in the summer of 2008. While there, there was a big situation with the prime minister publicly apologizing to the Aboriginal people for the atrocities they had endured by early Australians. The apology was well received by some and balked at by others, because, "I didn't do anything to them – That was generations ago!" This sentiment was rational in the minds of many, as truly, those individuals had likely done nothing to harm an Aboriginal person. The danger of this type of thinking, though, is that it's a closed-minded approach that speaks to the innate cultural perception of superiority that is pervasive among modern Western society, particularly among White folk. And it's virtually impossible to separate this example from our historic approach toward Indigenous Americans. We tend to believe that because we are "civilized" and have all sorts of sophisticated judicial processes, we must be smarter than the "savage" Indigenous peoples of the world. This mentality is dismissive of the centuries of the predecessor iterations of restorative justice that were common among Indigenous peoples before the world had court rooms and prisons.

Conversely, as Westerners are becoming further "enlightened," and begin adopting "new" ideas like restorative justice, the future of conflict resolution looks to be healthier and less litigious. I think back specifically to the case of the boys who burned down the historic bridge. That was a case where restorative justice gave the community the opportunity to express their feelings about the situation, the boys had an opportunity to own up to their mistake and apologize, and the end result was increased understanding and decreased retributive discipline. I can see a solution like this becoming more and more appropriate, as the current practice of settling legal cases out of court becomes increasingly more common.

Multiculturalism is essentially the ultimate goal of the American Melting Pot concept. The challenge with the concept is that is requires the individuals to not only be accepting of other cultures, but to adopt and incorporate other cultures, too. While we are making progress toward this outcome, the progress is slow, and far too many people continue to feel marginalized while we wait for everything to shake out. This is why there are people of color who some White folk would classify as "militant" in their approach toward equality – They've waited their whole lives and want to see progress happening not just eventually or in their children's lifetime, but now. If you have ever felt marginalized at any point in your life, you understand this sense of urgency. If you've never felt marginalized, you can now choose to understand why marginalized peoples may consider you "privileged." It is a privilege, in the minds of those who have been marginalized, to live without feeling marginalized.

★ ★ ★

As I was building a DEI module for The Leadership Mastery Program that Leadership Coaching for Results offers, I interviewed a series of experts and executives in the DEI space. I had always been passionate about diversity work, and believed it to be important and topical for those that we would be training. During each interview, I shared how in undergrad my peers and I had professional development programs we could attend during an annual career fair for hospitality students, and that there was always a program on diversity. I attended those programs religiously because I wanted to be exposed to what I didn't know that I didn't know. Interestingly, I was always the only White male in the room. It was my first experience being a minority, which was a lesson in and of itself. I also asked each of these individuals how they perceived my enthusiasm for helping others to understand the importance of DEI work. Each of them replied in some iteration of, "Based solely on who you are, if you don't choose to help others to understand this work, you're doing us a disservice. Not only should you do it, we need you to because you have nothing to gain and everything to lose. Your participation helps to reach people that we cannot." The point of this isn't to virtue signal or to imply that I was woke before it was cool, but rather to paint a picture: The people who needed to hear the messages the most – White people – are often the ones least likely to feel welcome enough to hear them. This is the piece that I have witnessed as missing in most DEI efforts – White folk may be talked at, but they aren't made to feel like they can be a part of the solution.

We don't need to tell a Black lesbian how hard her life is. She already knows that she's such a percentage more likely to be discriminated against for being Black, female, and gay – Let alone all three. Instead, we need more White people to know that by hiring The Other, they will have richer and more meaningful solutions for their diverse clientele. We need more White people to know that The Other is someone who will introduce them to experiences and perspectives that will improve their life. We need more White people to understand that The Other isn't all that different after all. And, DEI work is actually important for everyone to experience, because this Black lesbian may be just about as culturally unaware as a White male can be toward her, when it comes to her managing a paralyzed military veteran or a neurodiverse individual.

We're all unique in some way. We all have things we wish The Other knew about us. We all desire to be treated with respect. We are all humans.

★ ★ ★

As a college senior I had the unique and valuable experience of being assigned an alumni mentor who happened to be the CEO of the restaurant brand that I had dreamed of working for since I was 15. This CEO and future Chair of the National Restaurant Association, Phil Hickey, had recently closed the sale of the brand to the largest restaurant company in the world. I wasn't sure at the time if his mentoring me immediately after the sale of the company was going to help or hurt me secure my dream job, but I knew that I clicked with the man, and that I was inspired by his faith.

Phil gave me all sorts of incredible opportunities that helped prepare me for my first career role, and many that were just special. I attended an MSU football game with him in the

President's Suite; watched him give a keynote in Chicago at an annual Prayer Breakfast, where I first heard the phrase quoted from the Bible, JFK, and others, "to whom much is given, much is expected," and learned how he and his wife lived that statement by fostering nearly three dozen children; had the opportunity to execute a competitive analysis of 24 restaurants in Atlanta in a 48-hour period with a guy I barely knew who ended up becoming a wonderful friend for life, Jeff; and learned the importance of goal-setting which spurred my passion for developing and teaching whole-life vision setting to my clients. He has always had innumerable demands on his time, so seeing him move through an event space is like watching a tornado of activity, as the gravity of the room follows him around. Each conversation is given exactly the amount of time it needs and no more, but when Phil is with you in those moments, it feels like you're the only person in the world. He is truly an inspirational person, and someone that I've respected since the first time I met him. I never knew for sure what role he played, if any, in my being the only college graduate in the entire country in 2009 to be hired to work for that national restaurant brand, but I've always had a feeling that he was a variable in making my dream come true.

When I accepted the offer, I was told I'd train in Kansas City for a couple of months before moving to Minnesota to join a new management team at that location. Phil was quick to connect me with his mentor of decades, and the two of us had lunch while I was in town. It was another example of how thoughtful he is, and how eager he was to help me be successful.

When I arrived in Minneapolis, I was completely in my element and over my head. I was 24-years-old and had an out-of-control ego that I felt entitled to have based on past successes. I didn't realize how miserable of a leader I was at the time, because I was continuing to have tremendous success reaching the goals that had been set for me, like fixing our liquor cost productivity that had the bar ranked #45 out of 45 in the country. Within a year I turned it around to #1, which sounds impressive, and it was, but that ranking doesn't account for how many people I pissed off to make it happen. Where I struggled the most was in relating with others, and showing them respect. This was true in many areas of my work, but one: The Kitchen.

For a long time, I was intimidated by the Heart of the House. I had minimal formal culinary training, and apart from an internship, had spent all of my time up to that point working in the Front of the House as a server, trainer, or supervisor. For this reason, I showed more deference to the kitchen staff than anyone else in the restaurant. It was a unique experience for me, because for virtually everyone on that team, English was a second (or third) language. I could barely count to 10 in Spanish when I started there, but by the end of my time in that restaurant, I could tell a dirty joke with the best of them.

There were two things I enjoyed about working with our kitchen team – They busted their butts to be amazing employees, and they got a kick out of laughing at my expense. They'd often get me to say something stupid, like, "I have three balls," and everyone would crack up as they finished cleaning at the end of their shift before going to work their second job at another restaurant. These people were some of the hardest workers I had ever met, and they were super cool. The majority of that team was Ecuadorian, with a few Columbians and Mexicans, and they hustled every bit as hard as the Cubans I had come to respect in a previous restaurant.

Learning to speak Kitchen Spanish, a mixture of poor grammatic Spanish mixed with English for the more complicated words, made me popular with them. It allowed me to earn their trust, and learn more from them. They invited me to celebrate their cultural holidays in traditional ways, including eating Cuy (pronounced Coo-E). I had never before eaten guinea pig, but when they offered that I enjoy the meat from the skull and neck, a special piece reserved as an honor, I wasn't going to be rude and turn them down. My time with the kitchen staff turned out to be an incredible experience that I remember fondly. Then one day, I learned something that I wished I hadn't.

At the time I was on this management team, we had an incredible executive chef that I admired and respected. He was cool and calm 95% of the time, and seethed with inspiring intensity the other 5%. At this point in time I had similar behaviors, but mine were approximately 40% cool and calm and 60% unbridled intensity. I looked up to him, and believed that I wanted to behave more like him. We enjoyed working together, and we confided in each other. He was rediscovering his Christian faith at this time, and asked me to meet with him on our days off to hold a 2-person Bible study. We were close. At some point I was responsible for completing a task to ensure that all of the employees had all of their paperwork complete and on file. It was a crap shoot of a project that identified lots of missing documents that I was subsequently responsible for tracking down or getting produced. One day I casually asked the chef, "Hey, do you know that almost everyone who works in the kitchen is missing this certain document?" He just as casually replied, "That's because they aren't legal."

I felt my stomach drop, and it seemed for a moment like all sound stopped entering my ears. I immediately wanted nothing to do with the situation, as I wasn't sure what would happen to me if I were involved in employing illegal immigrants. It also seemed clear that, apart from our general manager, no one in the ranks above me was aware of this newfound information. I told him he'd have to handle the paperwork for his team on his own, and I pretended for years like I never knew anything about his comment.

I want to be clear; the purpose of this story is not to drag any person or organization through the mud – I've intentionally omitted the name of the restaurant brand that I was very proud to work for specifically for this reason. The parent company was doing their regular spot-check due diligence by having me execute the documentation review – They were completely unaware of the actions of this one individual. The chef soon left of his own accord, and everything staff-wise was made to be above board in the subsequent leadership transition. Those details are not the point of this story. The point I am trying to make is this: The hardest working people I have ever worked with were illegal immigrants. Each of these people wanted nothing more than to work, send some money home to their families, and have a little fun while spending 60-90 hours each week across multiple restaurants. Further, I have no reason to believe that the chef was behaving with criminal intent – He just wanted to give people a chance.

They were human beings. They were illegal immigrants. They were my friends.

★ ★ ★

In the years since, I've known a number of people who have shared with me their experiences entering our country illegally. Many of them had no choice, having been brought here as children. They served as translators for their parents, and many started working at a young age to help support their family. In all cases I've been privy to, the individual felt shame, embarrassment, and anger toward their parents for making them live in hiding. Interestingly, the individuals I've known who became naturalized citizens are often prouder to be Americans than many natural-born citizens.

Division aside, America is still the envy of the world. Whether we take it for granted or acknowledge our fortune, we are blessed to live in the greatest country on earth.

★ ★ ★

Much was made of perceptions of President Trump being a racist as a result of installing a physical barrier along the Southern Border. This always ignored the fact that Presidents Reagan, Bush, Clinton, Bush, and Obama all paid lip service to the importance of securing the border and controlling illegal immigration into the country. Not a single one of them did anything noteworthy to change the situation, though, except for Trump. For his action, he was painted as a villain.

I personally agreed with the physical border, as did most politicians and citizens before Trump's success, but I also acknowledge that appearances are what they are. This is why I believe if we feel the need to have a physical barrier to exclude individuals from entering our country in an unauthorized fashion along the Southern Border, we should have a physical barrier across the Northern Border, also. Currently we share with Canada a 40' clearing of trees as the official line of demarcation between our nations – Anyone who wants to enter either country illegally only has to sprint for a few seconds to avoid detection, and they're free and clear. If we truly feel the need to physically protect our Southern Border, we should protect all borders, otherwise anyone could rightfully and legitimately make accusations of racism.

In line with other policies that President Biden instituted in direct opposition to President Trump's, he unofficially opened the flood gate at the Southern Border, resulting at one point in over 15,000 immigrants residing in an unprotected outdoor holding area underneath the International Bridge in Del Rio, Texas.[71] The fact that so many individuals were concentrated in such a relatively small area should raise concern in a number of ways, but in the midst of a global pandemic, retaining these people together in this way didn't seem congruent with declarations of "following the science" – The phrase that so many politicians invoked any time they wanted to provide artificial credibility to support their actions. Further, at the point that all of the migrants were disbanded from the area, after the embarrassing national attention brought on the Biden Administration for Border Patrol Agents being photographed holding whips on horseback near migrants, Homeland Security Secretary Alejandro Mayorkas announced that the agency had removed all of the migrants with 2,000 being flown back to their home countries; 8,000 supposedly voluntarily returning to Mexico (although the calculus on that statement didn't seem to add up given reports from agents on the ground); and the remaining 5,000 being processed by the agency for next steps, which to date had included releasing the immigrants into the country with a Notice to Appear within 60 days at an immigration office.[72] Obviously this outcome had no teeth, which continued to amplify the crisis at the border.[73]

One of the most egregiously stupid and incongruent things that the Biden Administration had done, though, was to release these illegal immigrants into the country without mandating that they all receive a single-dose COVID-19 vaccine.[74] During a period of public health crisis that had led to the president instituting a mandatory vaccine requirement or weekly testing for companies employing more than 100 individuals, which encompassed some 100 million Americans, giving illegal immigrants an *option* to be vaccinated or not prior to their unofficial release into the country was insulting to American citizens and blatantly foolish. It was an action that pandered to the policy priorities of a sub-segment of his base, and came at the cost of undermining his credibility in regard to "following the science." It also further amplified vaccine hesitancy, as a logical-minded person would see this incongruency and think, "If the president doesn't think these people who are illegally entering our country need to be vaccinated, why should I?"

★ ★ ★

When I was in college, serving as the vice president of my campus ministry church, I would regularly wear a baseball cap to any and all events that I was a part of, including Sunday service. There were lots of times that people looked at me funny about it, but those same people generally gave me a pass when I'd remove my hat during prayer or communion. It was all intentional, though.

As a legacy project, I felt inspired to start a new church service for the un-churched and de-churched. It was called Wednesday ON FIRE. It started at 7:09 p.m., featured a rock band of student musicians, and very specifically did not feature a sermon from our beloved faith leader, Pastor Dave. The man was an incredible mentor to me, and to this day is someone that I count as a friend and confidant. When I told him that I didn't think he should give a sermon, he immediately agreed. The premise of Wednesday ON FIRE was not to be a rock version of church, but to attract those who did not feel as though they belonged in church at all. Instead, we featured student testimonial stories of their faith, and why God was an important part of who they were.

I served as the coordinator of Wednesday ON FIRE for the first two years of its existence, until my graduation in December of 2009. At that point, I chose to tell my story of why I always wore my hat to church.

The church served about 400 people, with approximately half being college students. Each year, Pastor Dave took under his wing two groups of five student leaders who were responsible for a variety of events and activities, and the vice president. As a young person who desired to lead others, Pastor Dave had inspired me in many ways. He held my feet to the fire when I made a foolish misstep, and was very patient with me when I wasn't ready to understand something that he saw as a missing piece of my future success. One of the things he did with all of the students he mentored, though, was to instill in us a sense of treating everyone equally. We were also responsible for making everyone feel welcome. In order to do that, we weren't allowed to use acronyms or tell inside jokes in the presence of those who wouldn't understand them; we were always to welcome and include a new person, particularly if they were alone; and we were always to have an extra chair at any table or circle, so if someone showed up late, they would feel as though they were welcome to join. We also didn't reference God with male pronouns, because there is no actual proof that the Christian deity has any gender, and there was no reason to make anyone feel negative or uncomfortable with such gendered pronouns in place. At the time the concept of pronouns seemed silly and unnecessary to me, but now I understand the concept very clearly – Why make anyone feel like an outsider if we can instead use language that makes them feel included? As a result, we simply called God, "God."

Kristy and I met at our church, Martin Luther Chapel, and as student leaders we both took Pastor Dave's lessons to heart. In reflection, his lessons are at the root of my whole belief system that we should treat everyone with care, kindness, and respect. Without him, I'm not convinced that I would have otherwise come to hold these beliefs.

I remember my last conversation with him as my undergraduate degree came to a close. I was about to move to Minneapolis and visited him one last time. When we were done, he walked me out of his office toward the front door and said, "I'm excited for you, and I'll miss you. We both know that you'll move back eventually. And when you do, things will be different." While neither of us said it, we both knew that what he was really saying was that our mentor / mentee relationship had reached its natural conclusion. I'd think back to his degree of awareness and selflessness from time to time as my mentoring relationships with mentees reached their natural conclusions. It always made me smile. Then one day I was watching the streaming show *Ted Lasso* with some friends. In the season 2 finale, one of the characters, Higgins, provides counsel to a staff member who has a career opportunity that is too good to turn down, but will cost her friend and mentor significantly through her absence. Higgins comforts the character by saying, "A good mentor hopes you will move on. A great mentor knows you will." Pastor Dave was a great mentor. I'm honored to have had the opportunity to learn and grow from him, and to share his lessons with you.

As I stood before the church for my final service of Wednesday ON FIRE, I held the lectern and explained why I had always worn a hat to church – Because some day a person who didn't know our etiquette would walk in, and instead of feeling ashamed or embarrassed, they would see someone else just like them "not following the rules," and would feel more welcome. It was simple and innocuous, but if it was the difference between someone staying to learn about God or leaving in embarrassment, I was willing to play that role. And it worked to help lots of people, including a guy who came up to me once and said that he was ready to follow God and live a clean life, free from a lot of negative things he had been hooked into. He came to me specifically because I was more relatable than someone dressed more "appropriately." We were able to help serve him because he had someone who he could more readily identify with in the room. That's inclusion – Creating a space for someone you don't yet know to feel comfortable when they show up.

★ ★ ★

Like many people in the early days of the pandemic, I chose to change my hair style. My wife had been cutting my hair for years, and was itching for me to change it up, too. I decided to rock a mohawk, as I had flirted with the idea a few times in the past. It was a cool style that seemed to be strangely fitting for my look and personality. It was cut in such a way that I could easily brush it to the side and turn it into a "normal" haircut, but I never ended up choosing to do that. People liked it, and I got lots of compliments, particularly from older White women.

The most stereotypical Karen personalities stopped me at events to make a positive comment about my appearance, which prominently features the most intentionally anti-establishment haircut in existence. And yet there are people every single day who fear being sent home from work for going into the office with their natural hair. I chose my hairstyle and get compliments, and Black folk can legally be sent home and fired over their "unprofessional" natural hair. It's sickening. Fortunately, there's a movement to change this type of discrimination in the form of legislation called the CROWN Act. The CROWN Act stands for Creating a Respectful and Open World for Natural Hair. It's a proposed law that would prohibit the discrimination of a person due to their hair texture or style. As of April 2021, 11 states have adopted the legislation.[75]

When I learned about the CROWN Act, I immediately decided to keep my mohawk permanently. I choose to wear it now in solidarity with those who must live in fear of losing their employment over a variable that they cannot and should not need to "control." Whenever I get a compliment about my hairstyle, it provides me the opportunity to share this story and to become a human prop to advocate for the need to make our world more equal and equitable. Virtually no White person I tell about the CROWN Act has heard of it, and they're all appalled that such discrimination can legally take place in offices all over the country. This is another example to me of how we're all ignorant to a lot of things, and when we learn about something that is belittling of another human's opportunity to live a happy and fulfilling life, we naturally object to it.

As a 6'4", 250lb, White male, I inhabit the body of Western

society's archetypal "leader." People look to me for advice when I should be the last to give it, solely based on my appearance. This reality has been a blessing in my life with little negative repercussions, which is really the definition of privilege. As a result, I do believe that I have benefitted both implicitly and explicitly from racism. You can choose to agree with that or not – I'm not trying to convince you of what I believe to be true in my life. I know the world we currently occupy was designed to benefit people who look like me, because for centuries it was designed *by* people who look like me. Acknowledging this reality, I seek to live up to Phil Hickey's role modeling from that Prayer Breakfast, because much has been given to me. As a result, I feel that much is expected, and that I am responsible for serving and supporting those who have made my privileged life possible. It's expected of me – If from no one else but me.

★ ★ ★

While I believe that I have a clear role to play in the conversation around diversity, equity, and inclusion, I do object to the notion that this body I inhabit automatically makes me racist. I don't object because I'm personally offended by the fact that someone who knows nothing about me would choose to label me that way, but because blanket labels like, "if you're White you're racist," vilify a whole slew of people that we need to enroll in this critically important conversation.

Telling White people that they're racist and there's nothing they can do about it, and that even if they try, racism will not end in our lifetimes is exactly the type of messaging that perpetuates a hopeless and ambivalent attitude toward racism. Nowhere in human psychological literature is there guidance that says, "then damn the person whose behavior you want to change, and tell them they can't make meaningful change even by trying, but that they still need to go out of their way to make changes that don't explicitly benefit them or they're a villain. And also, damn you anyway for trying." Plain and simple, that is not how we get a meaningful volume of White people, who do make up the majority of Americans, to enroll in the conversation and actions around diversity, equity, and inclusion. We need to include everyone – especially White folk – in the conversation that does not plainly benefit them, so that we can all work together to make a world that benefits everyone. We can start this process by not automatically excluding anyone from the conversation through the use of damning labels.

Excluding people, ironically, is the exact opposite of inclusion. This is not my attempt to object to the term "white fragility," which some could fairly attempt to accuse me of here. The term exists for a reason – I don't object to that. Rather, my intent here is to cast light on the blatant shortcoming of the messaging from those who want to see the world be more respectful and equitable for all. I share that passion, and I'm separated enough from it based on my gender and the color of my skin to be able to see from a different perspective that we won't achieve these goals by damning *anyone*. Instead, we need to get the buy-in of *everyone*.

★ ★ ★

Picture this: You are invited to attend a sporting event at a stadium location. You choose to participate and purchase a ticket next to your friend. You both pay the same amount – That's Equality. When you get there, you realize the seats are up in the nosebleed section. You both have to walk up innumerable stairs in order to enjoy the game from your seat. It's inconvenient, but someone has to sit there. The problem is, though, you are currently on crutches. While you and your friend both have the opportunity to enjoy an equal experience, you will personally have to work a lot harder than your friend to have the same benefit. Your friend may think it's unfortunate, or say something like, "Suck it up, buttercup," but your friend is unlikely to think much more about your plight, because they are not living it. You, however, will be acutely aware of how hard it is to enjoy the experience. In an Equitable environment, you and your friend would have the opportunity to enjoy an equal experience with a comparable amount of effort – Which is why we have elevators.

We can take this a step further, though. What if you weren't the only one with crutches? What if 70% of people who attend sporting events also had crutches? Would we continue to build stadiums with nosebleed sections? The answer is obvious.

Approximately 70% of the American workforce is made of up people who historically have not had the opportunity to design the way our workplaces function. For better or worse, White males have created our systems for generations, but they now only make up about 30% of the workforce. If we want to have true equality, we need to be mindful of the systems changes that are required in order to provide equal access to all who participate in those systems.

So how do we do this? It's actually far easier than it's made out to be. Through real-world, first-person research with a series of experts in the DEI space, we know that there are four things *all of us* can do that will demonstrate a commitment to including everyone:

4 Steps for DEI Success
Treat human beings like human beings.
Demonstrate empathy for the challenges each person faces.
Start interactions with the assumption that
The Other means well.
Give each other a little grace for screwing up.

Nothing there requires you to do anything but behave with decency. You have everything within you right now to be successful in any DEI initiative. Notably, these are not instructions to use just towards Black and Brown folk, or those in the LGBTQIA+ community. These are emotionally intelligent practices that each of us should choose to follow any time we're working with anyone who is The Other, which realistically is pretty much all the time. When we do these four things, what we're really doing is showing that we respect those around us. Respect is a prerequisite to being a Leader. Remember, I capitalize the word when we're referencing a person who motivates, inspires, and empowers those they serve. If you ever want to be a Leader, or truly believe that you already are a Leader, by focusing on respecting others, you have the capacity to seamlessly and consistently be effective at championing diversity, equity, and inclusion. Because at the end of the day, it's really all about respecting that a human being is a human being, just like you.

★ ★ ★

America will benefit from the increased engagement of populations equitable to their actual real-world representation. I believe that we really are better together, and that our motto, "United We Stand," is not a flippant three-word throw-away line, but a true assessment of how our country functions best. Natural disasters ironically bring out the best in us, and demonstrate how individuals helping one another in a time of great need is what makes us human. Black, White, male, female, democrat, republican, gay, straight... None of that *really* matters. Our unique variables inform our cultural identity and inform how we act and think, but at the end of the day, we're all humans. It should not take a natural disaster or act of terrorism to reunite us. We deserve to be, should be, and need to be united.

You and I already have the capacity to treat human beings like human beings. We just need to choose to be a little bit more like Pastor Dave and work to always make all people feel welcome in our presence. And we need to choose to be a bit more like Phil Hickey and recognize that, "to whom much is given, much is expected."

★ ★ ★
Politics

The responsibility of our elected officials is to represent the people. We have witnessed over the last several decades a transition in the behavior of politicians that demonstrates a desire not to truly serve those they represent, but rather to serve the politician's personal desires and those of their respective political party. Politicians like President Bill Clinton (impeached over the Monica Lewinski scandal), US Representative Anthony Weiner (resigned over sexting), US Representative Jesse Jackson Jr. (convicted of fraud), Governor Rod Blagojevich (impeached & convicted of public corruption), President Donald Trump (impeached twice), US Senator Al Franken (resigned over multiple accusations of sexual misconduct), US Representative Chris Collins (indicted over insider trading), Ohio Speaker of the House Larry Householder (expelled from the state legislature over $60M bribery indictment), US Representative Ilhan Omar (paid her husband's consulting business over $2.9M in campaign funds), and Governor Andrew Cuomo (resigned over numerous sexual harassment allegations) are just a few of the most recent and egregious examples of politicians misusing their power for personal gain.

Other politicians are equally unapologetic about their unwillingness to collaborate with those who work on the opposite side of the aisle, as they are to generally behaving irresponsibly. In 2016, then-Senate Majority Leader Mitch McConnell blocked President Obama's Supreme Court nominee, only to push through President Trump's nominee four years later under even more restrictive circumstances. President Trump's use of Twitter to bully those he disagreed with; President Biden's repeated contradicting statements and policies that run counter to his previous statements and voting record; Senator Ted Cruz going on vacation during the most severe snowstorm in his state's history, then blaming the trip on his daughters; Senator Rand Paul being caught with a year-late reporting of his wife's stock purchase in a pharmaceutical company days before the pandemic erupted in America; Senator Lindsey Graham's frequent and politically expedient tone changes regarding President Trump; the failed attempt by Democrats to impeach President Trump the first time over charges of soliciting foreign interference from Ukraine, even though an inquiry had already shown sufficient evidence was not apparent, in addition to the fact that there was no mathematical way the Democrats could succeed in that attempt at impeachment; the fact that Republicans who voted to impeach President Trump the second time were faced with Trump-endorsed and well-funded primary challengers; and how both party's leadership have publicly proclaimed that they would be "opposition" to the party in power. On an almost daily basis we see on the national news how our elected officials play politics with politics and are hypocritical in holding themselves accountable to the same standard they expect of others. While there are always outliers, the overwhelming majority of our powerful elected officials behave immaturely and inappropriately, all while supposedly being our country's "best and brightest."

The political system is inherently divisive, too, with the intentional exclusion of 3rd parties. Libertarians, the Green Party, the Constitution Party, the Communist Party, and others suffer from ballot access issues, and for all intents and purposes are unable to participate in presidential debates based on the rules that favor the Republican and Democratic Parties. The two primary parties get away with it, though, as long as their candidates pay enough lip-service to key topics during the election cycle, regardless of if they ever actually do anything to move the needle (See: Immigration).

So we have politicians, once referred to as "public servants," who are blatantly behaving in their own self-interest or the interest of their party. Their job is to represent the people, and ironically, we're the *only* ones they aren't serving. To say that they are representing us by prioritizing their party's agenda is unfair, too, because the priorities of a Democrat in the North are not explicitly the same as a Democrat in the South, and the priorities of a Republican in the East are not explicitly the same as a Republican in the West. To say, "I voted for a Democrat and therefore I subscribe to all of their agenda items," is not realistic or appropriate. We have 535 elected lawmakers because it's their responsibility to represent the localized priorities of the people, yet representatives from each party vote in unison with the party-line agenda on almost every single noteworthy issue. Our representatives are supposed to represent us. They're supposed to advocate on behalf of the individuals within the regions they serve – Both those who voted for them and those who didn't. They're not supposed to be blindly representing their party's agenda. And they're definitely not supposed to fall in line and do whatever they're told by the very few who seemingly call all of the shots. There are some politicians who are outspoken enough to get a lot of attention, like Senators Bernie Sanders, Elizabeth Warren, Mitt Romney, Ted Cruz, and US Representatives Alexandria Ocasio-Cortez and Marjorie Taylor Greene, but there are only a few that are actually setting the agenda: Senate Majority Leader Chuck Schumer, Speaker of the House Nancy Pelosi, Senate Minority Leader Mitch McConnel, and House Minority Leader Kevin McCarthy.

Our elected officials are supposed to be our representatives. They're supposed to help us by creating rules, laws, policies, and budgets on our behalf. They're supposed to be focused on all of the things that need to happen on the back-end so Americans can grow and thrive, enjoying the pursuit of happiness. They're not supposed to be manipulating things the way that they are to benefit themselves and their parties. These people are not Leaders. Sadly, they really aren't.

★ ★ ★

January 6, 2021 was the day that will likely live in American history as an infamous day of disobedience, disrespect, and many divergent parties feeling disrespected. It is also the day where we literally and very truly almost witnessed a coup d'état occur in our country.

On that day, President-Elect Joe Biden was to be certified as th next President of the United States through congressional action that takes place regularly every four years, as a normal and perfunctory task of Congress. The event usually involves very little pomp and circumstance, and as average Americans we don't even really pay attention to it taking place. What was different this time, though, was that the president in office, at that time Donald Trump, had refused to concede his loss to Joe Biden and was actively and very publicly advocating for his vice president, Mike Pence, to certify the election in favor of Trump instead of Biden. There was some reason to believe that Pence had this authority, based on the legal counsel provided to President Trump. There were lawyers and legal analysts who were reviewing the legality of such an act on behalf of both individuals, and ultimately both the president and vice president arrived at differing conclusions.

On December 19th, 2020, Trump tweeted out, "Peter Navarro releases 36-page report alleging election fraud 'more than sufficient' to swing victory to Trump. A great report by Peter. Statistically impossible to have lost the 2020 Election. Big protest in D.C. on January 6th. Be there, will be wild!"[76] On the 22nd, a leader of the Oath Keepers posted on Facebook, "Trump said It's gonna be wild!!!!!!! It's gonna be wild!!!!!!! He wants us to make it WILD that's what he's saying. He called us all to the Capitol and wants us tomakeitwild!!!! SirYesSir!!! Gentlemen we are heading to DC pack your shit!!"[77] It's clear with posts like this how Trump's words were being interpreted by his most ardent supporters.

On the 30th, Trump again promoted the rally by tweeting, "JANUARY SIXTH, SEE YOU IN DC!"[78] On January 1st, 2021, Trump tweeted, "The BIG Protest Rally in Washington, D.C., will take place at 11.00 A.M. on January 6th. Locational details to follow. StopTheSteal!" then he retweeted a supporter who wrote, "The calvary is coming, Mr. President! JANUARY 6th | Washington, DC" and the President replied to that retweet with, "A great honor!"[79] On January 3rd, Trump instructed his newly-appointed Acting Secretary of Defense, Christopher C. Miller, to, "do whatever was necessary to protect the demonstrators," who planned to attend the rally.[80] The next day, Miller order that no National Guard service members were to be deployed with gear or weapons without his direct approval.[81]

On the 6th, the President tweeted first thing in the morning, "States want to correct their votes, which they now know were based on irregularities and fraud, plus corrupt process never received legislative approval. All Mike Pence has to do is send them back to the States, AND WE WIN. Do it Mike, this is a time for extreme courage!"[82] On a phone call that morning, Trump said to Pence, "You can either go down in history as a patriot, or you can go down in history as a pussy." When asked by a reporter months later if the statement were true, Trump responded twice, "I wouldn't dispute it."[83]

During a series of speeches from notable Trump allies and supporters, Representative Mo Brooks challenged the crowds by asking, "will you fight for America," and referenced "kicking ass."[84] Shortly thereafter, Rudy Giuliani called for "trial by combat," a reference to the popular HBO show *Game of Thrones*, in which a defendant or plaintiff can win their case by killing the other party in one-on-one combat.[85]

At noon on the 6th, the president addressed the crowd. The following is a selection of notable statements made during his 70-minute speech.[86] All statements are sequential and have not been opportunistically edited to force a narrative. Some statements support the argument that the president encouraged his supporters to protest but remain peaceful. Others statements make a damning case for his inciting violence. I have bolded the phrases that stand out in either case.

> "We have hundreds of thousands of people here and I just want them to be recognized by the fake news media. Turn your cameras please and show what's really happening out here **because these people are not going to take it any longer.**
>
> "**We will never give up, we will never concede.** It doesn't happen. You don't concede when there's theft involved.
>
> "**We will not let them silence your voices.**

We're not going to let it happen, I'm not going to let it happen.

"**And Rudy, you did a great job.** He's got guts. You know what? He's got guts, unlike a lot of people in the Republican Party. **He's got guts. He fights, he fights.**

"**I hope Mike is going to do the right thing.** I hope so. I hope so. Because if Mike Pence does the right thing, we win the election.

"We're gathered together in the heart of our nation's capital for one very, very basic and simple reason: **To save our democracy.**

"We want to go back and we want to get this right because we're going to have somebody in there that should not be in there and **our country will be destroyed and we're not going to stand for that.**

"**If this happened to the Democrats, there'd be hell all over the country going on. There'd be hell all over the country.** But just remember this: You're stronger, you're smarter, you've got more going than anybody. And they try and demean everybody having to do with us. And you're the real people, you're the people that built this nation. **You're not the people that tore down our nation.**

"The weak Republicans, and that's it. I really

believe it. **I think I'm going to use the term, the weak Republicans. You've got a lot of them.**

"And you have to get your people to fight. **And if they don't fight, we have to primary the hell out of the ones that don't fight. You primary them. We're going to.** We're going to let you know who they are. I can already tell you, frankly.

"That election, our election was over at 10 o'clock in the evening. We're leading Pennsylvania, Michigan, Georgia, by hundreds of thousands of votes. **And then late in the evening, or early in the morning, boom, these explosions of bullshit.**

"But we look at the facts and **our election was so corrupt that in the history of this country we've never seen anything like it.** You can go all the way back.

"And you know what else? We don't have a free and fair press. Our media is not free, it's not fair. It suppresses thought, it suppresses speech and **it's become the enemy of the people. It's become the enemy of the people.** It's the biggest problem we have in this country.

"And Mike Pence is going to have to come through for us, and if he doesn't, that will be a,

a sad day for our country because you're sworn to uphold our Constitution. Now, it is up to Congress to confront this egregious assault on our democracy. **And after this, we're going to walk down, and I'll be there with you, we're going to walk down, we're going to walk down.** Anyone you want, but I think right here, **we're going to walk down to the Capitol, and we're going to cheer on our brave senators and congressmen and women, and we're probably not going to be cheering so much for some of them. Because you'll never take back our country with weakness. You have to show strength and you have to be strong.** We have come to demand that Congress do the right thing and only count the electors who have been lawfully slated, lawfully slated. **I know that everyone here will soon be marching over to the Capitol building to peacefully and patriotically make your voices heard.**

"Today we see a very important event though. Because right over there, right there, we see the event going to take place. **And I'm going to be watching. Because history is going to be made.** We're going to see whether or not we have great and courageous leaders, or whether or not we have leaders that should be ashamed of themselves throughout history, throughout eternity they'll be ashamed. **And you know what? If they do the wrong** thing, we should never, ever forget that they did. Never forget. We should never ever forget.

"We will not be intimidated into accepting the hoaxes and the lies that we've been forced to believe.

"More than 10,000 votes in Pennsylvania were illegally counted, even though they were received after Election Day. In other words, they were received after Election Day. Let's count them anyway.

"And think of what you're doing. Let's say you don't do it. Somebody says, 'Well, we have to obey the Constitution.' And you are, because you're protecting our country and you're protecting the Constitution. So you are.

"You will have an illegitimate president. That's what you'll have. And we can't let that happen.

"I've been telling these Republicans, get rid of Section 230. And for some reason, Mitch and the group, they don't want to put it in there and they don't realize that that's going to be the end of the Republican Party as we know it, but it's never going to be the end of us. Never. Let them get out. Let, let the weak ones get out. This is a time for strength.

"By the way, you're talking about tens of thousands. If Georgia had merely rejected the same number of unlawful ballots as in other years, they should have been approximately 45,000 ballots rejected. Far more than what we needed to win, just over 11,000. **They should find those votes. They should absolutely find that. Just over 11,000 votes, that's all we need. They defrauded us out of a win in Georgia, and we're not going to forget it.**

"The radical left knows exactly what they're doing. They're ruthless and it's time that somebody did something about it. **And Mike Pence, I hope you're going to stand up for the good of our Constitution and for the good of our country. And if you're not, I'm going to be very disappointed in you.** I will tell you right now. I'm not hearing good stories.

"Then election officials pull boxes, Democrats, and suitcases of ballots out from under a table. You all saw it on television, totally fraudulent. And illegally scanned them for nearly two hours, totally unsupervised. Tens of thousands of votes. **This act coincided with a mysterious vote dump of up to 100,000 votes for Joe Biden, almost none for Trump. Oh, that sounds fair. That was at 1:34 a.m.**

151

"At 6:31 a.m. in the early morning hours after voting had ended, Michigan suddenly reported 147,000 votes. **An astounding 94% went to Joe Biden, who campaigned brilliantly from his basement.** Only a couple of percentage points went to Trump.

"So, I mean, I could go on and on about this fraud that took place in every state, and all of these legislatures want this back. **I don't want to do it to you because I love you and it's freezing out here.** But I could just go on forever. I can tell you this.

"**The Republicans have to get tougher. You're not going to have a Republican Party if you don't get tougher.** They want to play so straight. They want to play so, 'sir, yes, the United States. The Constitution doesn't allow me to send them back to the States.' Well, I say, 'yes it does, **because the Constitution says you have to protect our country and you have to protect our Constitution**, and you can't vote on fraud.' And fraud breaks up everything, doesn't it? **When you catch somebody in a fraud, you're allowed to go by very different rules.**

"So I hope Mike has the courage to do what he has to do. And I hope he doesn't listen to the RINOs and the stupid people that he's listening to.

"We won in a landslide. This was a landslide. They said it's not American to challenge the election. **This the most corrupt election in the history, maybe of the world.**

"**In fact, it's so egregious, it's so bad that a lot of people don't even believe it. It's so crazy that people don't even believe it. It can't be true. So they don't believe it.**

"**This is not just a matter of domestic politics — this is a matter of national security.**

"With your help over the last four years, we built the greatest political movement in the history of our country and nobody even challenges that. I say that over and over, and I never get challenged by the fakeness, **and they challenge almost everything we say. But our fight against the big donors, big media, big tech, and others is just getting started.** This is the greatest in history. There's never been a movement like that.

"**We must stop the steal and then we must ensure that such outrageous election fraud never happens again, can never be allowed to happen again.**

"We will finally hold big tech accountable. **And if these people had courage and guts**, they would get rid of Section 230, something that no other company, no other person in America, in the world has.

"All of these tech monopolies are going to abuse their power and interfere in our elections, and it has to be stopped. **And the Republicans have to get a lot tougher, and so should the Democrats.** They should be regulated, investigated, and brought to justice under the fullest extent of the law. They're totally breaking the law.

"And we fight. We fight like hell. And if you don't fight like hell, you're not going to have a country anymore.

"So we're going to, we're going to walk down Pennsylvania Avenue. I love Pennsylvania Avenue. And we're going to the Capitol, and we're going to try and give. The Democrats are hopeless — they never vote for anything. Not even one vote. **But we're going to try and give our Republicans, the weak ones because the strong ones don't need any of our help. We're going to try and give them the kind of pride and boldness that they need to take back our country. So let's walk down Pennsylvania Avenue."**

At 12:58 p.m., moments before the 3rd layer of barricade around the Capitol Building was penetrated, United States Capitol Police Chief Steven A. Sund formally requested a declaration of emergency and the deployment of the National Guard. He made the request again at 1:05, 1:28, 1:34, 1:39, and 1:45.[87] The National Guard deployment was approved by Acting Secretary Miller at 4:32 p.m. – 15 minutes after President Trump released a video asking rioters to go home.[88] Sund resigned on January 7th.

5 individuals died during or as a result of injuries sustained during the siege. Over 100 police officers were injured. 4 officers involved in protecting the Capitol committed suicide.[89]

★ ★ ★

This was a tragic day for a whole lot of reasons. But one of the things that we didn't really explore as a people was *why* so many individuals would take it upon themselves to risk being arrested and charged with crimes, as nearly 700 rioters were by October 2021.[90] Why would people be willing to risk their lives for Donald Trump, in attempt to have him to be reinstated as president? The media painted this entire experience as a coup attempt. As a tragedy. As an experience that is anti-American. Arguments that I agree with. But what the media did not share, was the other side of the story. They did not seek to understand or explain why the rioters believed what they believed, thought what they thought, and behaved the way that they behaved.

I remember watching the Capitol Riot taking place as it was happening live. I was texting with friends that were in offices and hospitals who couldn't see what was happening, though they were getting news alerts on their phones. A few of us started finding videos posted to on different social media channels and started to get a clearer picture of what the media was not yet reporting, or in some cases were not able to show, like a woman being shot and killed by Capitol Police. As we were watching the news and sharing updates with friends, my friends and I openly started to wonder if we were witnessing the birth of a new American Civil War.

It was an emotional day for me, as what I was witnessing goes directly against everything I believe. The anger and hatred, from the protestors and those who criticized them alike, was unreal. That individuals would be so violently convicted about something they believed in without first seeking to understand the opposing side is the exact opposite of what I advocate for in this book. In fact, this event was a catalyzing moment for me, as I realized then that this book needed to be published more than ever, and I signed the publishing contract soon after. But why did it happen?

Those I was texting that afternoon included a number of individuals whom I care about and respect, and who voted for Trump in 2020. They were similarly working in environments that prevented them from watching what was happening. As I updated them, I got one response that said, "Well, it's necessary." And that stood out to me as equally appalling. "It's necessary. This is what needs to happen," was the attitude of these individuals. This reaction was backed up by pointing out the Black Lives Matters riots that had taken place the summer before, and how supporters of that movement had similarly expressed an attitude that those riots "were necessary." So some of these individuals that I was texting with were essentially approaching this tragedy from the diametrically opposite worldview, and ironically a similar attitude, as those who participated in BLM riots and protests. Their argument was essentially that this behavior was not just necessary but justified and, "They broke windows and burned buildings to get their message across last summer, so why is this so bad?"

This was another moment of real tragedy in my mind, that people would think more death and more destruction and more civil disobedience and more extreme disrespect and disregard for The Other was the acceptable path forward. "It was good enough for you, so it's good enough for me. More death, more harm. Oh well. This is what it takes to be heard." That was the attitude. But why was that their attitude?

One argument made by those who supported the rioters, or were unwilling to allow blame to be cast on the former president for inciting a riot, is that Donald Trump at no time explicitly told his supporters to riot. There is truth to this statement, though the extreme literalism ignores that most individuals "hear" messages and the intent of messages based on the tone and context provided. So, while Trump did not use the words, "Go march to the Capitol, push through barriers, break windows, and once inside desecrate the building," his messages in the days before and on the day-of were clearly full of intent designed to instigate his supporters into some form of action. The repeated use of words and phrases like "fight," "challenge," "weak," "strong," "tough," "courage," "stand up," "never give up," "save our democracy," "national security," and others carry a very distinct tonal message. He may not have told them what to do, but history speaks for itself – His message was clearly understood by those who listened.

Garrett Epps is a retired Professor of Law at the University of Baltimore. He is an American legal scholar, and had this to say about Trump's involvement in inciting the riot:

It's quite rare that somebody can be convicted of incitement. In applying that to the president's speech at the rally, it's an agonizingly close case.

It's pretty goddamn imminent because he's telling people to march to the Capitol and I will march with you. There wouldn't be any time for better counsels to prevail because you're just going to leave the Ellipse and walk down Pennsylvania Avenue.

He said we have to fight and show strength, but he also said we're very peacefully and patriotically going to ask, so he's covering himself. In the end, I think it's a jury question.

I'm not sure he's entitled to a dismissal of charges as a matter of law. There's some discussion that government leaders have more leeway, but I don't know how that would play out.

He clearly knew there were people in that crowd who were ready to and intended to be violent, and he certainly did nothing to discourage that. He not only did nothing to discourage it, he strongly hinted it should happen.[91]

I did not support Trump's 1st impeachment, as the facts were not sufficient to demonstrate that he had definitively acted in such a way to deserve to be removed from office – The whole attempt smacked of vindictiveness from the Democrats who disliked him. His 2nd impeachment, however, I did support.

Some thought it was frivolous and unnecessary to impeach an outgoing president with only days remaining in office, but I supported it specifically because of the statement it made. It showed that America will not tolerate an elected official, regardless of office, working to subvert the democratic process. It's unfortunate that more Republicans did not take the opportunity to stand up for America, and instead chose to stand up for a 1-term president who manipulated his followers. If anyone deserves to be primaried in 2022 and 2024, it's the Republicans who cowered in fear of the wrath of a vindictive politician who threatened their jobs.

★ ★ ★

President Trump claiming that the election was stolen from him and rigged is based in either a very clear misunderstanding or complete ignorance as to how the election process takes place. For example, the ballots that were mailed in prior to Election Day, the vilified mail-in ballots, were not included in the immediate totals that started showing up in the news coverage on election night. The reason for this is that many states did not have legal mechanisms in place to begin counting the mail-in ballots prior to the close of the polling booths. Remember, this election took place during a global pandemic. In a typical year, mail-in ballots were not used nearly as extensively as they were in 2020, so the rules that had long been in place typically had relatively little bearing on the overall outcome of the election results in any given state. For reference, in 2016, approximately 33 million people voted by mail.[92] In 2020, that number ballooned to nearly 66 million. With repeated attacks on mail-in voting by notable Republicans in the lead-up to the election, Republican voters overwhelmingly showed up to the polling booths in person. This means that those mail-in ballots that couldn't be counted until after the polling locations closed were logically going to be overwhelmingly in favor of Joe Biden. While it looked like Trump was winning when most folks went to bed, over 40% of the overall ballot count was either only just starting to be processed, or entirely unaccounted for until late into the morning or in the days after. President Trump claiming that "bags of fake ballots" were being dropped off overnight was a completely inaccurate statement. Many bags of ballots most certainly *were* dropped off overnight, but that in no way implies that those ballots were fake – It means they were finally able to be legally counted. If this information is publicly available to interested civilians, it's logical to assume that the office holder who counts on this information to keep their job would be privy to the process. President Trump claiming that "ballot dumps" proved the election was rigged, stolen from him, and invalid, shows his complete ignorance to the process at best, or his blatant lying to the American people at worst.

One of the arguments against mail-in ballots was the opportunity for fraud, as the ballots had greater opportunities to be tampered with. This ultimately was found to be untrue, aside from extreme outlier situations, and nothing of statistical significance. The situations of mail-in ballot fraud that were proven ironically included cases of individuals fraudulently voting for President Trump.[93]

An argument for mail-in ballots was to alleviate the perceived concerns of individuals opting not to vote for fear of the pandemic. Those who followed pandemic safety protocols most stringently were often Democrats, so in attempt to prevent an artificial landslide win for the Republicans, Democrats pushed very firmly for mail-in ballots to be accessible to as many voters as possible. Some may take umbrage with this notion. It's important to remember, though, that it is the sacred right of all eligible Americans to vote for our elected officials. The method of voting is not what makes our ability to vote sacred, it's that we have the opportunity to do so. In 2020, politicians ensured all Americans, regardless of their personal comfort level with in-person voting, were able to vote. And a record 155 million individuals did vote that cycle. This level of engagement in the democratic process is something that we should all be proud of and hold up.

One argument that was made and relatively ignored was that the summer of 2020 saw months of protests and rioting in the wake of the murder of George Floyd. Governors, specifically Democrats, who mandated stay home orders for the sake of public safety created loopholes for "peaceful protests." Whether or not the protests were appropriate is not the point of this example – The point is that the politicians were hypocritical and contradicted themselves on public health measures and "following the science" when it was politically expedient. For those individuals who lost their livelihood due to the pandemic, or did not fully understand or appreciate the perceived need for the George Floyd protests, it looked to those folks like super spreader events were being condoned for the sake of political points. And to be fair, there's no other legitimate way to categorize the decisions of those governors. Pair that impropriety with a previously unheard-of attempt by Democrats to provide mail-in ballots to as many voters as possible to ensure that no votes were lost due to individuals staying home – many of whom were happy to join the protests – and it becomes more understandable that Trump voters felt as though they were being silenced, punished, and ignored.

Another argument made by President Trump was that typically on election night we know the winner of the election by the end of the evening. Historically there was a fair amount of truth to this, with some outlier situations, like the 2000 election between George W. Bush and Former Vice President Al Gore, which took months before it was officially concluded that Bush had won the election. While there is some value and sense of closure in having the results within hours, there is no rule or law that requires it to be that way. This was another attempt by the former president to influence his voters and potential voters away from mail-in voting. Interestingly, in 2016, the mail-in votes were pretty evening split between Donald Trump and Hillary Clinton. This implies, ironically, that President Trump actually caused himself harm in 2020, making his own arguments a contributing factor behind the mail-in ballots being so disproportionately in favor of Joe Biden.

In the subsequent months, President Trump and his legal advisors continued the drum beat of "evidence," and "more evidence to come," and "surprising evidence," and "proof of widespread election fraud." None of these extreme claims ever came to fruition, but why they never came to fruition is another source of frustration for those who voted for the former president, and which contributed to the events of January 6th.

Over 60 lawsuits were filed by the former president and his legal team. There wasn't a single case that gained them any positive ground. Most of the cases were dismissed on the face, including by a number of judges that President Trump himself had appointed to uphold the law. This is important to note, because it informs one of the reasons why many of those who voted for President Trump were unwilling to accept the outcome of the 2020 election – The overwhelming majority of the cases were never actually heard in court. I spoke to one supporter who said, "Well, I'll never really know if he actually lost or not, because they weren't willing to even look at the evidence. They had it out for him since the beginning, and tried to impeach him even when they knew it would fail anyway. They were always trying to stop him and get rid of him. Since they never looked at the evidence, I'll never really know if Joe Biden truly won the election. This is just another example of how unfairly Trump has been treated since the beginning."

While there may be factual errors and assumptions in that statement, there is factual truth there as well. Donald Trump was and always will be the 45th President of the United States. The media was unapologetically uneven in their reporting of him before, during, and after his time in office. The accomplishments he did achieve, like a historic peace treaty in the Middle East in the Abraham Accords, record low unemployment for Black and Brown folk, criminal justice reform, and the strongest economy ever in the modern world, were all covered with minimal fanfare, while his missteps and mean tweets, of which there were many, were reported ad nauseum. When these folks saw the court cases dismissed and essentially ignored, they felt themselves to have been dismissed and ignored. They felt as though they weren't given the opportunity to have their case heard. They didn't feel respected. They didn't feel as though the fact-finding and due diligence to prove or disprove the evidence was given its metaphorical day in court – Because it wasn't.

★ ★ ★

If you voted for President Trump in 2020, it is entirely logical to question the integrity of the election, given all of these variables. It's also entirely logical to assume or want to believe that there were nefarious forces in the background colluding to oust the highly impactful president. And it's entirely possible that a nationwide conspiracy involving Trump opponents, allies, and appointees alike were all able to keep a massive election fraud initiative a secret from the public. But with the spoilers of unreleased Marvel movies being commonplace, the thought of so many self-interested players keeping such an incredible secret from leaking seems pretty unlikely. Even assuming that an election conspiracy was true, without any actual evidence to prove that to be the case, the factual reality is that innumerable Trump allies and appointees all determined that the president did in fact lose the election. Even in September of 2021, almost a year later, the outcome was once again proven, this time by a pro-Trump group. The Arizona votes, that were in this case hand-tabulated, did in fact show that Joe Biden as the official winner of the state. The Arizona Senate President, Karen Fann, a Republican, said, "Truth is truth, numbers are numbers." Trump actually ended up losing by *more* votes as a result of the forensic audit.[94]

But facts don't always matter to us. As humans, we are emotional creatures. We "trust our gut," even when there is no evidence-based reason to do so. And when we feel cheated, or ignored, or pushed aside for The Other, it makes us angry. When we're angry, we say and do foolish things. When we trust and believe in someone who we respect, admire, or appreciate, we are more likely to turn a blind eye to the missteps, "accidental" falsehoods, and even outright lies. Think to yourself now – Most of us have been manipulated by someone we trusted at some point in our lives. For some untold amount of time, we ignored the bad, assumed the best, and continued to fall in their trap until it cost us so much that we finally said, "enough is enough," and ended the relationship. This is what President Trump was so masterful at achieving – Blind faith. This does not diminish his accomplishments, which I've already stated were dramatically and unfairly underreported by the media. But it does demonstrate the reality of the situation: Those who participated in the Capitol Riot on January 6th were manipulated, just like you and I have been manipulated before.

I was absolutely disgusted and appalled by what I witnessed that day. As a conservative and pre-Trump Republican, it was embarrassing. As an American, it was horrifying. As a human, it was tragic. Those of us who condemned that behavior would be justified in attempting to disassociate ourselves from those who supported it. Those who supported it, though, believed it to be necessary to uphold the very fabric of our democracy. As citizens, we are entitled to criticize their individual actions and behaviors, but we can also choose to respect the core of their intent. They truly believed themselves to be patriots who were protecting America. Regardless of your personal attitude toward the situation, this was their belief – They wanted to protect you, your freedom, and our democracy, because they were led to believe that it had been hijacked. Instead of damning their intent, we should appreciate their passion and enthusiasm for our country. We can choose to respect the fact that they were willing to invest time and energy to defending our democracy. We also have the power to choose to empathize with the fact that they were manipulated by the most powerful elected office holder in the world – Our President.

★ ★ ★

In January of 2020, before all of this election turmoil, I had the incredible honor of being invited by the White House to attend a 400-person event in which President Trump celebrated the United States-Mexico-Canada Agreement (USMCA). While I disagreed with much of his behavior, I did agree with and support many of his policies. Democrats and Republicans agreed that the USMCA was a huge win for America, and it was another underreported accomplishment of the president. Whether I agreed with everything he said and did or not, it was an honor to be invited to attend such an intimate event with the President of the United States. Anyone who has attended a Trump speech or rally can attest to the charisma of the man. When he goes off script, he truly is funny, self-aware, and larger than life. After seeing him in person, it was no longer a surprise to me why so many people felt compelled to blindly follow him. He's no Ronald Reagan in terms of decorum, but he was the president, and I was honored to have the opportunity to be in his presence.

When I was a child, Reagan, George H. W. Bush, and Bill Clinton served as the president. I remember that when they would come on the TV it felt like the whole world stopped to listen. I remember the reverence we afforded those who served us in the role of President of the United States. Agree or disagree, that was the president, and you stopped to listen. I don't remember when that changed, or maybe it changed gradually, but I do know that it isn't true anymore, as fans in sports stadiums now openly chant, "Fuck Joe Biden," or the PG-rated synonym, "Let's Go Brandon."

Sometime in late 2020, my daughter, Bree, who was 6 at the time, asked me, "Daddy, who is that angry man?" I told her that he was our president, Donald Trump. She asked why he was so angry. I don't remember what he was inflamed about that time in particular, but I do remember it being something remarkably trivial. I took it as an opportunity to explain to her how some people show their passions differently, then sent her out of the room. When I was a child, you stopped and listened to the president, and here I was protecting my child from what she might hear from one. President or not, Donald Trump is simply not someone that I want my children to emulate. It saddens me to say such a thing about the person who is supposed to be the "Leader of the Free World." Whether we liked the policies or not, we all deserve better from the behavior of our nation's highest representative and global role model.

Historically, I have voted for individuals that I feel will do the best job of working collaboratively with others, as opposed to who will do the best job representing my party of choice. As a result, I typically vote for candidates from a variety of parties, major and minor alike, for the sake of attempting to elect the individual best suited to represent the citizenry as a whole. Trump created some of the most incredible policies that were wonderful for our country, but culture matters more. His policies and best economy ever evaporated in a matter of months as a result of the pandemic. His legacy of vitriol and disrespect have permeated our cultural identity, and have exacerbated the division that was already present in our society. That, if nothing else, is the reason why I voted for a Democratic presidential candidate for the first time ever in 2020. Policies matter, but culture matters more.

★ ★ ★

President Trump's behavior played a direct role in the division our country currently faces, but he is in no way the only source of the problem. During the 2016 Presidential Primary season,

Hillary Clinton was asked a question that proved to be more revealing than it should have been. As a former first lady, senator, and secretary of state, Clinton was asked along with the other candidates, "You've all made a few people upset over your political careers. Which enemy you are most proud of." Her response was, "Well, in addition to the NRA, the health insurance companies, the drug companies, the Iranians... Probably the Republicans."[95]

Republicans. Nearly 40% of the country identified or leaned Republican at that time,[96] and she was publicly proclaiming her pride about making enemies out of them. Now, it's important to remember that this was a Democratic Presidential Primary Debate, so she was absolutely pandering to her base, but the reality remains the same – The person who almost became president in 2016 was proud of making enemies out of the party that nearly half of the people she would have represented associated with. That is not leadership – It's disgusting.

In Barack Obama's post-presidency memoir, *A Promised Land*, he was relatively fair in calling out his own faux pas. One that stood out as particularly problematic, though, was when he and Hillary Clinton were vying for the Democratic nomination back in 2008. In a moment of unscripted, off-the-cuff commentary, then-Senator Obama was asked about those in the Midwest who relied on industrial jobs that were mostly eradicated during the Great Recession, and responded, "They get bitter, they cling to guns or religion or antipathy to people who aren't like them or anti-immigrant sentiment or anti-trade sentiment as a way to explain their frustrations."[97]

What's interesting about this comment is that it is both dismissive of the American people, and simultaneously pre-cognizant of the playbook Donald Trump utilized to activate his followers only 7 years later. Here let's focus on Obama's remark, and how it was lacking in empathy. In 2008, there was a notable amount of fear amongst White folk, particularly in the South or rural areas, that if Obama were elected to serve as the first Black President, he would usher in an era of dramatically different policies and approaches than had been the historic norm in America. There were concerns of what some deemed would be overreaching efforts to support the Black and Brown communities, the intensification of affirmative action efforts that would exclude White folk, and conspiracy theories of starting reparations or a race war. Some would aggressively refer to these concerns as racism, others would more gently refer to them as the fear of the unknown. Either are likely fair assessments based on your worldview, though the reality remains the same – People didn't know what to expect from the first Black president in US history. So when this statement was made, it triggered those who were already unlikely to vote for him, but it also cast light on his worldview.

Those who had lost their livelihoods during the Great Recession and wanted nothing more than to get back to work were being trivialized as common folk with basic understandings of the challenges they faced. Disregarding these individuals and characterizing them as a demographic whose concerns were not worth intentionally acknowledging made Obama into a villain among that population. He was already The Other for the color of his skin, and now he made himself out to be an elitist and uninterested in solving the problems of those he would be charged with serving. The division in our country was already simmering beneath the surface, and Obama helped to exacerbate it with this single comment. It's no wonder that the division continued to increase over the years as voters felt supported and emotionally attached to the messaging of Donald Trump – He served as a direct counterpoint to this sentiment from President Obama.

★ ★ ★

If Donald Trump's messaging and election was a reaction to Barack Obama's presidency, Joe Biden's messaging and election was a reaction to Donald Trump's presidency.

In the 2020 presidential cycle, Joe Biden represented "normalcy," in the expected behavior and temperament of the Leader of the Free World. Trump never prioritized this sense of normalcy, and often characterized it as part of the reason why politicians "get so little done." In this regard, his approach was effective, but it was also divisive. There were those who found a sense of joy or entertainment as the president eviscerated his opponents via a 3 a.m. tweet. Those who didn't appreciate this behavior felt that it was unnerving, and that it risked accidentally (or intentionally) starting a war. Joe Biden had a nearly half-century track record of how he behaved as a politician. While he gaffed frequently, one of his biggest selling points was that the American people could reasonably anticipate what to expect from his actions and behaviors.

The 2020 election was an amplification of the division we witnessed in 2016, where people posted on social media, "if you're voting for Hillary, you should unfriend me," and "if you're voting for Trump, let me know so I can unfriend you." People literally ended relationships based on who they felt was the most appropriate person to represent them. That's how we know this conflict has gotten out of control: Politics has become an argument not for the sake of which candidate will make our country better off, but over the personalities of ultra-wealthy celebrities who are supposed to be public servants. It has become all about them, and not about us. Instead of being represented, served, and protected, as our elected officials should be most primarily concerned, they are focused on reelection and signing eight-figure Netflix and book deals after they leave office. Politics has become a path to wealth and power instead of being about serving the people, and we're being used by them through the media (who benefit through ad revenue when chaos increases viewership) to fight with one another and drum up further ratings and engagement. It's become a massive game about making money, and has ceased to be about service to the greatest country in the world.

Name-calling has become so commonplace amongst our "political leaders" that terms like "Quid Pro Joe," "Sleepy Joe," "Crooked Hillary," "Lamestream Media," "Do Nothing Democrats," "Pocahontas," "Crazy Bernie," "The Squad," "Agent Orange," and "Lyin' Ted," became acceptable and normalized. The problem with this is that our elected officials are supposed to be our "best and brightest," and instead we are subjected to their childishness on the nightly news by talking heads who profit off of the chaos and further amplify the disrespectful behavior. And we wonder why America is so divided...

Culture matters. We have allowed a series of individuals to lead us in directions that we should not desire to be lead. We see their poor behavior and think, "well, that person that I (dis)respect is doing it, so I can do it, too." And then we get on social media and start calling our friends "sheep" for living the way they feel is appropriate. It's an increasingly vicious downward cycle of disrespect and animosity, and we're allowing it. By not demanding better from our elected officials and media journalists, we indirectly condone and approve of their fanning the flames of division. To be fair, not all politicians are bad or self-interested, particularly at the local level. But increasingly, more state-level and federal politicians need to take a good hard look in the mirror and remind themselves of why they have chosen to *serve the people.* We should be holding them accountable to the standards we expect of these figureheads, and vote them out, with our ballots and viewing habits, when we feel that they are not behaving in the best interest of the nation. Spoiler Alert: It's most of them that need to be voted out.

★ ★ ★

One of the reasons why people liked Donald Trump was that he had no previous political experience. While there is a cost to not intimately understanding the legislative process, there is value in having a fresh perspective that does not include the baggage of being a career politician. It's one of the reasons why I always admired and respected Michigan Governor Rick Snyder. The Republican known for "Relentless Positive Action" was elected to office while I was living in Minnesota and campaigning for the successful re-election of US Congressperson Erik Paulsen. I was back in Michigan by 2014, and had the opportunity to vote for Snyder during his re-election that year. He later appointed me to serve on the State of Michigan Board of Respiratory Care. As a life-long asthmatic, it was an honor to have the governor entrust me with that responsibility, and to have the opportunity to serve my state in that way.

In 2010, the US Census showed that the state had lost nearly

55,000 citizens since the 2000 Census.[98] This loss was mostly attributed to the fallout of the Great Recession, and was regularly referred to within the state as "The Lost Decade." 2020's Census demonstrated an increase in population of more than 193,000, bringing the new total population of the Great Lakes State to a record of 10,077,331.[99] Snyder served as Governor for 8 of those 10 years, frequently referring to Michigan as "The Comeback State."

By the time Snyder left office, among other notable accomplishments, the following was true of Michigan:
- 1st nationally in new job creation for manufacturing, up from 48th
- 2nd fastest economic recovery in the nation
- Unemployment was reduced from 14.9% to 4.6%, the lowest since 2000
- The state's Rainy Day Fund increased from just $2 million (enough to run the state government for 30 minutes) to nearly $1 billion
- The state budget was balanced and signed months in advance seven years in a row, defying a trend of last-minute signing or government shutdown that had become the norm in the state
- And maybe most importantly for our purposes here, over 90% of the bills he signed into law were voted on with majority bipartisan support from both the State House and Senate

★ ★ ★

Michigan was in a much healthier position by the time Snyder left office, but not everything about the state was healthier. The Flint Water Crisis took place on his watch, where the city's water supply poisoned those who drank it with unsafe levels of lead. Twelve individuals lost their lives, and more than 80 were sickened with Legionnaire's Disease. His official participation in the decisions that lead to the crisis has always up for debate, with arguments about his role ranging from being informed that the situation was identified and contained to a single home, all the way to the criminal charges of willful neglect of duty.[100] The formal legal proceedings were plagued with missteps by the prosecution and perceptions of the case being politically motivated by the Democratic attorney general who had a reputation for being unnecessarily antagonistic to those she deemed to be political rivals. Some 7 years after the crisis, the case is not yet closed.

Though he was villainized by many for being the executive in charge at the time, what I respected about his handling of that situation was that he owned it. In his State of the State address in 2016, he said, "No citizen of this great state should endure this kind of catastrophe. Government failed you — federal, state and local leaders — by breaking the trust you place in us." He went on to add, "I'm sorry most of all that I let you down. You deserve better. You deserve accountability. You deserve to know that the buck stops here with me. Most of all, you deserve to know the truth, and I have a responsibility to tell the truth."[101]

He and I had dinner with his wife Sue and a friend on Mackinac Island a few months after he left office. We spoke of many things, including the Flint Water Crisis. It was clear to me that the pain and suffering Michiganders faced as a result of the crisis truly weighed on him, and that he wished different decisions had been made. Take it for what it's worth, but when you break bread with a person and look into their eyes, it's hard to ignore the sincerity behind the words they say.

One of the things I always appreciated about Governor Snyder was his balanced approach to navigating conflicting vantage points. He would almost certainly not be a recipient of a 100% perfect Republican policy score, and for that, I respected him. He looked at all of the evidence with the analytical mind of an individual who holds an MBA, JD, and a CPA, and made decisions that he believed to be in the best interest of all Michiganders. He sought to understand the opinions of those who both agreed and disagreed with him, and made decisions that pleased and displeased those who opposed him nearly as much as those who supported him. In effort to find common ground items that all parties could not only agree to, but be successful in accomplishing, he vetoed bills that were Republican priorities (myself included), just as easily as he vetoed bills that were Democratic priorities (myself included). He developed a track record of collaboration through focusing on Relentless Positive Action. This behavior and attitude even led to the surprise move of his writing an op-ed for *USA Today* endorsing Democrat Joe Biden for president, saying, "For years, I mentioned in most of my speeches the need to bring back civility to our nation. We will not continue to be the greatest nation in the world if we can't get along among ourselves. We have only become more divided over the past four years. We need a leader who believes in civility and bringing Americans closer together."[102]

What impressed me the most about the Governor was his consistency in making "common sense" decisions, as he called them. At one point in an interview during his tenure, he was asked if he was an "equal opportunity pisser offer." Laughing, he replied, "I don't use those words, but that's a fairly accurate assessment."[103] This statement in particular stood out to me, and increased my respect for the man. He owns his behavior in making decisions that appear to him to benefit the majority of the people, not his party.

None of us are perfect, and there are things we all wish that we could do differently, but when I think of a politician who most authentically lives the lessons and behaviors advocated for in this book, it's Rick Snyder. His success acts as a real-world example of the success that you and I can have by similarly embodying these behaviors.

★ ★ ★

For all of the balance and consistency Governor Snyder brought to Michigan, his successor, Governor Gretchen Whitmer, brought dramatic contrast.

Early in the pandemic, Michigan was the most hard-hit state in the country. While it was incredibly undesirable, lockdown seemed like the only reasonable solution to many. Governor Whitmer quickly started acting unilaterally, and was dismissive of the legislature's co-equal role in protecting and representing the people. At one point, Whitmer introduced executive orders on a daily basis, and incurred the wrath of the legislative body to the point where the law was ultimately changed so that future Governors cannot have the near unlimited power she chose to wield in increasingly meaningless ways. For example, one executive order required one-stop shop stores like Wal-Mart to close individual sections of the store, like the garden section. Another mind-bogglingly unnecessary executive order that I personally witnessed in the wild made it so stores could sell regular paint, but not spray paint located in the exact same aisle. Compared to Governor Snyder who prided himself on "common sense decisions," Whitmer's authoritarian decisions were the diametric opposite.

Whitmer became the poster child of governors who locked down their states. She was held up by many for "taking bold action to protect the people." She was equally reviled for "attempting to destroy small business and the livelihoods of Michiganders." The people also became increasingly angry with the double standard in her behavior (and that of governors like Gavin Newsom who faced a recall election in California over his behavior), like repeated unnecessary trips to Washington D.C. and Florida during her declared periods of stay home or restricted travel orders, and being photographed violating gathering limits with a large group at a bar. All of which seemed to translate to "do what I say, not what I do," or the frequently quoted, "rules for thee but not for me."

To Whitmer's credit, Michigan quickly became one of the least infected states in the country, though the costs to businesses, worker livelihoods, and the mental health of individuals were great. Unfortunately, those costs didn't seem to justify the actions taken, as Michigan ultimately returned to being the most heavily infected state in the nation just before Thanksgiving of 2021 – Not only regaining the undesirable title, but breaking the previous record the state had set.[104] In early-mid 2020, protests about her rules were a common occurrence, with armed protestors once storming the State Capitol and roaming around the viewing gallery with AR-15s. The threats of violence grew so intense, legislators resorted to wearing body armor to work.[105] Trump fanned the flames of dissent by tweeting out a series of negative and infuriating comments including, "that woman from Michigan,"[106] and

"LIBERATE MICHIGAN!"[107] Everything reached a boiling point in October of 2020 when the FBI announced that they had arrested 13 individuals in a domestic terror plot to kidnap and "try" Governor Whitmer, which was reported to be code for executing her.[108]

Compare all of this with individuals like Republican Florida Governor Ron DeSantis, who actively attempted to defund or fine local governments, school boards,[109] and cruise lines who sought to act in the best interest of their respective constituents over the implementation of mask and vaccine mandates. The "let the people protect themselves" approach made DeSantis a rising star in the GOP, and a frequently mentioned future presidential candidate.

Florida was a model of success for much of the beginning of the pandemic, with increasing arguments that a laissez-faire approach to public health may actually be more effective than more aggressive measures. Trump rallies, gathering tens of thousands of people, were ever-popular with mask usage being a rare sight amongst the crowds in spite of the potential danger of such an environment. Then the Delta variant showed up as the source of the Fourth Surge, and Florida became a hotbed of illness, hospitalization, and death. All while DeSantis continued to make himself into a hero or villain based on your perspective, as he threatened to remove funding for the salaries of school superintendents who allowed mask mandates to be implemented in their districts.

Each of these examples of noble intent and foolish missteps, and the way the citizens of each state had (dis)approval rating of their state's executive that mirrored the percentages of the voting population for that individual, shine a light on the real issue of our nation faces: In a world of 51% election wins, playing to the needs and desires of one party at the detriment of the people as a whole is the direct root of the divisiveness prevalent in our society.

There are the occasional outliers, like Governor Snyder, and you may feel differently about any specific individual, but on the whole, our elected officials are not Leaders. Our elected officials are not the inspirational figures who give us hope for a better tomorrow. Our elected officials do not demonstrate aspirational characteristics that we can highlight to our children. Our elected officials do not behave with the thought and concern of all constituents. Our elected officials are not Leaders.

★ ★ ★

While President Joe Biden did represent a return to normalcy, he quickly proved to be surprisingly inept in his policy work. His response to COVID-19 overwhelmingly mimicked Trump's with the only difference being that he claimed to "follow the science" until it wasn't politically convenient. Trump oversaw the most rapid production of a vaccine in history, not Biden. Biden oversaw the mass distribution of the vaccine, but that doesn't mean he did anything "better" than Trump in that regard – Trump had already made purchasing agreements with the pharmaceutical companies to vaccinate every American. Ironically, Biden and his team caused problems with vaccine hesitancy just as much as Trump did. When then-Senator Kamala Harris was featured in a Vice Presidential Debate with Vice President Mike Pence, Harris was asked if she would take the vaccine that had not yet been approved for use. Her response was, "If Dr. Fauci, the doctors, tell us that we should take it, I'll be the first in line to take it. But if Donald Trump tells us we should take it, I'm not going to take it."[110]

Like Obama's throw-away line about "clinging to guns or religion," this off-the-cuff retort did nothing but pander to her base, and invite increased vaccine hesitancy amongst anyone who already had an inkling of doubt about a vaccine that was produced faster than any before it. This comment was unhelpful, and likely played a role in unnecessarily costing American lives by encouraging some individuals to not follow the science in the name of political points.

President Biden should get credit for the speed at which Americans were vaccinated, but again, that isn't something that we can fairly and clearly say differentiates him from Trump. Biden proudly proclaimed that he wouldn't shut down the country, and again, that doesn't differentiate him from Trump. The media consistently framed the more than 400,000 deaths from COVID as being on Trump's hands, but they have not held Biden similarly responsible for the fact that over 375,000 additional Americans have died (as of November 2021) since Biden took office – With a vaccine in his arsenal.[111] While Trump was a poor advocate for masking and mask mandates, Biden has had to backtrack from the vaccines being a magical cure that would eliminate the need for masking, to advising even vaccinated Americans to mask up. So, when we stack Biden and Trump side by side on the topic of COVID, neither of them has been specifically better or worse than the other – They performed very similarly, with the only differences being stylistic.

Biden also should not get a free pass on the numerous mistakes he made that we should expect not to happen with someone who has as much expert counsel as the President of the United States. In the summer of 2021, Biden announced with the United Kingdom and Australia that the US would be sharing sensitive nuclear submarine technology in a new alliance deal that immediately infuriated China and France. The French Foreign Minister, Jean-Yves Le Drian, went so far as to call the deal, "unacceptable" and "incomprehensible," as the deal essentially terminated a previous agreement with Australia to sell them a dozen submarines using diesel power – A deal that was valued at $66 billion. Drian went further to say about the US, "this unilateral, sudden and unforeseeable decision very much recalls what Mr. Trump would do."[112]

President Biden also massively fumbled the exit from Afghanistan, which resulted in a rare showing of bipartisan criticism. He claimed that the deal with the Taliban was Trump's deal, and that's true, but what he omits from that statement is how he used the tool of executive order to systematically undo virtually everything he could that Trump had previously done. In his first 100 Days in office, Biden signed over 60 executive orders, 24 of which reversed policies that Trump enacted. When called out on his record pace of using the unilateral power of executive orders Biden said, "And I want to make it clear — there's a lot of talk, with good reason, about the number of executive orders that I have signed — I'm not making new law; I'm eliminating bad policy. What I'm doing is taking on the issues that — 99% of them — that the president, the last President of the United States, issued executive orders I felt were very counterproductive to our security, counterproductive to who we are as a country, particularly in the area of immigration."[113] This means that seven months before the botched exit from Afghanistan, Biden either agreed with Trump's deal with the Taliban, or did not see it as counterproductive. In either case, blaming Trump for the chaos and loss of life is inappropriate, and works only to cast blame as opposed to President Biden owning his role in the decisions he made that unnecessarily cost the lives of Americans.

★ ★ ★

In the aftermath of the murder of George Floyd, Black Lives Matter murals were painted on roads throughout the country. In Lansing, the capital city of Michigan, where I have worked for nearly two decades, there was a desire to create an inspirational piece of art that felt more inclusive of all people. It was similarly painted on the road, and read, "Power to the People." A collaborative public art piece, artists were asked to paint whatever they'd like that represented this theme within a single letter that was some 20 feet high and 10-15 feet wide. I selected the "W" for its symmetry, and used spray paint to color the left and right sides purple, with the left center being blue, the right center red, and a starburst in the middle to represent the political conflict that our nation is seemingly marching toward. Here's the description of the piece:

> Our Executive Branch officials are meant to be the representatives of the people. They are meant to be visionaries for a better future. They are meant to be aspirational Leaders. They aren't.

> The reality is, the Federal and State Executive Branches have grown to have too much power. They bully the Legislatures that represent the people in order to serve their party's demands, or ignore them altogether and sign executive orders. Republicans and Democrats are all guilty of this, and the losers are the people they are charged with serving and representing – Us.

> "Power to the People – W: Depower the
> Executive Branch," showcases this reality by
> demonstrating the people, who truly want
> to live in harmony as friends and neighbors,
> as the purple outsiders; the elected officials
> on the Left and Right represented by their
> respective political colors; and the clash that
> is impending represented by the starburst of
> white. It's time to return Power to the People
> and depower the Executive Branch.

As unfortunate as it is, this is even more true now than it was when the piece was created.

What this issue really brings to light is the extreme and overpowered nature of the executive branch being able to create rules and laws almost at will, without the oversight and consent of congress. It also demonstrates how division is taking place within our country at a policy-level, when the executives we elect have the power to make and break any policy the previous executive has made with nothing more than the stroke of a pen. It's both the most powerful and most fragile way to influence the policy direction of our country, and it's massive abused by both Democrats and Republicans, at both the federal and state-levels.

★ ★ ★

The dyadic two-party system we have in America is a significant source of division. It's natural to have an "us against them mentality," as we are highly individualistic in Western society. The success of individualism is predicated on there being a winner, which implies that there must be a loser. But what if we stopped looking at the world through a lens that only makes us happy every 4 or 8 years when our preferred party is in power? What if we expected that our elected officials ALL worked for us at all times, instead of working for the party they serve? What if we used cancel culture to eliminate those who do not behave in a way that leads to unity and collaboration for America? What if?

★ ★ ★
COVID
_____
_____

At the beginning of the global pandemic, I was the executive director of a mental health nonprofit focused on proactively preparing teenagers to be mentally resilient and increase their emotional intelligence. I had been asked at the end of 2019 to become the first full-time leader of the nonprofit I had been representing. The work was to support all sorts of kids who were passively or actively contemplating self-harm or suicidal ideation, and those who weren't but would benefit from greater mental resilience. It was important work that resonated with me deeply.

I had been working with a lobbyist who is a good friend and neighbor, Jason. He knew the Michigan legislative body inside and out. He knew who to talk to, in which order, why, and what topics or key phrases would light up the politicians. He helped me to secure dozens of meetings with the individuals whose buy-in I was seeking. We were trying to raise $1.5 million in state funds to do a broad-scale pilot of the program I had implemented in a school district in 2018. In early March, I got the phone call that the key legislator whose word was gold had given us verbal approval for a $3 million line item in the state's upcoming annual budget. It was an enormous win. COVID officially hit two days later.

We held out hope that the funding for the pilot would survive the pandemic, but almost immediately there was talk of amending and shrinking the current year's budget. I didn't need to wait long to know that the initiative was dead in the water. It was at about this time that the conversation started for the federal relief package that went on to become the CARES Act. I called my lobbyist and asked what opportunities he believed we had. To his credit, Jason was always honest with me. He wasn't optimistic about attempting to solicit congress, but he was encouraging that if I wanted to give it a go, it couldn't hurt. My other fundraising efforts were rapidly drying up, so I didn't have anything to lose. I took a voluntary 1/3 pay cut and got to work trying to get funding included in the CARES Act.

I worked with Democratic Congressperson Elissa Slotkin's office in Washington D.C. I had already met her a couple of times during her first term, and had started to lay the foundation of working with her team before the pandemic started. It wasn't a straight-up cold call, but no one in the D.C. office knew anything about me or this nonprofit yet, and the timing couldn't have been worse to try to get the attention necessary to make this ask. Except... the positioning of my ask hit a chord with the D.C. team. Mental health was already an issue that was gaining momentum, and the initial wave of lockdowns had created a tsunami of articles and fledgling research about the perceived and anecdotal impacts on youth and adults. I was in exactly the right place at the right time.

It took a while – I don't remember how long exactly, because time felt like it moved differently then – but after LOTS of phone calls, I got the word that the congressperson would be including a $3 million allocation for youth mental health recovery work that would fund a COVID-specific modified version of the program we were originally seeking to fund. She went on the news after the CARES Act passed to tout the great work these monies would be doing to help the youth citizens of her district. I still appreciate and respect everything that she and her team did to make this possible. Unfortunately, big things like this take time, and the clock was running out for the financial health of the nonprofit. At the end of July, I agreed with the board chair that it was the most financially prudent decision for me to lay myself off.

I was literally at the peak of my career in 2020. I had recently finished my 2nd graduate degree, and had just been recognized as the #1 Corporate Trainer in the World. I was asked to lead a non-profit for work that I believed in. Twice in less than a month I was told that we were approved for government financial support of $3 million to fund the programming we would offer youth to who desperately needed it. At no point did I fail, screw up, or make a career-ending decision. And yet here I was, unemployed for the first time in my 19 years of work after having to lay *myself* off, because of a fucking germ.

It was a dizzying experience. I felt lost, angry, confused, and sad. I knew this wasn't a reflection of me or my abilities, and yet, it felt like it was. I also felt badly for all of the other people who had similarly lost their jobs. Many of my friends from college found themselves unemployed after struggling to find work only a decade earlier when we all graduated in the middle of the Great Recession. It all felt like a bad joke. Honestly, it felt like complete bullshit.

★ ★ ★

Lockdown was hard for me. I was still working at that time, but I was an extreme extrovert who was used to being out 2-4 nights a week for networking events or teaching at a national Fortune 400 company's corporate headquarters as their dedicated Dale Carnegie trainer. I was in no way conditioned to spend 100% of my time in my house with my wife and our 2-, 4-, and 6-year-old children. The first three weeks were agonizingly difficult, and I very clearly understood why there were mounting reports of increased drug and alcohol abuse – Reports that ultimately ended up demonstrating the highest overdose deaths on record in a single year in the United States, up nearly 30% over 2019 according to the CDC.[114]

Spring turned to summer, and my relationship with my wife became healthier than it had ever been. I was able to witness special moments of my children doing trivial things that made me smile. I was able to pause and reflect on who I was, and what I believed I was here on this planet to do. COVID was terrible for lots of reasons, but our family worked hard to find and appreciate the parts that have forever improved our lives.

I turned down the only job I was offered. It was a cool role working in the president's office of an international university. As the sole income-earner for our family, it was a strange experience to not have a job and to then turn down an income. One of the problems was that I would be making about 60% of my prior salary as a consultant. I watched a lot of people – a lot of friends, too – ignore this reality and grab the first thing that came their way. I don't fault their knee-jerk reaction to get back to work, but I sympathize with the fact that they may have made one of the worst financial decisions of their lives by resetting their income indefinitely for the sake of a faster paycheck. Hopefully my concern proves to be unfounded and everyone who lost their jobs will get back to pre-pandemic economic parity quickly, but there is little reason to believe that will actually happen for the majority of those who accepted reduced income in their new roles.

There was another reason why I turned down the role, but I couldn't articulate it at the time – It just didn't feel right. I told my wife that, and that I was contemplating turning it down, and she encouraged me by saying, "You always make the best decisions you can for our family. I trust you. Trust yourself." Trust yourself. That simple statement became the theme of a virtual speaking tour that I did all over the country in 2021. I listened to her.

★ ★ ★

You know that sinking feeling you get in the pit of your stomach when you look down from a high ledge? That's what it felt like when I laid myself off. That's the feeling I've had every time I had to make a major shift in my life. It's like knowing what the best course of action is, but also knowing that it requires a leap of faith. In order to take a leap of faith, though, you have to trust that you won't fall.

I had the opportunity to share my experiences during COVID with individuals all over the country in 2021, speaking to groups small and large. I was interviewed on podcasts, in magazines, and shared the story of hope and inspiration with the employees of big companies like DoorDash. It was a really cool thing to be able to do, but it was even cooler to know what it meant to people.

The first time I gave the talk was to a Rotary Club with about 20 people in virtual attendance. Admittedly, that first talk didn't seem like anything special or noteworthy to me, but that wasn't their experience. A superintendent friend of mine invited me to share my story of being recognized for an award I received in the fall of 2020 for accomplishments from 2019. I didn't much care about bragging to the group, so I decided to tell them all of the ugly parts of my journey, and bring it back full circle to something positive and action-oriented. By the end, there were actual tears, and I received numerous phone calls and emails thanking me for sharing the message. The superintendent shared that it was exactly the message of hope that his club had been missing and needing to kick off the new year.

I always ended the 25-minute talk looking straight into the camera and sharing some ad-libbed iteration of this message:

> Whatever challenge you're facing right now is real. Whether its financial insecurity, health insecurity, job insecurity, or just plain insecurity in general, I want you to know that you have within you everything you need to face this challenge and overcome it.
>
> You have been successful in your life lots of times. LOTS of times. And you have been less successful than you would have liked lots of times, too. You've learned from every single one of these experiences. They're like LEGO blocks in your mind. If you trust yourself, those experiences are parts and pieces that you can put together and recombine to resolve your issue, and successfully overcome the challenge that you're facing.
>
> When it feels like you're standing on the edge of that proverbial cliff, if you trust yourself, you'll find that you aren't falling, but you're flying.

★ ★ ★

About six months after turning down the job offer, I realized why it wasn't the right fit for me. At this point I had already started Leadership Coaching for Results. As I was building the curriculum for The Leadership Mastery Program, I had an epiphany. In the beginning of the program, each person goes through a guided process of identifying the type of Leader they need and want to be. The exercise is powerful and liberating, and informs many of the subsequent decisions a person makes in their life and career. In the end, they have what we call their Leadership Statement. It's a one sentence affirmation of who that person is as a Leader. Mine is, "I am a Leader who develops other Leaders."

When I finished building that exercise, I realized that the reason why the offer I had turned down didn't feel right was because the role wasn't in alignment with who I am and what I am here to do. That role would not have afforded me the opportunity to serve others and help them to become the Leader that they need and want to be. I feel blessed to have learned this, and that I don't regret the decisions that I made during that incredibly difficult time in my life.

★ ★ ★

Before I started Leadership Coaching for Results, I had another experience that was profound. I consciously chose to be open and vulnerable about my employment status with a number of people that I respected, and sought their counsel. It felt a bit embarrassing to admit in the moment, but everyone was very supportive and encouraging. What was a surprise, though, was that they were almost TOO encouraging! Everyone had tremendous faith in my ability to bounce back and land on my feet, and deep down I knew it too, but I wasn't in that mental headspace yet.

I knew I needed to process what I was experiencing. I also knew that I was cut-off from my extroversion outlet of being with people. Fortunately, at this point in the pandemic the caseload was cooling down and there was hope (as well as dreaded fear) that the autumn of 2020 would be different than the spring. I took the opportunity to invite a handful of trusted friends to my home to have their favorite cocktail on my front porch and catch up.

Each of these individuals was well aware of my situation, but none of them knew the gory behind-the-scenes details of how it came to be – Details I've chosen to omit here, as they would only serve to disparage others, and don't add anything of value to this story. Sharing my story was cathartic and allowed me to move on from the frustration and pain of the experience, and allowed me to shift my mindset to what could come next. It was with this renewed mentality that I was able to explore what I really wanted to spend my time doing, with whom, and how.

When I graduated with my undergraduate degree, I had the opportunity to be my class' student commencement speaker. Before some 5,000 people, I shared a message that was essentially, "We've been given so much by our family, friends, and this university – Let's get to work serving others." During one of these conversations on the front porch, I was reminded of that message, and how it has always been a core element of who I am. I knew that I wanted to be of service to others, but what that looked like was less important. One of those folks suggested that I reach out to a bunch of my old clients who had friended me on social media, and ask them to share with me the biggest impact I made on their life. It was brilliant counsel. Thirty-five people sent me videos sharing what I helped them to realize about themselves, or that I helped them to feel empowered, or that I held them accountable not to me but to themselves. Thirty-five people shared the difference I made in their lives. That was incredibly powerful. That was exactly what my battered psyche needed. That was a gift. And that became the basis for how I built my business. I didn't build the company I wanted to build, I built a company that was focused entirely around the successful and positive outcomes other people respected and appreciated me for helping them to achieve. I built a company that allowed me to be of service.

★ ★ ★

The company was thriving enough that I was able to pay myself for the first time just before Thanksgiving in 2021. Being without an income for 16 months is really hard. Kristy was willing to get a job to help out, but it was best for our family that she maintained responsibility of our children and household. We were fortunate that we had already made a bunch of financial decisions in the years leading up to COVID that made it possible. We were also fortunate to have the help and support of an incredible friend and confidant, our financial advisor, Ryan Kiernicki. I will actively and shamelessly plug him until the day I die. If you don't have a financial advisor, Google him – He can serve you in Michigan or elsewhere. Ryan was the counsel I leaned on the most throughout this experience. I had a number of individuals helping and supporting me in a variety of ways, but virtually every decision I made was run past Ryan before I pulled the trigger. He had answers to questions I didn't even know to ask, and he had recommendations that made my life easier and more cost-effective when I couldn't afford to waste a penny, like when I had to have an emergency appendectomy in January of 2021.

Our medical insurance was very good before I laid myself off. We were fortunate with the very generous coverage that we had. Paying to continue to maintain that coverage would have cost us almost $1,400 per month through COBRA. I was prepared to pay it until Ryan advised that I go to the Healthcare Exchange and purchase coverage there. It was one of the simplest recommendations he made, but it had tremendously positive impact. Unrelated entirely to Ryan, this decision also caused me a lot of headaches.

In 2009 I was a staunch opponent of the Affordable Care Act. I graduated with my undergraduate degree that year, and felt entitled to having insurance because I completed college and got a good job. I said on more than one occasion, "If these people want insurance, they should work hard and go get a job that provides it for them." I was even so bold at the time that I wore a t-shirt that had a big "OBAMA" written across the chest, but in place of the "O" was a hammer and sickle. In 2012, while I was rebranding the 70+ year-old professional trades small business, I worked directly with the owner, Rich, as we decided to reduce the level of healthcare coverage offered to the employees because the new prices were so prohibitive that we couldn't afford to provide the platinum-level coverage anymore. It physically pained Rich to have to reduce the offering to the employees he cared for like family, but we both knew there was no other option at that time. I had a really negative perspective of the ACA. And now I was using it. Thank God it existed.

Getting on the Healthcare Exchange isn't exactly hard, but it is labor intensive. Every phone call took 45-120 minutes. The people were all surprisingly nice, helpful, and knowledgeable. We were able to maintain a very comparable level of healthcare coverage not for $1,400 per month, but for about $350 per month. Saving this much money every month immediately changed the financial projections I had made, and allowed us the opportunity to have our situation go the way that it did. Then I discovered how difficult it is to use government welfare services.

There are a plethora of services provided to individuals who are low or no income, but none of them come easily, and all of them feel like they were actually created solely for the purpose of supporting other government-funded services to continue to provide jobs for more government workers. I can't speak to this actually being true or not, but it sure as hell felt like it. One of the services provided to low-income families is a child-specific version of free insurance. Since we had no income at all, we qualified, but I had budgeted to pay for comparable insurance to what we were used to, so using the free stuff was unnecessary. I attempted to decline the service, but was told that I was automatically enrolled as a function of being on the Healthcare Exchange at the income level I was at. In order to not use the free service, I was told that I needed to call that organization and request that it be deactivated. This made no sense to me, but I did as I was told and called to turn off the service. Forty-five minutes later, the kind gentleman on the other end of the phone said, "You're all set." You'd think that would mean that I was all set. But I wasn't.

It turned out that in order to make this deactivation official to the Healthcare Exchange, I was required to request a physical copy of my proof of deactivation, because, you know, fax machines, emails, and shared systems that can turn things on automatically were apparently incapable of turning them off in 2020... I didn't realize that this was a requisite step until another 75-minute phone call. At that point it was too late, as I had lapsed past an arbitrary deadline, thinking all along that I was "all set." This meant that I had broken the terms of my agreement, and the $350 per month premium jumped to almost $1350 per month. To drive this point home, I had to pay an extra $1,000 per month for the exact same thing because I didn't turn off the thing that I didn't ask for, nor did I need in the first place.

I was furious. It took four months and an untold number of hours before a formal appeal to have my issue overturned was declined. At one point, as the issue was being explained to me by the person who really wanted to help but couldn't, I finally lost my cool and said, "I have two masters degrees and I can't figure out how to work with you all. How the hell do uneducated people do this?" The individual on the phone punted before asking, "Would you like me to make this declined appeal official, or would you like to take this to a federal hearing?" I quickly asked for a federal hearing. I actually had to swear under oath that I was a victim of my own ignorance to the complexity of their system. Fortunately, it was clear to the federal officer that I had done my due diligence and truthfully made a mistake, and everything was reset back to where it was, saving me nearly $4,000 up until that point, and a $1,000 per month thereafter in the process.

I share all of that frustration to say, for better or worse, I'm thankful for the Affordable Care Act. When I had sudden and increasingly intense pain late one January evening and my doctor told Kristy that I needed to go to the ER, I suspected what the issue was. Not even an hour later it was proven that my appendix was on the precipice of rupture, and I required immediate surgery. Thirty minutes later I was in an operating room, and two days after that, I returned home. That experience had a total cost of over $40,000. But with the ACA, the bills came in at just over $3,000. And after a humble request to the hospital because I still had no income, they waived those outstanding fees. I texted a friend about it all afterward, and closed the story by writing, "Thanks Obama." She laughed and said she had never heard anyone use that phrase in a positive context. If I could thank him in person, I would.

I was vehemently opposed to the Affordable Care Act when I didn't personally see the value of it. It wasn't until I needed it and it was there for me that I came to appreciate it. I damned what I didn't understand until I finally understood its value. In how many instances is that reality true for each of us?

★ ★ ★

It became obvious that there was no choice but to lay myself off about two weeks after the federal unemployment bonus of $600 per week expired. It was really crappy timing for someone with a reasonably high salary to not have the opportunity to utilize the program. I'm glad it was there for those who needed it, but it created a giant unforeseen problem that was then bastardized and used as a political weapon. Offering someone like me an additional $600 per week would have been helpful in my time of need, but it no way came close to replacing my salary. Conversely, the high school and college students who teach at my kids' swim school were now making nearly triple their normal income by being unemployed.

As the $300 per week federal unemployment bonus was being intentionally rejected by Republican governors all over the country, and as the conservative media was making baseless claims of laziness, I started to see small business owner friends on social media sharing memes and writing angry tirades about "entitlement," and "sitting on their asses instead of working."

The irony I saw in all of this was that these same individuals were the ones who gladly accepted federal handouts in the form of the Payroll Protection Plan (PPP). There are organizations that I was intimately aware of actually being financially *better* off because of the federal support they received, and yet, here they were damning their own laid-off employees and prospective employees on public forums for not returning to work. I was appalled, and shared this message:

> Unpopular Opinion:
>
> If you took a PPP loan, how dare you complain about not being able to hire "entitled," "lazy people," "looking for a government hand-out."
>
> The PPP *is* a government hand-out.
>
> These workers have done the math. Working for you isn't the fiscally responsible move at the moment. If you want to be mad at anyone for the fact that you don't have workers, either look in the mirror, or blame the government. No one should have ever gotten over 100% of their prior income for being unemployed. But, since the government screwed up, the workers are making the decisions that are appropriate for them. They're not lazy, they're being smart.
>
> If you want workers now, try incentivizing them with the fungible dollars you saved due to your tax-payer funded, 100% forgivable, PPP loan. Or, stop complaining like an entitled lazy person and get back to work.

My opinion turned out to be not that unpopular. Admittedly, my own personal experience with being unemployed impacted my view of this issue and the vitriol being spewed at those who shared my circumstance hit very close to home. But I felt it was important to cast light back on the individuals who consciously chose to ignore the reality of the argument they were making, which was that they had been the recipients of a government bailout intended to offset the government-mandated lockdowns, and they had similarly benefitted for "doing nothing" just like those they were damning. It wasn't their frustration that I found offensive, but their blatant hypocrisy and demeaning attitudes toward The Other that really pissed me off.

★ ★ ★

It's a dangerous road when we damn someone for doing things differently than us. It's also entirely commonplace and generally accepted within close company to cast blame, name call, and belittle those who are different from us or who we do not yet know. The problem with this is that it doesn't change anyone's behaviors, and serves only to demonstrate our own ignorance to other viewpoints. It also opens up the opportunity to show the world our own blind spots and hypocrisies. Certainly you've identified some of mine by now. These are our inherent biases.

A prime example of these hypocrisies is the usage of slogans that are common to one side an argument being hijacked and used as an attack by the other side. Here we need to resort to stereotypes, while knowing full well that stereotypes are not truly representative of whole groups of people. This argument remains the same: Those who protest against vaccination are stereotypically the same individuals who oppose abortion, and yet they have hijacked the slogan, "My Body, My Choice" as a defense against vaccine mandates. The problem with doing this is that we can't have something be true when it's convenient for us, and untrue when we don't like it. If it's your body and your choice what happens with your body, that is true for The Other who makes choices you disagree with, like abortion. And if abortion is about one person's choice of what to do with their body, we also need to accept that there are individuals who will choose to remain unvaccinated, because that's what they believe is right for them. We can't have it both ways, or we're behaving like hypocrites. If we want to make a point by waving a sign that says "My Body, My Choice," everyone else gets that right, too, regardless of if we agree with the choices they make with their body.

★ ★ ★

Those responsible for making the toughest decisions during the early days of COVID were not in an enviable position. We may all disagree on what the best course of action should have been, but the one thing that I think we can all agree on is that the elected officials at the state and federal levels all got a lot wrong. They tried; I truly believe that. There was no modern era precedent that informed a single best practice. I believe that the Presidents Trump and Biden and the governors all did the best they could from their unique vantage points. That said, as a Monday Morning Quarterback, they all screwed up far more than they got it right.

The biggest thing that was bungled during this entire crisis was in the messaging. From Trump to Dr. Anthony Fauci to Biden to the CDC, the messaging from the federal government was abysmally inconsistent and confusing. Compilation videos of Fauci contradicting himself abound on the internet. From telling people not to wear masks, to advising that they do, to recommending double masking, to boldly proclaiming that the vaccine would allow individuals to not need masks, to implementing federal mask mandates even for the vaccinated, to not needing booster shots, to "definitely needing" boosters while the scientific evidence was still unproven, to the FDA directly contradicting the need for boosters, to his denial of the NIH funding Gain of Function research in Wuhan, to there being proof that he should have been fully aware of that funding... The messaging was tremendously inconsistent. Like him or not, Dr. Fauci's messaging played a very direct role in adding to the skepticism of those who didn't subscribe to the notion that COVID was an actual crisis.

One reason why it would be fair to cut Fauci some slack is the fact that we have witnessed the scientific process occurring in real-time. From hypothesis to testing to (dis)proving the hypothesis, the scientific process of understanding how best to live with COVID played out for all to see. Transparency is good, but messaging is important. Throughout this whole process, people were given conflicting messages that fueled confusion, anger, and skepticism. From a scientific standpoint, it is completely and entirely normal to expect that not all hypotheses would be proven, which means it should be completely and entirely normal to expect that guidance given at one point in the pandemic would be revisited and updated accordingly. The problem, though, is that every. single. thing. was explored openly in front of the public in daily presidential briefings. What should have been a source of authoritative information became a source of confusion, misinformation, contradiction, casual and flippant advocacy from President Trump about merits of bleach and hydroxychloroquine, and a series of guesses and assumptions by Fauci and others that were shared in 3-second sound bites on talking head shows that were later proven to be wrong. This is all because the federal government, under both Trump and Biden, failed miserably at messaging.

In hindsight, adopting the Obama Administration's use of "czars" would have been the best course of action for COVID messaging. Nothing would be shared unless it came from that singular authoritative individual. If an answer was unknown, an assumption or half-known answer would not be giving, but added to the list of answers that need to be found and shared at a later date. With this approach, information would have been released slower, but it also would have been far more broadly accepted, as there would be little to no "noise," and only the best and reasonably proven guidance would be provided.

Another area where the federal government missed the mark was in convincing individuals to actually have faith in science when the government actively ignored the science behind natural immunity developed by those exposed to the virus. Vaccine mandates for employers, federal employees, and threats of being excluded from movie theaters, restaurants, public transport, and the like gave many the feeling that the government was more concerned about people having a vaccine injected into their bodies than they were with actually following the science. There was little to no acknowledgment that those who survived the virus were equally safe to participate in society as those who were fully vaccinated. This exclusion of a massive portion of the population created a perception of impropriety and made it appear as though the elected officials responsible for guiding the people successfully through the global public health crisis were actually sales people for the pharmaceutical companies that lobby them and donate to their political campaigns.

At no time was this more obviously transparent than when the conversation around booster shots heated up in the fall of 2021. Questions of long-term vaccine efficacy existed back to the original testing of the protective serum, and there was always reason to believe that annualized shots may become a reality similar to flu shots. The conversation became more eyebrow raising, though, when Biden declared that Americans would be eligible, and strongly encouraged, to get a booster shot 8 months after completing their original vaccine course. Then it was announced days later Americans would be eligible to get a booster shot at 6 months. Then the World Health Organization Director-General, Dr. Tedros Adhanom Ghebreyesus, came out in strong opposition to "rich nations" providing booster shots when the rest of the world was still dramatically under vaccinated due to production and distribution chains.[115] Then the CEO of Pfizer, Albert Bourla, wrote an open letter touting internal findings and the value and importance of individuals receiving a booster shot, all while ignoring the obvious reality that offering or requiring booster shots plays a direct role on the pharmaceutical company's stock price.[116] To punctuate it all, the FDA determined that the scientific data did not support the need for booster shots for individuals under 65, or those without comorbidities.[117] Boosters were eventually approved for all adults, though there was never a public declaration that the scientific data had changed in such a way to favor this outcome.

If you are an individual who felt receiving the vaccination was personally uncomfortable, not personally realistic, or unnecessary, it makes sense that you would have felt that way. If you survived COVID, as an overwhelming percentage of infected individuals did, it's also entirely logical to see vaccination as being unnecessary or wasteful. And, there are a lot of people who think differently than you for similarly valid reasons.

★ ★ ★

One of the unintended consequences of lockdowns and stay home orders is what it did to the psyches of individuals. I previously referenced the increased incidence of drug and alcohol abuse, which will likely have some sort of long-term implications for our society. Lots was said in the media about the impact of learning loss and negative social impacts on youth, so much that the science of child development ruled that it was of greater importance than the science of avoiding being exposed to the virus.[118] The conversation around mental health bubbled up and died down with regularity, almost as if it was assumed that everyone's mental health had been negatively impacted, therefore it wasn't a problem worth focusing on until we concluded the pandemic (or ever).

As an aside, a study conducted by the *American Journal of Preventative Medicine* found in the fall of 2021 that due to their more stringent public health policies, Democrat-led states had an 8% lower incidence of COVID-19 spread than Republican-led states.[119] While the politicization of public health was the focus of the study, there should be a real and valid question in regard to the impact on those subjected to the more stringent public health measures, and an attempt to quantify if the 8% reduction in viral spread had a net positive or net negative impact on the overall health and wellbeing of the rest of the population, but such an intensive study will likely not be concluded for years.

What was dramatically under-reported, or possibly unknown, was the impact of individuals caught in situations of domestic abuse; the impact of ignoring health concerns like "a new lump," that couldn't be diagnosed in the early stages; and deaths of despair, which are either intentional or accidental deaths that were directly connected with the negative psychological impact individuals experienced as a result of isolation, loneliness, and persistent stress.

My focus at the beginning of the pandemic was on helping young people to not become a statistic tied to deaths of despair. I worked with peers in the space to provide programming in partnership with other nonprofits, and spent a lot of time delivering programs and building new programming that was specific to the needs of the moment. I was concerned with the low degree of adoption we were seeing so early in the pandemic, and in the end my concerns were verified, as that work proved to be provided too soon. The immediate chaos of the pandemic and lockdown created a tidal wave of confusion, stress, and distraction from long-term needs. People weren't thinking about the future at all – They weren't even thinking about the next day. They were living hour by hour as breaking news alerts flashed across every news station and cell phone push notification with increasing frequency. The mental health impact for young people was barely considered broadly until after I was no longer working in that space. To some extent I feel like I abandoned that work entirely, which I feel badly about, but I also know that I needed to protect my own mental health, and needed to create space between me and the source of my pain. Fortunately, there are lots of good people and organizations still championing that important work.

★ ★ ★

One of the ways I protected my mental health and processed the experience of lockdown was by creating art. I had started investing time and energy into creating art in 2015, and found success early and rapidly. By 2018 I had a permanent installation of my work in an innovation incubator, and in 2020 expanded my reach into exhibits all over the country, earning a Best in Show honor in a national juried exhibit for artists under 40.

I created a number of pieces during lockdown and the subsequent stay home orders. Here I'll outline three of them. Two were intended to be public art, and another that was a more personal reflection of my mindset at the time. The first piece of public art is a variation of this book's cover art. I've created *The Flag* many times for individuals and other projects. It's done using various applications of spray paint on particle board. It gives it a rugged and messy texture that I believe is representative of the current state of our nation. The description for the cover art has its own dedicated section at the beginning of the book, titled Art, for you to read at your leisure.

The second piece of public art is a very simple yet bold swirling white semicolon on a stark black background. The piece is called *Semicolon*, and represents the symbol used by those who have contemplated and overcome suicidal ideation. On the sides of the piece are words of support, like "Your Story Isn't Over," the phone number for the National Suicide Prevention Lifeline, and the description, "Semicolon: When an author could end a thought and chooses not to." I have the symbol tattooed on the inside of my left wrist as a reminder to myself of what I've overcome, and in solidarity with those who are still struggling. My hope with wearing the tattoo, and in creating the art, is that it will be a symbol of hope at the right moment in time for a person who feels hopeless.

★ ★ ★

**If you or someone you know are struggling with suicidal ideation, know that what you're feeling is not abnormal, and there are people who are committed to helping you.
Call the National Suicide Prevention Lifeline
800-273-8255**

★ ★ ★

The third piece was kind of an accident, but it ended up making the theme even more powerful. I had two pieces of 24" x 24" wooden board that were left over from another project, and I had some leftover red and blue spray paint that I had sprayed into cups for *The Flag*. I didn't need the remainder of the paint for that project, so they were going to go to waste. I decided to pour one of the colors over each of the spare boards. I originally planned for that to be a base coat for some other inspiration that would present itself, but instead, the finished yet unfinished look seemed to be a perfect analogy for how myself and so many others felt in the early days of the pandemic. I called it *Red / Blue*. Here's the description for you:

Red / Blue
Spray Paint / Wood
Toxic / Natural
Anger / Depression
Social Distancing / Feeling Isolated
Stay Home / Zoom

No School / Distance Learning
Republicans / Democrats
Don't Waste Masks / Masks for All
Flatten the Curve / Protest
Work from Home / Record Unemployment
Stimulate the Economy / Generational Debt
Small Business / Amazon
Public Safety / Civil Liberties
Vaccines / Second Wave
Deaths by Illness / Deaths of Despair

COVID-19 has created limitless confusion, anxiety, and contention.

Red / Blue, created during quarantine, is designed to create a similar sense of unease and frustration over the perception of being "too simple" or "incomplete," much as the governmental and media messages about the virus have elicited these emotions. The aim of this piece is to physically represent these conflicting reactions, and manifest in the viewer the uncomfortable feelings of the pandemic.

Clearly the message resonated with the way individuals all over the country were feeling, as it was featured in numerous virtual exhibits that were held throughout the nation.

★ ★ ★

Being forced to lay myself off because of COVID had a very direct impact on my mentality toward the virus. Through my experiences as a coach, I know that no single individual is truly unique in their thinking and behavior. If something is true for one person, it is almost certainly true for many. Therefore, I believe it is safe to assume that many of those who lost their livelihoods due to COVID are inclined to share my personal perspective. Conversely, there are countless individuals who did not lose their ability to provide for their families, nor were they negatively impacted in any notable way. As a result, it is reasonable that those folks would find it to be foolish to support new and uncomfortable measures, like masking, staying away from loved ones, and vaccination.

I was elected to serve on my children's school board right as we had to figure out how to keep the private Montessori alive through the extreme loss of students. The school was approaching its 40th anniversary, and we were truly concerned that permanent closure was a potential reality. We worked through all of the chaos of closures, ad hoc online learning, losing immunocompromised teachers, and an enrollment headcount that was completely unsustainable. We ultimately voted to approve a Return-to-School plan for the fall of 2020 that I agreed with for the school as a whole, but that I also knew would not be an appropriate solution for my young children – Another example of disagreeing with yourself for the sake of the greater good. As a result, Kristy and I pulled our kids out of the school and used my lay-off as the elegant excuse to save face. We hired a teacher directly with three other families, converted our garage into a permanent classroom, and created a pod of five children that absolutely thrived. It was an incredible outcome that was unfortunately not the norm for many children around the country.

Given the nature of the pandemic at that time, we all agreed to dramatically limit our exposure to others outside of our little bubble of families. In honor of that agreement, we named the Montessori-esque pod school the Bubble Casa. We all agreed to follow the wishes of the teacher, and the children were masked unless they were eating or outside. If there was an exposure, we closed the Bubble Casa for the recommended number of days. The families all had healthy relationships with one and other, and there was not even one instance of common cold amongst the kids throughout the entire year. We all sacrificed for one another, and consciously made difficult decisions around introducing potential infection into our bubble, including experiencing the holidays without extended family. Our family actually celebrated Thanksgiving in 2020 with one of the families from the Bubble Casa as opposed to our respective extended families.

While all of this was happening, I had three guys in my neighborhood that became very close friends. We bonded over a streaming show that we all enjoyed, and quickly had a standing appointment to spend Friday evenings together on one of the guy's back patio to watch the newest episode of whatever show we picked up next. We were outside, masked, wearing double coats and taking turns huddling near the fire or under an umbrella heater. In the deep of winter, we built a 3-sided structure out of tailgating tents and had multiple heat sources active at the same time. It was both miserable and fun at the same time, and memorable. We bonded deeply, made lots of great food and drink, and laughed. It was a really helpful and healthy outlet to have when we were each closed off from the rest of our individual friend circles and families.

Kristy and I were vaccinated at the very beginning of the Johnson & Johnson vaccine availability. The guy whose patio we occupied regularly and his wife were vaccinated at the exact same time and location. Our other guy friends and their families were already vaccinated. We were all very heavily engaged in reading, researching, understanding R-values, efficacy rates, side effects, and journal-level literature of the vaccine development (we're all pretty nerdy). We were all well aware of the fact that the vaccines took 14 days in order to be fully effective, but the euphoria of finally being able to see the light at the end of the tunnel, paired with the lack of incidence for months within our small group, we threw caution to the wind that night and celebrated. We ordered a bunch of food, drank more than normal, and spent the whole evening outside and unmasked. The next day we all felt shitty, but between the vaccine side effects and the items we had consumed the night before, it seemed logical. Until Patio Guy and his wife got worse the next day, then they both ended up in the hospital the day after that.

Patio Guy stayed in the hospital for a few days on oxygen and required an antibody infusion before he was released and went into isolation for weeks. It was a nail-biting period of days while we waited for the appropriate amount of time to pass in order for the drive-in testing site to be able to get an accurate read on if I was now infected or not. I wasn't, and neither were the other guys. But Patio Guy ended up with Long COVID and dealt with its effects for months before he started to feel normal again. It was an extremely close call that scared all of us back into behaving intentionally and cautiously.

As the school year came to a close, Kristy and I decided with the teacher to keep the Bubble Casa open for one more year. The incredibly low student to teacher ratio had resulted in the kids having learning growth that was unmatched compared to their peers. The other families all moved on for a variety of reasons, but we were uncomfortable with our children returning to school with the Delta variant in full swing and youth vaccines not yet available. I was personally less concerned about the kids contracting the virus itself than I was about them having the long-lasting and unpredictable side effects of Long COVID, which had been studied to affect as many as 46% of child COVID patients.[120] If I could prevent my children from experiencing brain fog, extreme fatigue, gastrointestinal issues, and the sensory distortion that many of my friends had experienced for indefinite periods of time, like Kristy's early-50's primary care physician who ended up on long-term disability for a year because of it, I was willing to do what it would take. Plus, the advanced learning our kids experienced the first year led us to be in favor of longer exposure to the teacher who became like a family member.

One of the other reasons why we decided to keep our kids out of school for a second year was based on the vitriol we saw on social media in videos of parents violently shouting about the Nuremberg Code at their school board members. I remained on the private Montessori board and witnessed how these issues were not happening within that school's population of parents, but I still felt uncomfortable with my children being exposed to the choices and decisions of strangers. I could not rationalize in my own mind that the choices and behaviors of strangers were not a potential threat to their safety. With countless news stories of parents aggressively arguing to make their own children's learning environment intentionally less safe by fighting mask mandates that were intended to protect their kids and others, the math just didn't prove out. Since we couldn't control the safety of their environment, we chose to control the safety of their environment.

Some individuals may have an attitude that the choices Kristy and I made were borne out of fear. Others may think that we made the best of a bad situation and found that it was so good, and that we were so fortunate to have it, that we kept it going. Others still may believe that we're recluses who used this as an excuse to hide from society, or will make other entirely different assumptions and judgments about our choices. The simple truth is this: My children are more important to me than anything else, and I will not allow the choices of others, particularly those who have a far more casual or intolerant attitude toward safety protocols, to threaten their wellbeing.

This is where we reach an impasse. About half of the population in America supports the intentional and unilateral implementation of public health measures. Approximately the other half of the population supports the notion that the virus is an inconvenience, but not worth adding further layers of inconvenience. Stereotypically we may assume that the first group disproportionately voted for Joe Biden in 2020, and the second group disproportionately voted for Donald Trump. But COVID has made strange bedfellows. I have a friend who is a long-time liberal and regularly makes social media posts that speak out against vaccines and vaccine mandates. I also know very conservative families that have remained almost exclusively in isolation since the first lockdown. While the camps are heavily scrambled, the reality stays the same: The country is split almost equally in opposition to one another.

★ ★ ★

When I was in graduate school, I was exposed to a whole bunch of content that I was previously unaware of. I realized during that time that not knowing about these things didn't mean that I was dumb, but rather that I was ignorant to them. Ignorance is often used in a disparaging way, but the definition of the word is actually, "lacking knowledge or awareness." Therefore, ignorance isn't a negative word, it simply means that we don't know what we don't know.

I consider myself to be a pre-Trump conservative, or more accurately a Libertarian. I believe that all individuals should have the right to do whatever makes them happy and that they find to be personally fulfilling. I say that with only one caveat: No one has the right to impede the happiness and fulfillment of others. If a person wants to shoot heroin in their arm, as long as they do not negatively impact anyone else (like stealing, causing harm, or making their mother cry), I believe that a person should have the right to do what they feel is the most appropriate thing for them. But if they impede the happiness or fulfillment of others, game over.

The formal definition of this attitude is called the Non-Aggression Axiom, which is the philosophical belief that aggression or interference in the lives of others is inherently wrong.[121] We'll explore this more in the Metaethics chapter, but for now, know that this is essentially the root of Libertarianism, and is an incredibly individualistic mentality. Individualism is a core component of Western society, and it is so deeply engrained into our culture that we rarely even think about. It's like water to fish – It just is. America is great because individualism has fueled generations of decisions and actions that have advanced our nation and world. Individualism is very healthy and valuable to society up to and until the point that it impedes the ability for others to live happy, fulfilling lives.

I was only tangentially aware of the concept of collectivism prior to my degree work. That is to say, I was ignorant to the meaning and value of a cultural approach different from the norm in Western society. Individualism, at the core, is about prioritizing the individual over the collective. Collectivism, on the contrary, is about valuing the individual in such a way that they are cared for as a part of the whole. If the whole is in jeopardy, so is the individual. If the whole is happy and healthy, almost certainly so too will the individual be. Both approaches have their own inherent merits and shortfalls.

The real root issue with the response to COVID-19 is that it is a conflict of Individualism vs. Collectivism. It's fair and logical for any person to think, "I'm healthy, so this shit isn't my problem." Realistically, that's probably entirely true for some people. It's also fair and logical to expect that in a civilized society, everyone has a role to play. Sometimes the role has minimal impact on others. Sometimes the role has monumental impact. But at virtually all times, we are engaging with one another in some way. Public health is an issue that doesn't respect individual rights, because we are social animals and we do not live in isolation from one another. The very nature of being a human requires that we interact with other humans. And through those interactions, the individual has an impact on the individuals they are interacting with. Public health cannot be controlled with individualistic behaviors and ideals, particularly when the issue is invisible and can be spread before the infected individual is even aware that they are ill.

★ ★ ★

I was in undergrad at Michigan State studying Hospitality Business when cigarette smoking in restaurants was banned.

Prior to this time, restaurants had Smoking and Nonsmoking sections, then shifted to a norm of allowing smoking only on patios or in the bar areas. As an industry, we were terrified of what would happen when that fateful day arrived and the clientele would be told they could no longer smoke anywhere inside the restaurant. There were case studies and research focused entirely on this seismic shift in leisure culture. We were positive that the industry would be negatively impacted by 10% or more in the first year, and there was deep-seated fear that the industry would never recover from such a dramatic change in behavior. None of that proved to be true.

I worked in a relatively high-end restaurant during this time – The one I previously referenced with all of the insane behavior. Our brand made the conscious decision to do something that many deemed to be foolish: We ended smoking in the restaurant two months before it was required by law. The first days and weeks were strange as we had to, somewhat uncomfortably, explain to guests that they could no longer smoke like they had during their last visit. But something happened that we didn't expect – Our sales increased!

When news got out that we eliminated smoking in the restaurant ahead of all of the others in the market, guests who were not regular diners due to a distaste for being exposed to second-hand smoke started to visit in increasing numbers and frequency. Instituting the smoking ban early actually lead to making our restaurant more profitable, attractive to guests, and enjoyable for the staff, and the effects lasted far longer than the two-months of early implementation. Doing something that was designed to benefit the collective did exactly that by making life better for everyone. And the individuals who smoked were not excluded from anything. They were just no longer allowed to impede the happiness and fulfillment of others, and were instead asked to step outside to enjoy their cigarette. Inconvenient? Sure. But thinking back now, how barbaric does it seem to you that we used to allow individuals to smoke right next to nonsmokers while they were trying to enjoy a celebratory meal? While each individual has every right to allow toxins into their bodies if they feel so inclined, they do not have the right to make that decision for others. Behaving as if some of our actions did not have a negative impact on others is disrespectful and harmful to the collective, so we stopped the practice. It's the same thing with public health.

While it may be unpopular with about half of the country, just as ending smoking indoors once was, creating expectations of new behaviors in social settings will not only protect our public health, but it will also create an environment for the other half of the country to start to feel comfortable enough to begin participating in the economy again. This will help to resolve the employment gap that's plaguing the country with the Great Resignation, and will return buying and travel decisions to sustained pre-pandemic norms.

★ ★ ★

There is a group that we should be more mindful of supporting and including in the conversation around the implementation of public health measures: The Recovered.

The vast majority of individuals who have contracted COVID-19 are walking amongst us today. They contracted the virus unintentionally because they were exposed to another individual who either was unaware that they were sick, or was so disrespectful of others as to engage in society knowing full well that they were spreading disease. In either case, millions got sick, recovered, and returned to living their lives. A truly unknown number of individuals contracted the virus, were asymptomatic, and have no idea that they have antibodies today that protect them from re-infection or severe illness. And yet they all remain unaccounted for in government reporting of vaccinated populations.

This reality serves to cause more problems than just being an oversight. It leads some to question if our elected officials are truly "following the science," and leads others to question the intention of those politicians who so aggressively proclaim that vaccination is the only path to ending the pandemic. It also paints an entire group of individuals, who by rights could probably be just fine without vaccines, as second-class citizens in the eyes of those who are vaccinated.

I've worked hard to keep my own opinion at bay unless it's expressed through a story that helps illustrate a point. Here I share it intentionally and willingly: I support public health mandates that include masking in a variety of environments and a form of proof that demonstrates complete vaccination or prior recovery from COVID-19.

This does not mean I support vaccine mandates. I don't. I don't believe anyone should have to get a shot if they don't believe it's the right thing for them. It is each person's individual right to choose to become vaccinated or not. With that said, the individual rights of one person do not carry more weight than the individual rights of anyone else. Just like I can't sit in the booth next to you at a restaurant and blow marijuana vape pen vapor at you, my children who are not old enough to be vaccinated have the right not to be subjected to the virus that you don't realize is in your body. While I do not support vaccine mandates, I 100% fully support Immunity Passports.

An Immunity Passport would be different from a Vaccine Passport, in that it would include those who have been fully vaccinated *and* The Recovered. It would allow the holder to live freely, while being able to attend movies, concerts, dine indoors, fly on planes, and so forth. Notably, none of these activities are *necessary* for any person in order to live a happy and fulfilling life. This means that if an individual feels that becoming vaccinated is unimportant in their life, they are welcome to continue living happily, though they will be excluded from some activities for the sake of the collective. This is no different than what we've done to smokers. They can continue to choose to slowly kill themselves if they want to, but they do not have the right to poison the lungs of those around them.

An Immunity Passport would provide more individuals with confidence in returning to a physical workplace, to resume travel, to resume participating in the economy, and to return to a semblance of normalcy. Those who do not find value in these activities will be able to continue living their life with their individual rights intact, because not a single one of these activities is a right – They are each a privilege.

We expect decency and appropriate behavior from individuals in order to engage in our civilized society. No Shirt, No Shoes, No Service is a public health measure. Seatbelts are a public health measure. Legal drinking limits are a public health measure. Not being allowed to misuse free speech by shouting "FIRE!" in a crowed environment is a public health measure. We have LOTS of public health measures that we accept every single day. If we don't like them, we choose not to engage in those activities. An Immunity Passport would do nothing more than add new behaviors that individuals get to choose if they want to support and engage with or not.

From a civil liberty, capitalistic, and individual rights context, this is actually the most individual rights option we could provide within a public health solution: A choice to participate or not. Capitalism will win the day with individuals having the opportunity to choose where they spend their dollars, and businesses and industries will rise or fall as a result. If those who prioritize remaining unvaccinated make up a big enough voting bloc with their dollars that the airline industry collapses, that will be the power they wield. If they choose not to dine indoors or attend concerts and movies because remaining unvaccinated is more important, they will have the power to force businesses to adapt how they operate. If businesses want to cater specifically to those without an Immunity Passport, they would be entitled to do so. And if unvaccinated individuals happen to contract the virus and recover, they will become immediately eligible for an Immunity Passport.

Those who are not The Recovered or vaccinated are not a second-class, but they are the 2020's equivalent of a smoker: They get to live just like everyone else, but their individual right to allow toxins in their body is not more powerful than the right of those who desire to keep toxins out.

★ ★ ★

You may completely disagree with my opinion on this topic, and based on public opinion, approximately half of those who are reading along with you will. But, you'll likely be hard-pressed to damn me for my opinion now that you understand why I have it. That's the key! When we stop and listen to The Other, and understand why they believe what they believe, we can't help but respect why they believe it. We don't have to agree, and likely we won't, but at least we get it.

When you choose to be curious and ask questions, and listen to understand instead of listening to respond, you'll find that The Other will answer. As the conversation continues, and as you listen and ask more questions, you'll gain a deeper understanding of The Other. When we stop and listen, the person who is different from us feels heard. When they feel heard, they become calmer and more rational. When cooler heads prevail, the conversation becomes even more valuable still.

When we stop and talk to the person whose vein is bulging out of their forehead as they scream about mask mandates in front of children at a school board meeting, we'll likely be surprised to hear *why* they feel so passionate about their beliefs. And, if someone asks us to wear a mask in their presence, like immunocompromised Florida Senator Tina Polsky did of the state's Surgeon General Joseph Ladapo, we should not follow in Ladapo's footsteps and ignore or belittle the request.[122] When we finally accept and understand that The Other is actually just like us, its transformative in how we think about, act toward, and treat those around us. The reality is this: We're all humans who are just trying to live happy and fulfilling lives. When we remember this, we can't help but to respect The Other, if for no other reason than that we understand where they're coming from. We don't have to agree with them, aspire to be like them, or be their friend, but when we intentionally strive to understand The Other, we can't help but to respect them. And with that respect, we can choose to work together in spite of our differences. It's a choice. It's your choice.

You use this power of choice every single day. You already have it within you. When you choose to use it to become more understanding, you can influence relationships in such a way as to work together with those that you disagree with. Or you can choose not to and say this suggestion about choice is all a bunch of bullshit. That, also, is your choice, but if you keep doing what you've always done, you'll keep getting what you've always gotten. If you follow my recommendation to work to be more understanding, you will be able to overcome the divisiveness that occurs in your conflicts with others. Either choice is legitimate, and can be the "right" choice for you. You can choose to stand on your moral high ground and keep fighting with the wind, or you can choose to have a greater pool of people around you who you can collaborate with to improve your life and our world. You have the power to choose the kind of life you want to live, and the type of world we have. It's your choice.

Results

We all have opinions. Watching politicians on the nightly news, we regularly hear some iteration of, "Your opinion is wrong, and mine is right!" But where do opinions come from? They are formed in each of us as a result of our upbringing, family culture, life experiences, actions we've taken, things we've been subjected to, and countless other external forces that occur throughout our lives. This means that our opinions are formed by, and are a reflection of, the sum of our lived experiences. If those experiences truly define our beliefs, attitudes, and opinions, the opinions that we hold to be "right" cannot be in our own minds be "wrong." In that regard, claiming that a person's opinion is "wrong," is tantamount to damning that person's life experiences as wrong. Clearly this isn't possible, nor is it appropriate behavior for responsible adults. It also demonstrates a complete lack of emotional intelligence. Therefore, there can be no such thing as "right," and "wrong," as the entire notion is based on an individual's personal perspective.

When we add to that reality that we've already knocked down the ability to draw moral hard lines because they move based on time, culture, and popular opinion, we start to find ourselves in a sticky situation. Accepting that morals are not universally accepted by all individuals around the world, and the situation becomes stickier. The logical next step is to ask, "How can we function without morals?" or "Is your next argument going to be for anarchy in place of generally accepted social norms?" The answer is neither of those. The solution to the problem of having no such thing as "right" and "wrong" is not accepting the absence of morals, but rather to collaborate with The Other to achieve results together.

★ ★ ★

When I was growing up, my mother often found conflict whenever The Other (usually me) claimed to be right about something, as it implied that she was wrong. As a highly opinionated and outspoken teenager, this didn't sit well with me when I knew that I was also not wrong in a situation. As things came to a head, the only thing I wanted my mother to realize was that I, too, was solving a problem correctly, but differently from her. That didn't make me wrong, and ironically, her attitude towards other people doing things differently from her was what I often felt she was wrong about. These arguments were intense and emotionally charged. I knew going in that if I reached a tipping point, I could force my mother to see things differently. It was a highly aggressive play, but after much yelling, crying, and apologizing, I was successful in creating the mindset-altering change I was looking for. In conflict management, this is considered to be, "competition with the aim of being constructive by achieving cooperation." It definitely isn't the most effective way to resolve conflict, but it was my preferred method until I learned otherwise.

★ ★ ★

I graduated from Michigan State University in December of 2009. In 2012, I was asked to join *The* School of Hospitality Business' Alumni Association, making me the most junior graduate of the largest and most active alumni board at Michigan State. In early 2013, I experienced the Dale Carnegie Course, and coincidentally took the class with seven Hospitality Business students, one staff member, and one alum with whom I had graduated. Together, the 10 of us agreed that the opportunity for students to learn the lessons the course provides was not just valuable, but game-changing in terms of their marketability while acquiring their first job. I knew and respected the donor who funded the students and staff member, and anticipated that he would support the initiative a few more times before eventually redirecting funds to support another important endeavor. If this opportunity were to continue indefinitely, some sort of endowment would need to be created. Being on the alumni board, I also knew that endowments started at $30,00, which at that time I could not raise or fund myself. I decided instead to create an unofficial endowment, and committed to each current student that I would write a check in their name each year, if they agreed to support the initiative and write a check every year once they graduated. All 9 of these new friends signed on immediately.

I asked for a meeting with the 26-year Director of *The* School of Hospitality Business, Dr Ronald F Cichy, O.M. Ron was kind enough to write the Foreword of this book at my request. He and I have co-authored numerous nationally-published articles together, and have grown to have a deep and trusting friendship. Prior to this meeting, we already had a long and friendly relationship, dating back to my time as a student in 2007. I still look up to Ron, respect him, and call him a friend. He has shared wisdom and counsel that has been helpful in many aspects of my life. In that meeting, I shared with him what I was planning to do by creating an unofficial endowment. While I didn't know it at the time, the stars were aligning, as he was in the process of stepping down as director to begin a transition to retirement. He had recently been courted to see if he'd like a professorship in his name, or a bust, or some other form of legacy marking for his service to *The* School and the university. Ron was also a Dale Carnegie graduate from some decades earlier. I shared this idea to permanently support a handful of our students to become more emotionally intelligent before their graduation, which is something that would have been a difference-maker in my first job when I earned the nickname, "The Hammer," for my utter lack of emotional intelligence. He loved the concept and asked if we could use his name to pump it full of money and support more students than I envisioned. A few months later I signed the documentation for the fastest growing endowment funded by more than one person in the university's history, as it immediately raised nearly $100,000. With all of that context in play, my passion and support for the hospitality program should be evident.

A few years later, the alumni board found itself in a slow boiling conflict with other factions within the university. The transition from Ron to a new director was quite bumpy, and fundraising was down dramatically. All the while, MSU was dealing with the fallout of the Larry Nassar sexual assault scandal. No one was the villain in this conflict, but differences of opinion on the path forward, combined with external variables that heightened tensions, were at the root of the issue.

A communication went out to the alumni board that, when read with background knowledge, was received very negatively. Specific details are too revealing and unhelpful to those still involved, but when I learned about all of this, I was immediately angered. I decided that I had two options: Quit the board in protest, or act. Thinking about it over the weekend, I decided I cared too much for the students to just walk away. If enough actively engaged alumni walked away, as three immediately did, then the whole board would collapse. I instead decided to fight for what I believed in. In my bullheadedness, I intended to utilize my preferred method of conflict from disagreements with my mother and force such intense conflict that some form of reunification would become necessary on the other side.

After outlining a plan, I shared it with a person whom I respected, and asked for an opinion. They thought it was well laid-out, and asked what I anticipated as an outcome. I expected to gain the anger of the less engaged board members and create a vocal uprising against the proposed action. None of the likely outcomes were desirable for me personally, but I was willing to accept the consequences if the objective was met. Like Snowden and Assange, I was working against my own self-interests in the name of the greater good. My experience wasn't nearly as harrowing or life-threatening as theirs, but the concept was the same.

My confidant asked me to think about what I was prepared to do, especially if I wasn't fond of the outcomes for myself. They suggested I talk with other highly engaged board members to get their input before acting so dramatically. The coaching and counsel seemed wise, and in line with the concepts of conflict management that I had been learning for the previous few years in grad school, so I decided to attempt that path.

Over the next few weeks, I spoke with over 20 members of the board, the executive committee, and faculty. I was now the most knowledgeable person about the topic, and knew all of the players, motives, blind spots, and the whole playing field. I realized that I didn't need to be an antagonist and attempt to cause problems with the proposed action, but that I could instead ask the right questions that would cause other board members to ask questions. In the next board meeting, the conversation was heated, but it was respectful. Again, the details, while very interesting, are not important or helpful to those involved. The moral of the story is that by seeking understanding instead of inciting conflict unnecessarily, a mutually agreeable solution was found and all parties ended up being better off for it – Especially the students.

It was in a moment of reflexive action that I paused long enough to allow someone to remind me to be thoughtful and diligent as opposed to reactionary. This was a moment that demonstrated to me the value of conflict coaching, and helped to solidify into practice the theories I had studied. Sometimes we're just too caught up in the moment to pause and reflect on what we should really do – REST.

★ ★ ★

You hear it dozens of times a week: "Oh, I'm really busy." You've been guilty of saying it, too: "Business is great! We're so busy!" You know what phrase is equally redundant? "I've been breathing a lot of air lately." We all breathe air – It isn't special. If we all say it so flippantly, "being busy" isn't special, either. This is even more true when the words "busy" and "productive" are not synonymous.

Here's the deal: Managers are busy. Leaders REST.

Management and Leadership are not synonymous. Management is about overseeing a team of people, following processes, reaching goals and KPIs, and making sure the clients are happy. Management is a job.

Leadership is about motivating, inspiring, and empowering others. Leaders give others the opportunity to grow, succeed, and become Leaders for themselves and others. Leadership is a behavior. Leadership is a choice. To do this effectively, Leaders cannot afford to kill themselves by working unnecessarily long hours. Leaders rest. Leaders rest to role model to their teams the importance of taking care of themselves. Leaders rest so that they have mental clarity and space for creative thought, because Leaders are knowledge workers. Also...

Leaders REST
[Give] Respect
[Demonstrate] Empathy
[Are of] Service
[Build] Trust

Managers will say, "**Respect** must be earned." Leaders give respect to others, regardless of if they feel like The Other has earned it. When respect is freely given, it is reciprocated more rapidly, which allows us to get things done faster and easier.

Leaders demonstrate **Empathy** by being human with other humans in their time of need. They let their guard down, take the titles off, and share an intimate moment of compassion when someone says, "I'm sorry I missed the deadline. My mother is extremely ill."

In the 2020's servant leadership is dead. Long live Leaders who are of **Service**! If you don't have others as your primary focus in every single decision you make, you aren't a Leader – You're a manager. Leaders are expressly concerned with being of service and building up those they have the opportunity to serve.

We all want results, but most people don't realize that there are a series of steps necessary to get results. It all starts with **Trust**. When we build trust, people become more engaged in their work. When our people are more engaged, they're more inclined to put differences aside and behave in collaborative ways. When our people collaborate, we get healthy, diverse, and meaningful results for our clients and organizations.

We're all busy – You aren't special. If you *want* to be special in someone's mind, you already have the power to do that. You just need to REST, and one day, someone will share a story about how you were their favorite Leader!

★ ★ ★

I was halfway through a 12-month project working with the executive team of a statewide insurance firm. The first 6 months were dedicated to diagnosing a problem and the second 6 months were dedicated to executing a prescriptive solution to improve the organization's highly toxic culture. I was reporting results and next steps to the CEO, who had refused to participate in anything up until that point (Guess where the culture issue stemmed from...). With just the two of us in a large and beautiful conference room on the top floor of the building, I was gently introducing the need for one-on-one coaching to serve his individual needs when he suddenly stood up and shouted, "How much do we still owe you?! $40,000?! I'll pay you $40,000 to get out of my office!"

It was a stunning moment unlike anything I had ever experienced. And to be honest, I actually entertained the idea for a moment. This guy was offering me more money than he paid his average employee in a year just to avoid improving himself for the sake of serving his company. That isn't the type of person that is particularly enjoyable to spend time coaching. I remember thinking, "What the hell is going on?" followed immediately by, "He's emotional because he cares. You can work with that. Just trust yourself."

After a few moments of intentionally not allowing myself to react, the CEO looked at me confused as I continued to sit calmly in my chair. "You're not leaving?" he asked. "I don't believe you really want me to. Am I wrong?" He invited me to meet for breakfast the next morning and we finished the project with dramatic success.

★ ★ ★

In business and life, we all want results. You have specific results you want to see. The Other has results they are focused on. Your friends, family, colleagues, and employees all have results that they care about. And we all have results we're concerned with achieving in our personal lives. What we often forget, though, is that there is a process to achieving results, and it only works if all of the steps are accomplished. It all starts with building trust, like I did with the angry CEO.

Honesty is crucial to building trust, which ultimately leads to results. When we are in the position to have to deliver difficult news, hiding details or sugar-coating it leaves opportunities for The Other to later learn that we weren't entirely honest. If that happens, trust is damaged or lost, which directly impacts our ability to get results down the road.

Over the years, I have learned that virtually everyone would rather know the truth of a situation than find out that the bad news just keeps getting worse because of omissions made at the beginning. So be honest. If you make a mistake, own it. Be open and honest about your commitment to seeing everyone through the issue. By expressing that you're going to be "with them" throughout the process, trust is further built.

One of the ways trust can be established relatively quickly is by recognizing The Other for their contributions, and what those actions show about who they are as an individual. Once trust is in place, all of the next steps that lead to results can take place. But trust is necessary in order for the next steps to be possible.

I have worked with men, women, youth, and elderly individuals of all races and sexes, and the process is the same for every person. Therefore, I would recommend following this process and utilizing these steps as you are working to build trust with The Other. It's called The Results Equation.

The Results Equation
Recognition leads to Trust
Empathy leads to Trust
Trust leads to Engagement
Engagement leads to Collaboration
Collaboration leads to Results

Put differently:

Recognition & Empathy = Trust = Engagement = Collaboration = Results

If we want results, we first need an environment where individuals collaborate with one another in spite of their differences. This takes on many forms specific to each situation, but the bottom-line is the same: Nothing happens in a silo and homogenous thought-processes serve only to please those who fit within that homogenous demographic. If we really want to serve our diverse end-users, we need to ensure that our actions and decision-making includes diverse perspectives. Therefore, collaboration is a necessary step in achieving results.

To achieve collaboration, individuals must be engaged in their work. This is logical when we think about it. If our employees aren't concerned about their responsibilities or colleagues, they won't have a desire or reason to work to collaborate with those around them, particularly if that collaboration will include some iteration of decision-making conflict. Therefore, engagement, on the project-level and cultural-level is critical to successfully achieving results.

Engagement has been a corporate buzz word for two decades, and with as much emphasis as the topic has gotten, you'd be smart to assume that tremendous progress has been made during that time. Unfortunately, that isn't true. Nationally, workplace engagement peaked in 2018 with about 3/10 workers being fully engaged in their work, and 2/10 being actively disengaged (See: Borderline sabotaging the company). The pandemic has destroyed those gains, with real-world data still being calculated, but with The Great Resignation in full effect, it's safe to assume overall corporate engagement is dismal. The good news is, there's a way for you to develop engagement on the individual-, team-, and organizational-levels. You just need to create an environment where The Other feels as though they have psychological safety to try, fail, try again, succeed, and speak out against things that they don't believe are helpful, all without fear of negative consequences for their actions. Psychological safety comes from having trust in The Other (in this case, you).

Building trust is only accomplished in two ways: Recognition and Empathy. Recognizing the efforts, achievements, and outcomes of those around us on a consistent basis will, over time, build trust with those we serve. Similarly, demonstrating empathy toward those we serve, by stripping away our arbitrary titles and instead behaving like a human being with another human being, is a way for us to build trust. When we do either of these things, trust will begin to form. When we do them both, it forms even more rapidly.

Getting results may sometimes feel like a daunting task, but the reality is that you already have the ability to make it happen. By recognizing those we serve and being present with them when they're struggling, we get trust. With trust, engagement becomes a natural outcome. With engagement, collaboration with The Other will become possible. With collaboration, we will get meaningful, inclusive, and rich results. This is true for our organizations, end users, employees, and personal relationships. If you want results, you already have the power within you to make it happen, as long as you follow the process. Let's dig in deeper on each item.

★ ★ ★

Trust is sacred. It's the crux of all relationships, and relationships are the key to success in getting results with The Other. The two ways to develop trust in a relationship are by recognizing The Other, and demonstrating empathy. We'll first explore empathy:

"I'm sorry, sir, I just don't think I can work today," the critically important facilities supervisor says to the general manager of a country club.

"Miguel," the GM responds in shock, "I don't understand. You know how important this event is. We've been planning for this group all spring. What's wrong?"

"Well sir, my family in Ecuador..." he pauses, "A volcano erupted this morning. I'm not sure if they're okay or not. I just can't focus and be what you need me to be today."

This is a difficult situation. It's a fictionalized version of a real situation that actually happened to me. While the specifics may be different, everyone will eventually face a situation where they are negatively impacted and disappointed by the very real needs of someone else. The question becomes, how do we deal with it, and how do we leverage the challenge to build greater trust?

Some managers would take the easy way out, argue that there is nothing the employee can do today anyway, and "I'll let you out first tonight." Leaders will instead seek to be present, ask questions, and engage in dialog with the employee. They would also run a cost-benefit analysis, and determine if expecting the employee to help execute an important event is even worth attempting, or if it's better to let the employee have time to process the tragedy and work through their grief. Minimally, demonstrating empathy would look something like, "I'm so sorry to hear that, Miguel. I can't even imagine what you're feeling right now. Would you like to talk?"

Empathy is about being present. Listening, caring, and asking questions. It's about companionship and compassion. Empathy isn't about problem solving or utilizing toxic positivity to pretend an issue doesn't exist. It also isn't about wallowing in pain or regret. Empathy is about letting a person feel their feelings, and helping them get back on their feet. When done effectively, this show of emotional intelligence bonds two people together, and this new bond forges a degree of trust.

Being empathetic isn't as hard as it sounds. Every person has the capacity to demonstrate empathy if they choose to. The process of slowing down, asking questions, and truly being present for a few moments makes The Other feel cared about and valued. This experience, combined with others over time, will lead to developing their trust, which will lead to their increased engagement.

★ ★ ★

A manager cashes out each server at the end of a long, busy evening. Knowing that the hard night went smoothly and without any issues, the manager gives his go-to send-off as he shakes each person's hand and says, "good job tonight," and "good job tonight," and "good job tonight," and "good job tonight." Until one server finally responds, "What exactly is it that I did well?" With a long, awkward pause, the manager is both embarrassed and mortified. He's been publicly called out for paying lip service to his employees. The pause ends when the server says, "Yeah, that's what I thought," and walks away with the manager's hand still extended.

Again, this is something that actually happened to me, and I really was mortified because it happened exactly as stated.

Recognition is more than saying the things that we're "supposed to say," to The Other. Recognition is an opportunity to engage with another person about the things they do, certainly. It's also an opportunity to share with them, who you "see" in them, through your eyes, as a result of what they do. It's an opportunity to share a special moment that has the capacity to be flippant, but instead, because it's thoughtful, becomes meaningful and memorable.

Doing this is easier than most people think. It's as simple as the word, "Namaste."

When Kristy and I lived in Minneapolis, we had a cool apartment about 20 minutes outside of town in a city called Eden Prairie. Of the 500 units in the complex, we were one of five units occupied by non-South Asian Indians, and one of only two White couples. It was an amazing cultural experience that exposed us to new friends, food, music, and religious practices. The complex had all sorts of incredible amenities, like an indoor and outdoor pool, a steam room, sauna, and free yoga once a week. I had only experienced yoga tangentially until this point, but I knew that my back injury would benefit from the stretching and core strength, so I attended the weekly class religiously. Attendance quickly dropped off, but I remained, meaning I regularly had private lessons. By the time the service concluded six months later due to low participation, I was more flexible than I had ever been, could do headstands, and I was calmer overall. I also learned the meaning of "Namaste," the traditional closing statement in yoga lessons.

There are numerous variations of the meaning, but they all distill down to a similar intention. My preferred meaning is, "the god in me sees the god in you." The concept is that we all have a divine part of us that is imbued by our Creator, and that we can "see" that divinity in others. Seeing The Other for who they are based on their actions is a way to make them feel special and truly recognized.

What I could have done instead of spewing the same throwaway line to each server would be to say something like, "I appreciate the way you cared for the Johnson's this evening. They were looking for an extra special experience while hosting Mrs. Johnson's parents from abroad, and you delivered masterfully. You have a servant's heart."

Think if you received recognition like this from someone. It would knock your socks off! This type of recognition is specific, meaningful, and shares the way we "see" The Other. When we feel seen, we begin to have more trust in those we work with. This is the type of recognition that makes people want to come to work, engage with us, and over time, trust us.

The next time you have the opportunity to recognize someone around you, take a few extra seconds, think of what made that moment significant, and share explicitly with the person what it is that their performance tells you about that individual as a person. When you do this, you will begin to build trust with The Other. Namaste!

★ ★ ★

Trust is a critical component of engagement. In the workplace, when our managers and front-line workers don't feel trusted, they will automatically become disengaged, which sets off a chain reaction of behaviors that ultimately leads to turnover, either voluntary or otherwise. It's a natural psychological reaction rooted deep in our reptilian brain to protect one's self from harm. To combat this issue, and to work towards a collaborative environment that generates results, we must create a trusting environment. It is our responsibility, as Leaders, to challenge and encourage our managers to build trusting rela-

There's No Such Thing as Right and Wrong

tionships with our front-line workers.

Think of any time you were fully invested and engaged in the work you were doing – You likely felt trusted by those who bestowed responsibility upon you. They knew that you would execute, and they knew that you would win the proverbial war, even if you lost the occasional battle. You already know the benefit of complete engagement, whether you've felt it or witnessed it, and you know the benefits it will create for your organization and life to have a fully engaged people around you. This feeling of engagement leads to collaboration, which leads to results.

So the next time you engage with your employees, make sure they know you trust them, and encourage them to convey that message to their employees, and you will see more engagement and more productive outcomes for your organization.

★ ★ ★

When we have individuals working in our organizations, it is our goal and objective as Leaders that those individuals are highly energized, passionate, and engaged. It should also be our focus that the engagement they demonstrate is channeled at an achievable and mutually beneficial outcome through collaboration. Sometimes they are so engaged that they see another highly engaged person as a threat to their success, or view an alternative approach as an obstacle rather than a viable path forward.

The way we overcome this is by having the two engaged parties in conflict seek to truly understand one another. This is a conversation that is not about who is right and who is wrong, but rather, "Why do you believe that your idea is right," and "This is why I believe that my idea is right." This attempt at achieving understanding is the pinnacle of leadership, as it allows each party to feel heard, and forces them to set their personal perspectives aside for a moment to listen to a differing viewpoint from an objective position. When this takes place, both engaged parties have the opportunity to impact change together. This is an exercise in collaboration that provides Leaders with the best of all perspectives, and allows differing parties to identify the best path forward.

Next time you see two highly engaged individuals in your organization passionately arguing, challenge them to pause, seek to understand the other party's viewpoint, and encourage them to find a collaborative solution. The outcome will be that you will see greater results for your organization, and even more engagement from your team.

★ ★ ★

Picture a situation where an individual was planning to plant trees on his property. A neighbor shares that his family owns a tree farm, and that he'd be happy to coordinate access to the land, a vehicle for transport, and tools for removal if the first person would be willing to help him plant trees on his property, too. One party benefitted by not having to purchase trees or rent equipment. The other benefitted by having access to additional labor at no cost. Both benefitted by having more beautiful properties at no additional cost. This is a win-win situation, where both parties contribute and both parties benefit. Collaboration, where all parties are better off than before is what we should be striving for in all scenarios as Leaders.

In the popular movie series *Star Wars*, there are two rival groups, the Jedi and the Sith. While they are diametrically opposed, they both utilize the same mystical power source: The Force. The same power source is used for good or evil. Influence is The Force that powers Leaders. We have the ability to motivate people or manipulate them. When we motivate people towards win-win collaborative outcomes, we are using influence in its intended and positive form. When we manipulate people, so that there is a win-lose outcome, we have behaved in a negative, potentially "evil" way that betters one party and harms the other.

In our organizations and personal lives, we have the ability to seek collaborative outcomes that benefit both parties. We have the ability, as Leaders, to influence our employees to seek win-win solutions that benefit both the team and the end users. The outcome of this goal is that everyone, including our clients, are happier, more loyal, and invest more into our organizations. Collaboration leads to mutually beneficial outcomes, and results.

★ ★ ★

We all want results. You do. I do. The Other does, too. The problem is, only you and I are learning how to get results. The Other may not have the luxury of learning what you've learned. You cannot control the actions and behaviors The Other, but you can control how you respond to them. Putting our ego on the shelf long enough to understand The Other leads to our respecting their unique perspectives, and helps them to trust us. By asking questions and seeking understanding instead of damning those whose lived experiences have led them to completely different conclusions than we've arrived at, we can engage them in solving problems, and collaborate with them to get results.

★ ★ ★

Metaethics

There's No Such Thing as Right and Wrong

What we have discussed together throughout this book is a subject in philosophy called Meta-Ethics, or Metaethics. Metaethics is one of three tracks that philosophers studying ethics tend to explore. The other two are referred to as Normative Ethics, which explores how a person should behave, and Applied Ethics, which explores what is the right way to behave in a given scenario. Metaethics is less concerned with how we should behave and what is right, and instead focuses on questions like, "how do we know what is right or wrong?"[123]

From a philosophical standpoint, seeking to answer what is right and what is wrong is not really the purpose of asking the question. The purpose of asking the question is in exploring how we could arrive at either answer, or both. Metaethics does not judge something that is determined to be "wrong" as equal to being "bad," and similarly does not value an action that is "right" as being of greater value than something that is "wrong." Instead, philosophers have previously determined that there is no "one right way," and therefore, we live in a world not made up of black and white, but rather infinite shades of gray.

Within the field of Metaethics there are numerous sub-categories that philosophers enjoy debating ad nauseam for the sake of debating. They include terms like Ethical Naturalism, Ethical Non-Naturalism, Ethical Subjectivism, and a whole slew of others. Like the questions Metaethics attempt to explore, the field itself is littered with shades of gray. Ironically, though, philosophers will debate and argue endlessly that the assumption they hold to be true within this space is in fact the "right" way to look at the field. A better use of time is to determine how one can conclude if something is right or wrong, and seek to apply that in one's life, or, within the context of our thought experiment, how that can be applied to overcoming conflict.

The purpose of bringing all of this to your attention is to set a grounding point for the ethical journey we have been on during this book. The thoughts, arguments, and recommendations you have read are not the result of some casual belief held by some random dude telling you stories about the dumb mistakes he's made, but are in fact based in science, philosophy, and culture. The purpose of sharing this with you is to prepare you for the inevitable arguments that you may encounter based on the new way that you will approach conflict and collaboration.

For the sake of greater context, I will share a series of points and counterpoints within the Metaethics space. This will help you to more articulately explain yourself to anyone who may accuse you of living an amoral life because you choose not to damn others for their choices. Also, I'd like to impress upon you the fact that subscribing to this philosophical mindset adds you to the lineage of ethics-minded philosophers like Aristotle, Confucius, Noam Chomsky, Jesus Christ, Pope John Paul II, Martin Luther King Jr., Moses, Plato, Ayn Rand, and others.[124] I hope for you to be proud in your association with this group of individuals. I also hope for you to hold that pride close as it inspires you to keep persisting when you inevitably stumble through being successful the first bunch of times you attempt to approach conflict in this way.

Buckle up – This chapter is about to get pretty academic. If this content doesn't interest you, I suggest skipping a few pages to read about Moral Relativism, and then just move on to the next chapter. Moral Relativism is important for you to understand in order to effectively explain why you are so collaborative with The Other. The rest of this chapter is really interesting if you want deeper understanding of what we've discussed so far. If you don't care about this heady stuff, the next chapter, Understanding, is where you will learn exactly how to become very effective at collaborating with The Other.

★ ★ ★

One of the chief arguments people make when I say, "There's no such thing as right and wrong," is "Well, what about what God says?" Great point. There's a theory in Metaethics for that, and this book doesn't subscribe to it. The reason for this is simply because not everyone believes in God, or any other deity, and therefore, we cannot reasonably use the whims of deities as a measuring stick for the morality of all.

Regardless, here's the gist of the Divine Command Theory: For anything to be "right," a deity must endorse it, and everyone must follow that edict in accordance with the deity's commands.[125] The problem with this theory is that there are estimated to be more than 4,300 religions practiced throughout the world, so which deity's edicts must we all follow? As of 2020, Christianity is far and away the most predominate religion in America, and is also the most widely practiced religion throughout the world, with nearly 2.4 billion adherents. Islam is second throughout the world, with more than 1.9 billion followers. Approximately 1.2 billion are unaffiliated or subscribe to Atheism, and just over 1 billion are Hindu. The rest of the world's approximately 1.4 billion inhabitants subscribe to one of the other 4,295+ religions.[126]

While we could make assumptions and assertations that America is a Christian nation, that actual runs counter to the founding of America. The 1st Amendment of the Constitution is often referenced in defense of free speech, though the very first declaration is actually, "Congress shall make no law respecting an establishment of religion, or prohibiting thereof;" followed immediately by, "or abridging the freedom of speech, or of the press..."[127]

To claim that America is a Christian nation is not only incorrect and against the intent of our Founders, but it is also inaccurate. Americans who associate as Christians do make up about 78% of our population, but that means nearly 1 out of every 4 people you know does not associate with the majority. To assert that our morality must be based on the Divine Command Theory based on the Christian God, or any deity for that matter, ignores this substantial minority in America, and the overwhelming majority around the world. Therefore, we are not subscribing to this concept here. You're welcome to choose to subscribe to this sub-theory of Metaethics, but that choice will undo much of what we've explored already together, as you will be forced to put hardlines into your decision-making and understanding of others, which will limit your ability to respect their unique and opposing viewpoints, immediately limiting your ability to be consistently successful in collaborating with a non-religious The Other to achieve mutually beneficial results.

★ ★ ★

Another primary argument individuals make when rationalizing the theory that there is no such thing as right and wrong, is, "What about murder? Are you saying that it's okay to go around killing people?" Well, no... But yes, we already did, as long as the killing is in an appropriate context.

This argument is logical, as the average person has not been exposed to the philosophical thought experiment we are currently engaged in. Therefore, we need to address it here. This entails a few sub-theories within Metaethics, but you'll find that the conclusion we arrived at in the Killing chapter is backed and supported in research and the linage of philosophical debate.

First, we need to understand Universal Prescriptivism, which assumes that the statement, "killing is wrong," is equivalent to "do not kill other people."[128] While each declaration may have similar intent, the statements are in no way the same. One could believe that killing is wrong, but still find themself in a situation where the action is necessary or appropriate. To assume the two statements are the same implies that we must put ourselves in a box of equivalency to infinite other potentially unrelated statements. This also assumes that killing is universally "wrong," which we have already disproven.

Next, we need to understand Error Theory, which suggests that statements like, "killing is wrong," and "killing is acceptable," are in fact both false.[129] The concept here is that Error Theory argues that statements cannot imply morality, because morality doesn't actually exist. Here it is assumed that morality is a construct that individuals subscribe to. Another way to think of this is in regard to how we perceive the nobility of horses or the filthiness of rats. The reality is that, while some horses may exhibit behaviors that we associate with nobility, and while some rats may in fact be disease carriers, neither of these words is actually a true descriptor of either animal. Some horses are assholes, and some rats are wonderful pets. Further, in parts of the world both of these animals are considered foodstuffs and the cows we regularly consume in America are considered sacred. Under Error Theory, killing is neither wrong nor acceptable, as the context of the killing is what determines if killing is wrong or acceptable.

Some may mistake your adherence to Error Theory, or your subscribing to this book's belief that there is no such thing as right and wrong, as assuming that you do not value life. If someone suggests that, they are making an assertion that you are a Moral Nihilist. In my view, this suggestion is offensive, but we can't blame people for their ignorance to a subject they know little about. They very likely don't even know this term, but now you do. Moral Nihilism *is* a theory within Metaethics, but the argument in that theory is that nothing has any moral value.[130] Adherents to Moral Nihilism would suggest that killing a stranger on the street means nothing, and is neither right nor wrong. This is where folks get confused, because it sounds similar to "there's no such thing as right and wrong." We know that this is untrue because the act of unnecessarily killing a person inherently prevents them from being able to live a happy and fulfilling life. So rather than Moral Nihilism, this book actually advocates for Moral Relativism.

Moral Relativism is a Metaethics theory that is the core component of everything in this book. Those who are deeply entrenched in their religious dogma often struggle with Moral Relativism because it requires consciously accepting that not everyone believes said religion, and therefore should not be held accountable to said dogmatic standards. This is because Moral Relativism suggests that, while some people may subscribe to the notion of right or wrong for certain topics, there is not a singular and universal standard by which we can measure "right" and "wrong."[131] This is why at the beginning of the book I said we would not explore time as a social construct or "the sky is blue." In both of those cases there are universal standards that there are 24 hours in a day, 365 days in a year, and the color of the sky is blue unless the sun is obstructed.

What Moral Relativism allows for is the cultural, personal, and time-based variance of the morality of any issue. For example, in America we do not practice religious rituals that include cannibalism. To us, that's wrong. The Aztecs, however, did practice ritualistic cannibalism. They also practiced human sacrifice to their deities. They believed the sacrificed corpses to be sacred, so they consumed them.[132] This is an example of something you and I may find abhorrent in Western society in the 2020s, but at one time, and to one people, this was as acceptable and innocuous as eating the Body of Christ and drinking the Blood of Christ on Sunday morning.

This example is literally the definition of Moral Relativism – A thing may not be right for me, but it is right for someone else, and time may change both. This is why the morality of drinking alcohol is no longer a common concern, and the public opinion on the prohibition of drugs is changing. This is also why I can confidently and comfortably hold beliefs that abortion should be accessible to those who need it, but I personally find it wrong in my life. Further, that I can be a Christian who believes I will go to Heaven when I die, while holding beliefs for the greater good that are incongruent with spreading Christianity. I know that not everyone believes what I believe, even if I believe it to be true. And I know that imposing my beliefs on others presupposes that my beliefs are inherently more valid than their beliefs. If I were willing to impose my beliefs on others, The Other would be just as justified in seeking to impose their beliefs on me, which I am not interested in allowing unless I make that choice for myself. This is why, even as a Christian,

I do not subscribe to the Divine Command Theory, and do not see it as helpful in overcoming conflict.

I am a not a Moral Nihilist. I am a Moral Relativist. And if you are still tracking with me, so are you.

★ ★ ★

As with all of Metaethics, there are many shades of gray that each person must determine for themselves if they are true and valuable or not. Rather than further muddy the waters with concepts that *There's No Such Thing as Right and Wrong* does not subscribe to, I encourage you to study further for yourself the following items that you may agree with. A resource that I find to be overwhelmingly clean of bias and noise is the *Internet Encyclopedia of Philosophy – A Peer Reviewed Academic Resource*.

None of the following sub-theories definitively invalidate what we've discovered together, but all do create inherent conflicts by requiring that someone, somewhere, must be "right." The concepts worth exploring are: Consequentialism (What is right produces a "good" outcome – But who defines what is "good?"), Ideal Observer Theory (Moral facts can be known through rational deduction – But who defines what is rational?), and Deontology (What is right is determined by weighing if the correct series of rules were followed, not by the outcome of the action – But who defines the rules?).

The following are concepts that do further reinforce our thought experiment:
- Pragmatic Ethics, which, like the scientific method, assumes that what is known to be true today may be dis-

proven tomorrow, and therefore we need to be accepting of the fact that we do not currently have all of the tools our species will ever have to deduce what is right and what is wrong. There is inherent hope that future generations will improve upon what is believed to be true today.

Pragmatic Ethics focuses primarily on society at large as opposed to the individual; does not hold that anything within the space is so sacred that it cannot be improved upon; and what is morally acceptable today may be rejected as acceptable by future generations, like slavery.[133]

- The Principle of Permissible Harm, which suggests that it is permissible to harm another individual if that harm results in net positive good. The example of this is the stick figure morality dilemma image you may have seen on the internet. In it, a trolly car is rolling down the track with five people tied up on one fork, and one person tied up on the other fork, and an individual who is forced to make the choice as to which fork to direct the trolly. Logic dictates that, absent the ability to stop the trolly, one lost life is better than five. This is the Principle of Permissible Harm, and ironically, it is a subset theory of the sub-theories Consequentialism and Deontology that I have suggested are unhelpful to our ability to overcome conflict.

- Finally, the Non-Aggression Axiom, or the Non-Aggression Principle. This concept, which was referenced earlier in the book, is the core tenet of Libertarianism, and is my personal Red Line in what is and what is not permissible when we discuss what is "right," and what is "wrong."[134]

The Non-Aggression Axiom argues that aggression, force,

interference, or threat against another person or their property is inherently wrong. As I have stated numerous times throughout the book, each person is and should be free to live a life that brings them happiness and fulfillment, up to and until the point that their happiness or fulfillment infringes upon the happiness or fulfillment of another person. Put more plainly, you can do whatever the hell you want, but if you hurt someone else: Game Over.

Essentially, the Non-Aggression Axiom makes the case for de-regulating virtually everything, with the assumption that all peoples will participate accordingly. This informs the responsibility of individuals to behave with care and compassion towards others, and to seek to be mindful of their actions in the absence of rules, laws, and regulations. For example, drinking is okay, but drinking and driving is not. Speeding at 2 a.m. when the roads are clear is okay, but speeding at 2 p.m. in a school zone is not. Fishing and hunting without a permit is okay, but claiming all of the livestock for commercial sale and leaving none for individual use is not. Choosing not to be vaccinated is okay, but refusing to wear a mask around others is not. The unfortunate reality is that selfishness often gets in the way. In an economic conflict concept called The Tragedy of the Commons, individuals left to their own devices are prone to take more than their "fair share," ultimately spoiling the outcomes for all.[135] This is essentially the justification and rationale for regulations to exist: To protect the collective from the selfish individual.

★ ★ ★

While I fully recognize that my family, friends, peers, clients, and complete strangers will have a variety of responses to this book, which almost certainly will include both support and dissent toward different arguments made, the purpose was never to persuade anyone to do what I personally think is right. The objective was always to challenge individuals to arrive at the destination they find most appropriate for themselves. It is my belief that your decision-making in this context will play a critical role in your ability to help make our world a happier and more civil place. It is for this belief that I wrote this book, because, ironically, I believed it to be the right thing to do.

★ ★ ★

Understanding

There's No Such Thing as Right and Wrong

When I was a Dale Carnegie Trainer, I had the opportunity to attend a number of North American and Global Conventions. The President / CEO, Joe Hart, took the helm shortly before my first attendance. What stood out to me about him was his sincere interest in those he served, specifically the trainers. He held a first-ever Trainer Roundtable, where an overflowing room of global trainers had the opportunity to engage with him directly. It was scheduled for an hour, and went far longer than that as he listened to the thoughts and concerns of those who had their boots on the ground. I remember standing against the wall near the front of the room watching in amazement as he carefully wrote notes about the items each person shared.

Think of that – A global CEO *standing* because he gave his chair to someone else since the room was so packed, and physically writing notes in a book not for show, but because he truly wanted to understand what those who work closest to the end-user had to say. This simple but unusual act was very symbolic of the attitude that he continues to demonstrate today. I had the opportunity to share this memory with the board of directors when I dined with them after being recognized in 2019. By this point, Joe's behavior was understood to be sincere and consistent, but it was also the reason why we all were willing to follow him. He chose to be curious and to be of service, and people connected with that, particularly when he put himself through the grueling process of becoming a Dale Carnegie Trainer, which has a notoriously high failure rate. While I am no longer a Dale Carnegie Trainer now that I lead my own coaching company, I will always hold the work of Dale Carnegie and Joe Hart in high regard. I respect the work, the outcomes, and those who are committed to serving others. I wouldn't be who I am today if it weren't for taking that program and working to become a trainer.

Choosing to leave Dale Carnegie was strangely both difficult and easy. I loved the work and the content, but had realized for about 18 months that I was seeing opportunities to expand the scope of the content to deal with the realities of what I was finding in the classroom. It was borne out of the comments and questions from my students, but also from my own interest in my graduate studies, as well as what I was researching on my own in the leadership space. The Dale Carnegie Course that my peers taught was typically 3.5 hours per week for 12 weeks. The version I was teaching regularly went for 4.5 hours, and even broke 5 hours on numerous occasions. I was digging in deeper than was expected and sharing additional content that did not conflict with the core content, but rather added to it using additional resources. To be fair, I was rapidly approaching a point where I could jeopardize the integrity of the core content by adding external supports. This realization was one that made me take pause and contemplate if it was in the best interest of the brand that I continue training or move on. Ultimately, moving on was what made the most sense to me based on my interests and passions.

As I developed Leadership Coaching for Results, I knew that I wanted to provide individuals with the opportunity to "choose their own ending," as it were. I am of the opinion that Leadership in its truest and purest form is simply about motivating, inspiring, and empowering those the Leader is charged with serving. This means that there is no "one right way" to be a Leader, but rather infinite ways to be the Leader that each person needs and wants to be. This approach required a focus on the fundamentals in a way that seems different than any of the work that I had previously studied or delivered. By having a First Principles approach and breaking Leadership down to its constituent parts, I realized that it also resonated with more timely and topical focus areas that I had always found fascinating, but were outside of the scope of work that I had previously been responsible for teaching. I also knew that I wanted to have a strong focus on tangible outcomes, as one of the biggest challenges to selling development content was always, "This looks great, but how do we measure success?" With all of this in mind, I dug deep into researching, identifying, and creating the tools necessary to help my clients become the Leader not that I could prescribe as an outcome, but that they needed and wanted to be. This chapter shares much of what I discovered and teach my clients.

★ ★ ★

When Kristy and I were in college, we participated in a training program with our church to become lay counselors called Stephen Ministers. The training consisted of over 50 hours of direct instruction and practice, and then enabled us to work with individuals dealing with whatever in their life was causing them difficulty. We were by no means experts, but we were able to be helpful to those in need. One of the most important tenets of the program was that Stephen Ministers were not responsible for, nor expected to, provide solutions to those we cared for. Our responsibility was to ask questions and let the other person come to conclusions on their own, based on what they deemed to be appropriate for their life. This required extensive work in learning to be an empathetic listener, or the type of person who could be present with The Other without "adding value."

In conversation there are three primary ways listeners engage:

Listening to Respond, Listening to Learn, and Listening to Understand. Listening to Respond comes a from a position where the listener feels the need to contribute to the conversation because it is either socially appropriate, they believe their experiences can be valuable to The Other, or because, bluntly, they like to hear themselves talk. Listening to Learn is an activity where an individual is actively working to internalize information. This does not necessarily allow the person to engage emotionally with The Other, as they are focused on taking mental or physical notes as opposed to just being present. Listening to Understand another person is the primary example of empathetic listening. Listening to Understand requires the listener to be actively engaged (not looking at their computer or phone), focused on asking questions that go deeper than surface-level, and committed to listening without responding unnecessarily.

There is a time a place for each of these styles of listening to The Other, depending on the outcome you are seeking. When we are seeking collaboration, we need to be able to navigate conflict successfully. Conflict is either logically- or emotionally-charged. If you are in conflict with someone over a logical-based difference of opinion, you will likely end up having a conversation or debate. If The Other is emotionally connected to their opinion, the conflict you are entering will very likely end up in an argument. Logic-based conflict is easier to deal with, but it's also far less common. Let's be real, how many times have you ended up crying over something logical? The bulk of conflict is emotionally-charged.

Here's something important to know: When The Other is emotional in a conflict, it is for only one of two reasons. They are either very passionate about the topic you're discussing, or they are very passionate about you and are concerned for you based on their perception of your opinion about the topic. They're emotional because they either care about you or the topic.

Whether it's logically- or emotionally-charged conflict, we can't control the behavior of others, but we can control the way we respond to them. In order to have the success that we want, which is to overcome the conflict, understand The Other, and be able to collaborate with them, we just need to follow:

The ABC's of Conflict Management
Analyze
Breathe
Collaborate

When we're in conflict, the first thing we need to do is Analyze what's going on. Ask yourself, "What is this person seeking to achieve?" Do they want to be heard? Are they very passionate about this subject and you just accidentally walked into a conflict? Do they care about you, and they're really arguing about your stance on a subject? Deducing their agenda will help you to be more successful in navigating the conflict.

Next, we simply Breathe. Taking a moment to pause and breathe will help to override your Fight or Flight response. When we enter into conflict with The Other, our brain automatically reacts as if we are physical danger, releasing epinephrine to literally help us escape the situation. This is why some people experience a flush over their chest, neck, and face; their heart rate increases; they may feel the need to urinate; and may begin to tremor or shake. Breathing can help to control these subconscious physiological responses by intentionally recalibrating your brain. You brain reacts to your body as much as your body reacts to your brain. By slowing yourself down and breathing deeply, your brain starts to realize that you are not in danger, because otherwise your body wouldn't be behaving that way. Navy SEALs use a process called Square Breathing to ensure that they are fully in control of their bodies.

The process for Square Breathing is easy, and something I've taught individuals for years to regain control when they are psychologically overwhelmed. Simply breathe in for four seconds, hold your breath for four seconds, breathe out for four seconds, and hold your breath for four seconds. Repeat this process four times, and almost invariably, your brain and body will have calmed down. If not, do it again, and you'll be in great shape. I use this with my small children regularly to help them calm down when they're inconsolable, which allows for us talk through the conflict or injury they are crying over.

Finally, in conflict we are seeking to Collaborate. Work hard to be the bigger person and keep your own emotions at bay. Remind yourself that this person cares about either you or the topic, which means it is appropriate to demonstrate respect. And seek to find a Win / Win outcome that serves you both. Any time someone is passionate enough to argue with you, that passion can be redirected toward positive outcomes if you are thoughtful and intentional enough to influence them.

When I was in the conflict with the CEO who offered me $40,000 to get out of his office, this was the process I used. It was clear that he was emotional, but he didn't know me well enough to care about me, which meant that he cared deeply about the issue we were discussing. I then breathed while he seethed, keeping myself calmer than seemed reasonably possible in that moment.

It actually allowed for me to find the situation comical, though I kept that to myself. Finally, knowing how passionate he was about the issue, I was able to redirect and influence him toward a Win / Win outcome that allowed us to collaborate.

★ ★ ★

When you're working to overcome conflict and understand The Other, you can also remind yourself of statements and sentiments that have been shared throughout this book, like:
- We believe what we believe based on the sum of our lived experiences.
- The opposite of criticism is understanding.
- People live their lives for them, not for you.
- If you feel justified about something, so does The Other.
- When we stop trying to be right and acknowledge that The Other also believes that they are right for reasons just as valid as you, we can work with them in spite of our differences.
- The Other is actually *just like you.*

And then there's something that I alluded to when I shared my opinion about abortion – That I believe each person should have the opportunity to make the best decision for themself, and even though it isn't the right choice for me: We hold some opinions that are formed out of extreme experiences, making those opinions reliably immovable. In these cases, you will likely never change a person's mind, and they may not even care to hear about your opinion. Even though you are entitled to your own opinion, it's important to remember that to The Other, sometimes it just doesn't matter what you think.

In cases of immovable conflict, Listening to Understand is your best course of action. Instead of arguing endlessly and jeopardizing relationships, we need to work extra hard to understand The Other. Fortunately, the process is very straight-forward, and you have the ability to be successful at this immediately:

The Understanding Technique
Recognize The Other
Ask a Question
Shut Up
Repeat

When our son, Bryce, was four, he had to have a test that required mild anesthesia and a doctor monitoring the test in real-time at a hospital. This doctor in particular had previously worked with Kristy and I in an emergency situation with our daughter, Bree, a few years earlier and navigated that issue masterfully. He also took great care of my brother some 30 years earlier. This doctor doesn't have the warmest personality, but he's truly and expert in his field. I knew the test would be about 45 minutes long, and that the doctor's responsibility during that period of time was primarily to be present in case of an emergency. I had the choice to either sit there in silence next to the doctor or engage him in conversation. This situation was not a conflict, but The Understanding Technique works just as well out of conflict as it does in conflict.

I first reminded the doctor of how he cared for my daughter, and recognized him for the way he intentionally walked us through the crisis. I also commented on how he had cared for my brother. Receiving half-smiles on both accounts, I then asked him about the most miraculous case he ever worked on. Holding him up for his herculean effort and outcome, I followed by asking about the most tragic thing he witnessed, and how he handled it. I recognized him again, and before I knew it, he was telling me his whole life story. He told me about meeting his wife, their first date, the apartment they lived in during medical school, and on and on. He talked for 45 minutes with nothing but my occasionally interjection of support. When the test concluded, he shook his head, and was visibly confused as to why he had just shared so much, even going so far as to say, "I'm not sure why I told you any of that. That probably wasn't very professional," then shrugged and said, "Oh well." And when we were done, he HUGGED ME!

The Understanding Technique is an incredible tool to learn about The Other. Used in or out of conflict, you'll yield similarly powerful results, and will demonstrate a strong command of your own emotional intelligence. In order for it to work effectively, you must be a big enough person to put your ego on the shelf for the duration of the conversation; you must GIVE respect to The Other, even if you don't believe they deserve it; and you must reframe within your own mind the definition of "winning an argument." In this case, "winning" is not about getting the other party to acquiesce, but rather to get them to share enough with you so that you can find a way to influence them toward a Win / Win collaborative outcome.

If this concept makes sense to you, but you're struggling to envision how you'd put it into play, here are a few examples that are generic iterations of statements I use regularly with The Other:

> "What I appreciate about you is that you are so confident in sharing your opinion with me. If I were you, I'd feel the same way."

This works because if you were them, you absolutely would

feel the same way. Agreeing isn't the point here. Being agreeable helps you to calm The Other down so you can more effectively understand them.

> "It's clear that this topic is really important to you. I can't understand exactly what you're feeling, but based on my own similar experience, I can relate."

Under no circumstances should you ever say, "I know how you feel," because anyone can immediately counter you with a blind-side attack. I once had a hard day at work and asked a friend how he was doing. He replied, "Today sucks," to which I replied, "I know how you feel." Angrily, he looked at me and said, "No you don't. My dad just died." Instead of making an ass of yourself like I did, demonstrating empathy is the goal. You can do this by showing them that you are humble enough not to claim to understand, but savvy enough to "get it."

> "I respect how passionate you are about this. What experience did you have that led to you feeling this way?"

If nothing else, we can always respect the passion a person has for a subject. We definitely don't need to agree, but it is appropriate to acknowledge how important their opinion is to them. Asking where the opinion stems from may feel like it's probing, but if they're passionate enough about the subject, they'll have no problem answering. They'll feel heard, and through the uncovering process of engaging with them further, you'll be more understanding of the source of their passion.

It's important to note the use of "I" and "you" when in conflict.

The last thing you want is to set off an already agitated person by accident. Saying "I" in a way that claims ownership of your role in the conflict is smart and respectful. Saying "you" in a way that does not cast blame, but instead holds The Other up for something you see in them will make them feel seen, heard, and important. Remember Namaste.

★ ★ ★

There will certainly be times where you have no choice but to engage in conflict. This happens in professional environments and personal environments alike, particularly when you are charged with holding The Other accountable for something that they did not live up to. In this case, there is another tool that you can use in order to positively influence the outcome:

Transforming Conflict into Collaboration
Start with the End in Mind
Defeat Objections Before They Arise
Talk Like a Human
Replace Directions with Questions

Simon Sinek is a wonderful author and thought leader. His book, *Start with Why*, and the TED talk he did where he focuses on The Golden Circle are masterful works that everyone should understand. Essentially the lesson he teaches is to Start with the End in Mind. It's logical for anyone who learned as a child that solving maze puzzles is always easier when the pencil mark begins at the exit of the maze. When we know what we want to achieve, it's remarkably easier to be successful. So for you as you are intentionally entering into conflict, ask yourself, "What am I trying to achieve? Do I want compliance, buy-in, victory, or collaboration?" It's likely one of those four, so figure it out and plan accordingly.

Speaking of planning, you would be wise to plan to defeat objections before they arise. Use the process law students use, and pretend like you are making a defense case for The Other. Anything you would say if you were them, you need to prepare for them to say and have a way to overcome it. The more articulate you are in identifying the holes in your own argument, the more likely you will be to overcome their objections.

In all conflict, you have a choice: You can talk to The Other like a boss, or you can talk to them like a human. By choosing to behave like an ally instead of an adversary, you will be far more likely to get them to listen and engage with you. If they feel as though you are trying to help them to be successful, you will get greater buy-in, which will yield collaboration instead of compliance.

Finally, if you can give directions, you can instead choose to ask questions. Engaging The Other in this way allows them to craft solutions to their own behavioral problems, or to enhance the new initiatives you are implementing. People are far more likely to buy-in to what you want them to do if they're the one to come up with the way to achieve the outcome.

Taking us back to the parable of the fine dining managers in conflict, the general manager said, "The opposite of criticism is understanding." When we understand opposing viewpoints, we are no longer restricted by our inherent biases. This allows us to make educated choices to change our opinion when we feel that is appropriate, and it allows us to have a more receptive listener when they finally get around to asking us about our opinions.

Understanding is the key to averting conflict. Think of any

There's No Such Thing as Right and Wrong

situation you have ever been in where you were strongly opinionated but truly didn't know much about the topic. Now, think of that situation, or another, where you later learned more about the topic and switched your viewpoint. The difference is that you criticized what you didn't understand, and when you understood it, you could no longer criticize it, just like me and the Affordable Care Act. When we understand The Other, we will naturally respect them, which allows us to collaborate in spite of our differences.

★ ★ ★

Throughout this book, and specifically in this chapter, you have been exposed to a series of tools. *The 4 Steps for DEI Success, Leaders REST, The Results Equation, The ABC's of Conflict Management, The Understand Technique,* and *Transforming Conflict in Collaboration* were all items created in support of helping individuals to learn to overcome conflict and behave like the Leader that they need and want to be. Each of these tools is explored and practiced during The Leadership Mastery Program from Leadership Coaching for Results. They are shared here for your benefit, so that you can utilize them to improve your life.

Admittedly, there are times when I fall short of my own expectations and do not behave in the ways I have advocated for in this book. That doesn't make me a failure or a hypocrite, but rather a human being. I regularly realize when I'm facing self-imposed hardship because I let my emotions get the best of me and allowed myself to say or do something that I know is not helpful. The power in this is that each time it happens, I become increasingly aware in the future, so my mistakes occur less and less frequently. This will likely be your experience as well – You'll try something you learned here and it won't work the way you expected, or you'll remember in the middle of an ugly argument that you now have the tools to adjust your behavior for better results and forgot to use them. All of these things are normal and a healthy part of each person's development toward becoming the best version of themselves.

While I now have very few arguments with those who do not play an important role in my life, I do still occasionally have arguments with people that I care about. This is because of the emotional variable we identified – Those closest to me care about a topic *and* me, and are concerned for me. Just because I have a strong mastery over these skills does not mean that I am Jesus Christ and perfectly control my emotions every time I'm in conflict. Hell, even Jesus trashed a temple once. The approach I have advocated for you to adopt is highly effective, but even I can still be triggered, particularly if someone pushes one of my hot buttons. You and I will not be perfect at any point, but with each conflict we experience, we can hold ourselves accountable to being better than the last time. That said, when you fail, which you 100% will, don't beat yourself up – Know that I've probably failed in conflict more times than you've yet had the opportunity to attempt success. Being intentional and persistent will ultimately lead you to the outcomes you desire.

There's another important thing to consider as you are mastering your use of these tools: Is this person even worth the heartache? If you've ever allowed yourself to argue with a stranger in the comments section on the internet, you know that virtually all of those arguments are worthless. Sure, maybe it's fun to try to "educate" The Other, but how often is that the actual outcome? Rarely. So just don't allow yourself to be sucked into those types of conflict. A more difficult decision, though, is deciding if a long-time friend or family member is worth the heartache of conflict. Some people like to play Devil's Advocate to such an extent that there is little room left for a positive and supportive relationship. Others are just flat-out assholes. Just because they have been a part of your journey in life up until this point doesn't mean that you are chained to them for the rest of the journey. It isn't an easy decision to make, but sometimes the best approach to conflict is to avoid it altogether because The Other just isn't worth keeping in your life. When I finally made this decision and stopped engaging with those who added nothing positive to my life, the pointless conflict and drama I experienced immediately dropped to nearly zero.

As I said at the beginning of the book, you have the power to choose the outcomes you want from conflict. I committed then to showing you how. My hope is that you now make choices that make our world a happier and more civil place.

★ ★ ★

Think back to any point in your life where you held a strong belief that you no longer hold. It could be about anything that you were outspokenly opinionated about. It could even be about conflict itself, which hopefully has been positively influenced by what you've read here. Whatever the topic, that is actually less important than this next question: Why did your opinion change?

Thinking of your shifted perspective, what was happening? Who were you with? What did you say or do? Did you hurt someone, or were you hurt by someone? Was the other person actively seeking to change your mind, or were they resigned to the fact that you were likely never going to change your mind so they felt that they could freely speak? What happened next? What happened after that? Why did your opinion change?

As you think through these questions, your brain operates faster than you can read them. You have all of the puzzle pieces before you right now, and you may have already solved the puzzle by this point. The answer will always boil down to the same thing: You had a new perspective, and you understood something that you didn't previously understand. With that new understanding came the realization that you could no longer legitimately criticize that which you once damned. That doesn't mean you necessarily agree with the new realization, but you understand it, and you understand why others could think and feel this way. And with this understanding of yourself and The Other, you also realize that you've always understood that there is no such thing as "right" and "wrong."

★ ★ ★
Collaboration

As we have considered many of the ways America is currently divided, it seems clear that it is equally possible to reunite our nation by collaborating, respecting each other, and recognizing that our differences of opinion do not make one side "right" and the other "wrong," but that each side is right for different reasons, and we need to find a way to incorporate each side's perspectives.

One concern I had with writing this book was that I would be misconstrued as a cynic attempting to burn down everything, and that I advocate for anarchy. In fact, that is exactly the opposite of the objective of this book. While I did burn down both Trump and Biden's behavior (and many of the sides of each conflict topic we explored), the intention is not to be cynical of all politicians or policies. Rather, the intention is to advocate for better behavior that is respectful of contradictory viewpoints, opinions, and beliefs. The answer is not, "We should have no politicians," but rather, "All politicians should seek to serve *all* people." Therefore, in order to ensure that there is no confusion, this chapter is focused entirely on building everything back up in a way that respects and acknowledges the priorities of the two competing sides of the dyadic conflicts we have already explored, plus a couple of other common sense ideas that serve our friends and neighbors.

Certainly my personal biases will show here, but at this point they won't surprise you. The intention isn't to share what I think is best, but instead to find solutions to perpetually topical problems by seeking to serve as many people as possible. If I've done my job effectively, you'll love these recommendations as much as you dislike them, and you'll agree that they're logical regardless. I also hope that you will find them to be notably better than what is currently in place. I don't personally love everything here, but my affinity for any one idea isn't the point – The point is to serve as many people as possible.

It has long been my personal belief and attitude that an *actual* political Leader should have strong beliefs of what is right, based on their experiences and encouragement from their constituents, while also being willing to work collaboratively with those who have a differing opinion. *Real* political Leaders should have a personal mandate to be willing to sacrifice their own interests for the sake of the greater good, and should seek to hold The Other accountable to the same standard. Through collaboration, *true* political Leaders will ultimately agree on solutions that serve the majority. This methodology will require accepting occasional individual or party losses for benefit of all. Taking it a step further, I'd even suggest that if a politician were always winning and getting what they want, that would be a clear indicator that they are failing to represent *all* people.

With that, here are a series of policy recommendations that I hope our elected officials adopt, not for the sake of making their respective party appear innovative, but for the sake of all Americans they are charged with serving and representing. The intent here is not to have a series of full-fledged policies that have explored every single If / Then, but rather a series of strong starting points that take into consideration opposing viewpoints, therefore serving more people. Politicians who advocate for these policies will be responsible for bringing them to life and determining the specific nuances around their implementation. These recommendations are designed to achieve collaboration for the sake of unity.

★ ★ ★

Graduated Drinking License

What if, instead of hoping and praying that 21-year-olds will be smart about their choices when consuming alcohol, we educated young adults on how to safely use the legal drug? What if we adapted a formula that already works for teaching kids how to drive, and created a Graduated Drinking License?

The only reason why the legal drinking age is 21 is because the federal government has forced a mandate by tying highway funding dollars to the enforcement of a 21-year-old drinking age.[136] A better solution than a later starting point, though, is to educate young people on how to safely use and consume alcohol earlier. By creating an optional training program for individuals as young as 18, we can create a 3-year long learning curve that helps individuals to understand risks, best practices, and how alcohol personally affects their body. For example, in year one, an 18-year-old who successful completes the program will earn a designation on their driver's license that affords them the opportunity to consume beer with a responsible adult until 10 p.m. In year two, after more education and an updated designation, they can consume beer or wine with a responsible adult until 10 p.m. After year 3, and further education and a final endorsement, they can consume beer, wine, or liquor with a responsible adult until 10 p.m. Then when they turn 21, they can consume whatever they want whenever they want, like a responsible adult.

The program would be optional. No one has to take it, but if they choose not to, they would be required to wait until they're 21 to consume alcoholic beverages. Each level of the program would be fee-based, which would offset the cost of the programming and fund programmatic supports for those with substance abuse issues.

As counterintuitive as it may have seemed before reading this book, this is a solution that should be able to get the mutual support of Mothers Against Drunk Driving, the Fraternal Order of Police, and the beer and liquor lobby, as the solution leads to education for young people that will save lives, safer consumption that should result in fewer police interventions, and will create an increased customer-base for the companies that create and sell these products.

Instead of choosing a side, let's choose a cause: Less young people getting hurt or dying from irresponsible alcohol consumption. By choosing a cause, we can enroll people and groups from opposing sides to collaborate and serve more people.

★ ★ ★

Compassionate End-of-Life

What if, instead of forcing individuals to suffer at the end of their life, we give them the dignity and deference to make the choices that are best for them?

Let's educate doctors on how best to advise their patients on end-of-life options, which includes a Compassionate End-of-Life (euthanasia). If we first require formal counseling sessions with a trained psychiatrist, we can protect vulnerable individuals, and ensure that the individual is actually in the right headspace to make that final decision. We can then have an End-of-Life practitioner counsel the individual, and allow for the individual to make the choice that is the most appropriate for their individual circumstances.

This respects individual rights, provides options for those who desire them, protects families from the burden of caring for those who no longer wish to suffer, and ensures the dignity of the individual who decides that it is the best path forward in their journey.

★ ★ ★

Pardon and Appoint Snowden and Assange

Edward Snowden and Julian Assange have become martyrs of free speech. Both individuals, at the core of their actions, are Whistleblowers. Both became exiles because they blew the whistle on the inappropriate actions our government took, and continues to take, against you and I in the name of keeping us safe.

What if, instead of damning these two individuals, we pardoned and repatriated them and allowed them to continue their work? What if, even further, our president appointed them to leadership positions within our Intelligence Community? If our government feels the need to hide its actions from its citizens, it is only a matter of time before those actions have the ability to be used by a bad actor against our best interests. Instead of blindly trusting that our government is innocent, let's put those who are most well-known for holding our government accountable in roles that allow them to truly protect American citizens by keeping our government in check.

Doing this would demonstrate that America is open, honest,

and transparent to the people. It would show Americans that we can have faith in our government, because if they step out of line, we'll know about it. It would serve to make America safer from domestic threats, as confidence in the government would begin to increase. It would also show our friends around the globe that we're serious about being a role model and example to other nations by willingly holding our government to a high standard of accountability that they should also strive for.

★ ★ ★

Eliminate the Gas Tax, Invest in the Future, Make it Equitable

What if, instead of the federal government having legal ownership of our nation's highways, all roads within a state were ceded to said state for care and purview? What if we eliminated the gas tax, privatized every road, and paid for their maintenance and repair through user fees?

Electric vehicles will make the gas tax obsolete within a decade or two. Roads throughout the country are already in poor condition, as both Presidents Trump and Biden argued in advocating for each of their once-in-a-generation infrastructure plans. The problem with "once-in-a-generation," is that it ignores the gap in investment between generations. By ceding ownership of highways to the states, and allowing the states to lease the rights to tracts of roadway to private entities, a couple of things happen immediately. First, we would put the power and responsibility of roadway upkeep in the hands of those who stand to lose the most by ignoring their investment, therefore incentivizing them to keep the roads in healthy condition. Second, through the use of existing technologies like Electronic Toll Collection (ETC), we can easily ensure that those who are using the roads are paying for their use, and those who don't, never have to. Third, the cost to the average American would be Net Zero, as the average cost of usage would replace the average gas tax and federal infrastructure taxes the average American already pays.

With a lease agreement of something like 30 years, 10 years past the average lifespan of a typical roadway, the lessee would be required to improve their investment at least once during the life of the investment, and other regulatory concerns can also be mandated as appropriate. This concept generates revenue for states, encourages placemaking initiatives, incentivizes unique and clever uses of technology to capture wasted road energies, and creates competition for superb maintenance that will draw drivers to intentionally use or avoid certain roads based on state of care or per-mile pricing.

By using a model like this, we hold up those who advocate for competition and capitalism. We hold up state's rights. We create an environment for green solutions to be implemented and utilized. And we, The People, are the biggest winners as our costs will remain neutral while our driving experiences will become safer, more pleasant, and ready for the future.

★ ★ ★

Actual Immigration Reform

What if, instead of allowing every single presidential candidate to pay lip service to immigration, we actually solved the problem? What if we acknowledged that the illegal immigrants that we work with and live near are actually our colleagues and neighbors? What if we stated publicly, that there would be a window of time for any illegal immigrant to become a naturalized citizen, with no questions asked?

We could give a window of time, let's call it 18 months, to allow illegal immigrants the opportunity to go through the process of becoming legally recognized and naturalized American citizens, until say, July 3rd of a year. That way, on July 4th, all current illegal immigrants who live, work, play, and contribute to our country will have the opportunity to celebrate the pageantry and patriotism of the 4th of July as an American. This approach honors the life and dignity of all peoples who wish to positively contribute to our great country, and honors the rule of law that is an important precedent worth respecting.

This approach is again optional. In the event that someone chooses not to take up this opportunity, as they feel it may not be appropriate for them, if they are ever arrested for any reason and found to be living here illegally, they would be immediately deported to their nation of origin. This gives illegal immigrants the opportunity to start fresh and do things, "the right way," while also providing options and holding those accountable who choose not to follow our laws.

Some would say that this is amnesty. It is. I would also argue that Presidents Reagan, Bush, Clinton, Bush, Obama, Trump, and Biden have all provided amnesty by doing nothing meaningful to actually change the situation. All of these presidents have made bold statements about us being "a nation of laws," and follow that with their specific brand of spin and "solutions," though nothing has changed in regard to those already living in our country illegally. That's amnesty.

This solution treats human beings like human beings. Instead of going on a witch hunt to deport our friends, neighbors, and coworkers, we can provide an opportunity for them to live the life they want to live without living it in fear. They can continue to contribute to their communities, pay taxes like the rest of the citizens do, and they can be proud of their choice to become an American.

We can also make the process of applying for and receiving acceptance of immigration easier. Not simpler so as to serve a lower common denominator for admission, but easier so there is less incentive to do things the wrong way. This approach will create jobs, decrease criminal entry at the borders, and make America a more welcoming and inviting place to come and add value. It also reestablishes our Shining City on the Hill status by reinforcing our tenets of encouraging Life, Liberty, and the Pursuit of Happiness.

★ ★ ★

Bipartisanship or Bust

What if we expected collaboration as a non-negotiable behavior from our elected officials? What if we created environments where the display of respect for The Other was more important than "winning?" What if winning meant that as many Americans as possible are served and represented at any given time instead of just the party in power? What if we held our elected officials to the same standards that we hold their opponents? What if we made politics actually work for us by influencing a culture of understanding, respect, and collaboration?

What if, instead of allowing the state and federal executive branches to do and undo whatever they would like through unilateral executive orders, the president and governors were only allowed to use executive orders in situations or defense or emergency? What if the legislative bodies were expected to work collaboratively and swiftly so that executive orders were not necessary at all?

What if every single law that is ever brought to the House and Senate for a vote was required to be co-authored by a representative from both the Democratic and Republican parties? What if, even better, each bill that is passed required a majority of each party to vote in its favor?

Some may say that this a fool's dream and isn't possible in today's political climate. I say to that, it is for exactly that reason that a solution like this is necessary.

Presidents Biden and Trump, and Governors Newsom, Whitmer, Noem, DeSantis, and their compatriots all wield incredible power over those they are charged with serving. And in an environment where elections are won by only a couple of percentage points, this means that approximately half of those they represent will disagree with the party-influenced decisions these individuals make. And something as relatively innocuous as mandating or preventing mandates for mask usage has direct implications that may not be applicable, appropriate, or desired at the local-level.

Further, individuals like Nancy Pelosi, Mitch McConnell, Chuck Schumer, Kevin McCarthy, Alexandria Ocasio-Cortez, Bernie Sanders, Rand Paul, and Marjorie Taylor-Greene do not behave as representatives of the people. They behave as representatives of their parties, and their actions demonstrate that they are working with the primary focus of advancing the agendas of their party leaders and super donors, not with you and I as their primary focus and concern.

By limiting the scope of which executive orders can be utilized, while simultaneously expecting the state and federal Legislative branches to work collaboratively in spite of their differences on policy, we can have a government that is operated for the People, by the People. This doesn't change anything systemically, but at the same time, changes everything systemically. With our elected officials working together on our behalf instead of against each other for the sake of their party, we will have an environment of respect and unity that is sorely missing in Washington D.C. This will also attract our *actual* best and brightest who we can be proud to point to as Leaders and role models.

★ ★ ★

Institute a Flat Tax

Taxes are a mess. They're scaffolded in such a way as to be "equitable," but the reality is that those who are in the highest tax bracket (Like our elected officials and their mega-donors) are also the ones who have the greatest ability to pay experts to circumvent taxes in the first place. This is why Donald Trump, Jeff Bezos, and others in the highest tax brackets actually pay less in taxes as a percentage of earnings than you and I. Instead, what if all Americans were taxed equally, and no deductions or loopholes existed?

The concept here would be that a Flat Tax would replace the current tax bracket system, and each individual would be taxed at say, 10% of income and earnings. With the removal of virtually all deductions and loopholes, the outcome would be that every single person, from the minimum wage worker to Elon Musk, would all be taxed the same percentage of their income and earnings. Businesses would also be included in this system. The outcome of this would be that taxes would be incredibly easy to file; those who are the most likely to have the means to protect their dollars would lose that ability; the increased income captured from those dodging taxes would lower the overall necessary tax percentage for all individuals; and increasing the federal government's annual revenue would serve to pay down the national debt.

This serves the democratic call for those with the greatest wealth to "pay their fair share;" serves the conservative call for a simpler tax code; and with a proper analysis of what the percentage should be, will generate more revenue for the federal government without actually raising taxes on anyone – And potentially lowering them for everyone.

★ ★ ★

Hold China Accountable & Reduce the National Debt

It's clear that COVID-19 originated in China. The exact method of origination, whether it was through natural means or human engineering, is still up for debate at the end of 2021. What isn't up for debate, though, is that COVID-19 originated in China. Their failure to contain it led to the global pandemic that cost lives, livelihoods, entire businesses, massively disrupted the global supply chain, lead to trillions of dollars of lost productivity, and required the infusion of government funds into municipalities, businesses, and individuals in order to prevent further chaos.

All of this could have been prevented with responsible behavior, but it wasn't. Other burgeoning nations could see the lack of accountability as permission not to invest in safety measures to prevent such a colossal mistake of their own making. This is tantamount to testing a nuclear weapon and having it "accidentally" fall on a nation, which is to say it's utterly and entirely unacceptable. Without holding China accountable for their failure, intentional or not, there is little reason to believe that this type of crisis won't happen again in the future.

What if, instead of giving China a playful slap on the hand, a deep financial analysis was performed to determine the exact financial impact the pandemic had on the US economy, and the economies of the whole world? Let's call it a $10 trillion blow for the US, for the sake of argument. What if that number was used as the penalty to China for their lack of prevention? What if the US refused to pay the $1.1 trillion of the nation debt owed to China, and fined them for the rest?

This would serve to shore up the lost productivity, cover the expense of numerous stimulus and recovery bills, and would significantly reduce our national debt. Paired with this action taken by nations all around the world, China would become an example for all that living in a global economy requires that each nation has a responsibility to behave with the best interest of all humans in mind, or pay the consequences for disregarding those who may be negatively impacted.

★ ★ ★

Eliminate All Taxes & Institute the Freedom Dividend

Why are Americans even paying to support the federal government in the first place? We work to earn money, then we give a portion of that to provide for the government to maintain itself – Poorly, one could argue. What if, instead of paying taxes to support the federal government, American citizens were paid a Freedom Dividend *by* the government?

The premise behind this idea is that the federal government should be responsible for funding itself through the production and sale of goods and services, just like any other entity. With this model, the government would understand its annual financial expenses and price its products such that the expenses are covered, and that there is a "profit," which is paid out in equal portions to each legal American citizen in the form of a Freedom Dividend.

Potential products and services the government could explore as revenue streams include the investment in and successful harnessing of fusion energy, which could then be sold to nations around the world; asteroid mining for rare and expensive materials; and the direct billing to nations who require our military support.

Investments in new energy technologies would be extreme at the onset, but would literally pay for themselves if we made their utilization a priority. Mining asteroids sounds like science fiction, but with the clever use of intentionally landing them in safe locations on Earth, we could far exceed the investment of redirection or the attempt to mine and transport while in space. We do already bill our allies in what it called, "host nation support," but our investment cost far exceeds the monies and goods returned, and the reporting is intentionally murky, making transparency impossible.

By being intentional with our investments as a nation, we can not only generate enough revenue to eliminate the need to tax average Americans, but we can instead pay them a dividend for their patriotism of choosing to invest their lives and efforts in the greatest country on earth.

This concept serves the fiscal conservative priority of eliminating the national debt, the Libertarian preference of eliminating taxes entirely, and serves to support the liberal progressive goal of providing individuals with universal basic income. It requires the federal government to be fiscally prudent and responsible, and keeps hard earned dollars in the pockets of those who worked for them. Everyone wins by making the government work for us.

★ ★ ★

No Vaccine Mandates / Require Immunity Passports

What if we treated each other with respect? What if we trusted humans to do what's right for them, and allowed them to? What if we had an Immunity Passport that does not harm the individual who does not have one, while also protecting the overall public health of the collective?

No person should be excluded from living a happy and fulfilling life based on the opinion of a politician they may not have voted for. Similarly, no person should be excluded from living a happy and fulfilling life because there is not an expectation of basic respect for each individual's health and safety.

Instead of requiring vaccines that have varying efficacy and do not flat-out prevent infection, and instead of blatantly ignoring the science of natural immunity, let's allow individuals to make the best choices for themselves. Each choice comes at its own cost: Acquire immunity through natural or medical means and have free reign to participate in life circa 2019, or choose to be excluded from certain activities that have an increased opportunity to negatively impact the happiness and fulfillment of others, like flying.

This approach does all of the things I previously stated at the end of the COVID chapter, which includes providing individuals with the free choice to make the best decision for themselves. This solution provides an option for individuals, with those who opt not to participate losing nothing that is a natural-born right, only privileges they can consciously choose to live without.

★ ★ ★

Free Menstrual Hygiene Products for All Who Desire Them

Nearly 51% of our population, a majority, experiences menstruation at some point during their life. This recurring event requires hygiene products in order to maintain the health and safety of those you and I call friends and family. Some, particularly those who are low income, unhoused, or beginning their journey to adulthood, do not have access to the products they require. Instead of focusing only on the few for something that impacts the majority, what if we focused on serving the majority of individuals, as each of these recommendations calls for? What if we made menstrual hygiene products freely available to all who desire them?

Schools, universities, public buildings, and more can easily implement this solution as they all require some form of government support already. Private businesses could apply for a grant to offset the cost of offering the products in their restrooms. Individuals who do not have immediate access to the products they require could go to a variety of locations, including grocery stores that also sell more premium iterations of the products, and acquire the items they need without charge.

Caring for the health needs of the majority removes a barrier to ensuring health equity, removes a barrier to ensuring financial equity, and eliminates the concern of mental space necessary to care for a natural human function that sustains our species. This suggestion harms no one, and serves all who require it.

★ ★ ★

Utilize Technology for Increased Democracy

In the 2020s we have grown accustomed to casually voting for things and people that entertain us the most. Television shows, social media contests, and more are directly influenced by the votes of those who care to pay attention. What if we initiated policies based on the public opinion of the policy? What if, instead of damning politicians for "waffling" on a topic based on the evolving priorities of those they represent, or worse, allow that elected official to vote based on what is politically expedient, we allowed for the people to vote on individual policies?

A system with appropriate security measures could easily capture an individual's social security number, and allow for their single vote on issues small or large. Instead of parti-

san pollsters who seek to influence through their "research," would could actually keep our finger on the pulse of the people, and do as they say. We could vote on matters small or large from our phones, like we do while watching singing contestants, and have our voices heard more than every 2-4 years. For example, we could put forth the issue of the War on Drugs and allow individuals to vote:
- Keep all drugs illegal
- Decriminalize the following drugs
- Decriminalize all drugs
- Legalize the following drugs
- Legalize all drugs

This approach would improve the engagement we have in the democratic process, would increase the confidence we have in our government, and will remove the blockades party leaders put in place on items they don't want but the people do. The only losers here are the egos and accumulated power of politicians. The winners are Americans.

★ ★ ★

Legalize Sex Work

In the Media chapter, I damned media talking heads for not doing what their job is intended to be, and instead for serving as prostitutes who sow division. The piece I didn't address while damning their profession as it currently exists, is I didn't say this: Sex work is work.

The skills and abilities of any person should be legally and freely usable for the exchange of goods and services as each individual feels the exchange is appropriate. Virtually all people at some point trade their time, energy, function, and effort for something else. Discriminating against sex workers for what they believe to be an equitable trade of goods and services only serves to uphold a system that assumes some know better than others.

Returning to our exploration of Metaethics, treating sex work as immoral is inappropriate, because who defines morality? Further, this presupposes that the beliefs of some are of greater value than those of others, and that those who look down on selling one's body are "better" than those who choose to profit from such transactions. If someone wants to earn an income and has the skills and abilities to do so with either their brain or their body, no one but those engaged in the exchange should have a say in that transaction.

This approach supports the right of individuals to freely make choices for themselves, and it allows the free market to dictate what is or is not desirable for the trading of goods and services. It would also make sex work less taboo, and arguably safer for the worker.

To those sex workers who I may have offended by unfairly associating you with media prostitutes: I apologize. To those in the media who I offended by my declarations: Be better and demand better of your industry. For all our sake.

★ ★ ★

In late 2017, I was feeling "strange." I wasn't specifically depressed, but I wasn't excited about anything. Nothing was particularly bad in my life, and from the outside, anyone would be right to say that I had everything going for me.

Those around me at the time who defaulted to toxic positivity most certainly tried to remind me of this. But on the inside, I was feeling empty, exhausted, and lacking joy. As a result of the pandemic, we now know this feeling to be described as "languishing." At this point in time, I was already a highly effective coach, about a year away from being recognized as the #1 Corporate Trainer in the World, so I was well-versed in helping individuals who were in the situation I was facing. The troubling part, though, was that I couldn't solve my own problems with the tools I would use to help others. I decided to go to a counselor for the second time in my life.

While this was a different counselor than the one I visited when I was a suicidal teenager, it was again the perfect person for me at exactly the time that I needed him. He asked questions, listened, and shared stories that made me see parts of myself that I couldn't otherwise see. I realized while I was working with him that part of my problem was that I had come to the conclusion that I truly did not desire a future where I held political office. I was wrangling with envisioning a future where I ran a company for the rest of my career and lived happily ever after, as opposed to suffering and enduring through political campaigns and endless scrutiny that would cause my family pain. I had worked with and coached enough politicians to know that I didn't want to put myself or my family through all of that. I also knew that I felt a compulsion – or from a religious context, one could say a Higher Calling – to serve our country.

We talked at length over a period of many sessions for me to finally come to a conclusion: I no longer sought to be a public servant, but I was willing to subject myself to the pain for the sake of our nation's greater good. Through our work together,

I was able to come to peace with myself and the ambiguous nature of if I would eventually run for office. I was able to hold myself up for the big difficult things I had previously done, and understood that a more peaceful life could still afford me opportunities to serve others. I ultimately decided that if others called on me to serve, I would be ready and willing. Not to serve my ego, but to serve our country.

I hope that these policy recommendations are adopted by those currently serving our great nation. But even more importantly than policies, I hope our elected officials adopt the cultural behaviors advocated for in this book. I hope they choose to be more understanding, respectful, and collaborative. To that end, when you decide that you're done with this book, please don't just put it on a shelf – I encourage you to send it to one of your political representatives. Take a picture of the book and mailing address of who you're sending it to, and post it on social media to inspire others and influence a cultural shift. Over time you and I can influence progress and achieve the unity that we deserve as Americans.

And if these politicians don't decide to act in our best interest, you'll do the right thing, and we'll make it happen together.

Epilogue

When we think about American politicians, they can be defined in broad strokes as being self-serving, antagonistic, intolerant of opposing viewpoints, and judgmental of opinions. Imagine a world, though, where those representatives of the American people behaved as Leaders. Where they motivate, inspire, and empower all of us to be the best we can be. Imagine Democrats and Republicans sitting down together and recognizing *why* a member of the other party has the opinion that they have. What would happen if they dialoged for impact instead of monologuing for sound bites? Imagine the policy-making that could take place if both parties were to work toward collaborative solutions that serve and represent the best interests of the citizenry, instead of a party banner. What would happen in your piece of the world if, instead of having an opinion that you feel strongly about on a topic that you've not truly experienced or researched, you sought to understand the topic from someone who lives it?

The ultimate goal in conflict is not the absence of conflict, because conflict is inherent in life. The ultimate goal is to understand The Other, respect the passion and opinions each of us hold, seek to collaborate, and find the middle ground that serves everyone maximally. You and I have the power to make this ultimate goal into a reality. I said at the beginning that you already have this power, and throughout our time together, I've showed you how to use it. Now all you need to do is choose to use your power to positively influence our world. *You* have the power to choose. *You* have the power to influence change.

There is no such thing as "right" and "wrong." If by this point you still disagree with that statement... You're right.

References

1. The Columbine High School Shootings. CNN Special Edition. http://edition.cnn.com/SPECIALS/2000/columbine.cd/Pages/NARRATIVE.Time.Line.htm. Published 2000. Accessed February 19, 2019.
2. Rosin H. Columbine miracle: A matter of belief. The Washington Post. https://www.washingtonpost.com/wp-srv/WPcap/1999-10/14/026r-101499-idx.html. Published October 14, 1999. Accessed February 19, 2019.
3. Medal of honor: Meet 16 heroes of Iraq and Afghanistan who received the nation's highest honor. We Are The Mighty. https://www.wearethemighty.com/veterans/medal-of-honor-iraq-afghanistan/. Published May 12, 2021. Accessed October 14, 2021.
4. Landler M. Obama Awards Medal of Honor to former Army sergeant. The New York Times. https://www.nytimes.com/2013/02/12/us/politics/obama-awards-medal-of-honor-to-clinton-romesha.html. Published February 11, 2013. Accessed October 14, 2021.
5. Kurtzman L. Killing in war leaves veterans with lasting psychological scars, study finds. Killing in War Leaves Veterans with Lasting Psychological Scars, Study Finds | UC San Francisco. https://www.ucsf.edu/news/2016/12/405231/killing-war-leaves-veterans-lasting-psychological-scars-study-finds. Published October 28, 2021. Accessed October 14, 2021.
6. Davies M. Journal of Veterans Studies. https://journal-veterans-studies.org/articles/10.21061/jvs.v7i1.232/. Published May 31, 2021. Accessed October 14, 2021.
7. Eide M. 20 years of 'Forever' Wars have left a toll on US veterans. Texas A&M Today. https://today.tamu.edu/2021/09/10/20-years-of-forever-wars-have-left-a-toll-on-us-veterans/. Published September 10, 2021. Accessed October 14, 2021.
8. Dohrenwend BP, Turner JB, Turse NA, Adams BG, Koenen KC, Marshall R. The psychological risks of Vietnam for U.S. veterans: a revisit with new data and methods. *Science*. 2006;313(5789):979-982. doi:10.1126/science.1128944
9. Office of Public and Intergovernmental Affairs. VA releases 2020 National Veteran Suicide Prevention Annual Report. https://www.va.gov/opa/pressrel/pressrelease.cfm?id=5565. Published November 12, 2020. Accessed October 14, 2021.
10. Book of Joshua. In: *Holy Bible: NRSV*. San Francisco, CA: Harper Bibles; 2007.

11. September 11 Attacks. Wikipedia. https://en.wikipedia.org/wiki/September_11_attacks. Published October 29, 2021. Accessed August 20, 2021.
12. Savell S, Crawford N, Lutz C. Costs of the 20-Year War on terror: $8 trillion and 900,000 deaths. Brown University. https://www.brown.edu/news/2021-09-01/costsofwar. Published September 1, 2021. Accessed October 14, 2021.
13. Yergin D. In: *The Prize: The Epic Quest for Oil, Money, and Power.* New York: Simon & Schuster; 1991:401.
14. McWilliams WC, Piotrowski H. In: *The World since 1945: A History of International Relations.* Boulder, CO: Lynne Rienner Publishers; 2014:154.
15. Dionisi DJ. In: *American Hiroshima: The Reasons Why and a Call to Strengthen America's Democracy.* Victoria, B.C.: Trafford; 2005:40.
16. Six-Day War. Wikipedia. https://en.wikipedia.org/wiki/Six-Day_War. Published October 13, 2021. Accessed October 14, 2021.
17. Conflict in the Middle East (1947-2000). PBS. https://www.pbs.org/wgbh/americanexperience/features/hijacked-conflict-middle-east-1947-2000/. Accessed July 12, 2021.
18. Executive Orders. National Archives and Records Administration. https://www.archives.gov/federal-register/codification/executive-order/12170.html. Accessed July 12, 2021.
19. Penn N. 444 days in the dark: An oral history of the Iran hostage crisis. GQ. https://www.gq.com/story/iran-hostage-crisis-tehran-embassy-oral-history. Published November 3, 2009. Accessed July 12, 2021.
20. Iran–Iraq war. Wikipedia. https://en.wikipedia.org/wiki/Iran%E2%80%93Iraq_War. Published October 23, 2021. Accessed July 12, 2021.
21. Middle East | US pulls out of Saudi Arabia. BBC News. http://news.bbc.co.uk/2/hi/middle_east/2984547.stm. Published April 29, 2003. Accessed July 12, 2021.
22. President Clinton's address to the nation on military strikes in Iraq. Clinton Digital Library. https://clinton.presidentiallibraries.us/items/show/15978. Accessed July 12, 2021.
23. Innocence Database. Death Penalty Information Center. https://deathpenaltyinfo.org/policy-issues/innocence-database. Accessed August 13, 2021.
24. Mettler K. 'Father, please stop': Parents horrified after priest used teen's funeral to condemn suicide. The Washington Post. https://www.washingtonpost.com/religion/2018/12/15/

father-please-stop-parents-horrified-after-priest-used-teens-funeral-condemn-suicide/. Published December 15, 2018. Accessed February 18, 2019.
25. Gould MS, Marrocco FA, Kleinman M, et al. Evaluating iatrogenic risk of youth suicide screening programs. *JAMA*. 2005;293(13):1635. doi:10.1001/jama.293.13.1635
26. Memmott M. Dr. Jack Kevorkian, 'Dr. Death,' has died. NPR. https://www.npr.org/sections/thetwo-way/2011/06/03/136916881/dr-jack-kevorkian-has-died-his-lawyer-says. Published June 3, 2011. Accessed August 24, 2021.
27. Dram Shop Law. Wikipedia. https://en.wikipedia.org/wiki/Dram_shop. Published July 4, 2021. Accessed February 20, 2019.
28. Mittelstadt J. The war on alcohol: Prohibition and the rise of the American state. *Journal of American History*. 2017;103(4):1013-1015. doi:10.1093/jahist/jaw511
29. Joszt L. CDC data: Life expectancy decreases as deaths from suicide, drug overdose increase. AJMC. https://www.ajmc.com/view/cdc-data-life-expectancy-decreases-as-deaths-from-suicide-drug-overdose-increase. Published November 30, 2018. Accessed October 10, 2021.
30. Did Coca-Cola ever contain cocaine? NIDA for Teens. https://teens.drugabuse.gov/blog/post/coca-colas-scandalous-past. Published December 23, 2020. Accessed September 18, 2021.
31. Weiss JN. From Aristotle to Sadat: A short strategic persuasion framework for negotiators. *Negotiation Journal*. 2015;31(3):211-222. doi:10.1111/nejo.12091
32. Garcia A, Hanson K. State Medical Marijuana Laws. https://www.ncsl.org/research/health/state-medical-marijuana-laws.aspx. Published August 23, 2021. Accessed October 14, 2021.
33. Alcohol's Effects on the Body. National Institute on Alcohol Abuse and Alcoholism. https://www.niaaa.nih.gov/alcohols-effects-health/alcohols-effects-body. Accessed October 14, 2021.
34. NIDA. Marijuana DrugFacts. National Institute on Drug Abuse website. https://www.drugabuse.gov/publications/drugfacts/marijuana. December 24, 2019 Accessed October 14, 2021.
35. Seth P, Scholl L, Rudd RA, Bacon S. Overdose deaths involving opioids, cocaine, and psychostimulants - United States, 2015–2016. Morbidity and Mortality Weekly Report (MMWR). https://www.cdc.gov/mmwr/volumes/67/wr/mm6712a1.htm. Published March 29, 2018. Accessed October 11, 2021.
36. Waxman OB. Presidents and drugs-Bill Clinton didn't inhale 25 years ago. Time. https://time.com/4711887/bill-clin-

ton-didnt-inhale-marijuana-anniversary/. Published March 29, 2017. Accessed October 11, 2021.
37. Coleman PT, Deutsch M, Marcus EC. In: *The Handbook of Conflict Resolution: Theory and Practice, 3rd Edition*. John Wiley & Sons; 2014:3-28.
38. Van Green T. Americans overwhelmingly say marijuana should be legal for recreational or medical use. https://www.pewresearch.org/fact-tank/2021/04/16/americans-overwhelmingly-say-marijuana-should-be-legal-for-recreational-or-medical-use. Published April 16, 2021. Accessed October 12, 2021.
39. Slisco A. Two-thirds of American voters support decriminalizing all drugs: Poll. https://www.newsweek.com/two-thirds-american-voters-support-decriminalizing-all-drugs-poll-1599645. Published June 11, 2021. Accessed October 11, 2021.
40. Pew Research Center Media Bias Rating. AllSides. https://www.allsides.com/news-source/pew-research. Published December 26, 2019. Accessed October 15, 2021.
41. On 50th anniversary of "War on drugs," poll shows majority of voters support ending criminal penalties for drug possession, Think Drug War is a failure. American Civil Liberties Union. https://www.aclu.org/press-releases/50th-anniversary-war-drugs-poll-shows-majority-voters-support-ending-criminal. Published June 9, 2021. Accessed October 11, 2021.
42. Drug war statistics. Drug Policy Alliance. https://drugpolicy.org/issues/drug-war-statistics. Accessed October 11, 2021.
43. Whitelaw M. A Path to Peace in the U.S. Drug War: Why California Should Implement the Portuguese Model for Drug Decriminalization. Digital Commons at Loyola Marymount University. https://digitalcommons.lmu.edu/cgi/viewcontent.cgi?referer=&httpsredir=1&article=1746&context=ilr. Published June 2017. Accessed February 13, 2019:81-113.
44. Livingston MD, Barnett TE, Delcher C, Wagenaar AC. Recreational cannabis legalization and opioid-related deaths in Colorado, 2000–2015. *American Journal of Public Health*. 2017;107(11):1827-1829. doi:10.2105/ajph.2017.304059
45. Barber C. Public enemy number one: A pragmatic approach to America's drug problem. https://www.nixonfoundation.org/2016/06/26404/. Published June 29, 2016. Accessed October 11, 2021.
46. Waxman OB. Presidents and drugs-Bill Clinton didn't inhale 25 years ago. Time. https://time.com/4711887/bill-clin-

ton-didnt-inhale-marijuana-anniversary/. Published March 29, 2017. Accessed October 11, 2021.
47. Castuera I. A social history of Christian thought on abortion: Ambiguity vs. certainty in moral debate. *American Journal of Economics and Sociology*. 2017;76(1):121-227. doi:10.1111/ajes.12174
48. Keener E, Strough JN. Having and doing gender: Young adults' expression of gender when resolving conflicts with friends and romantic partners. *Sex Roles*. 2016;76(9-10):615-626. doi:10.1007/s11199-016-0644-8
49. Beckmann KB, Dewenter R, Thomas T. Can news draw blood? the impact of media coverage on the number and severity of terror attacks. *Peace Economics, Peace Science and Public Policy*. 2017;23(1). doi:10.1515/peps-2016-0025
50. Rothman M. Kathy Griffin breaks down, says Donald Trump 'broke me'. https://abcnews.go.com/Entertainment/kathy-griffin-breaks-donald-trump-broke/story?id=47794134. Published June 3, 2017. Accessed February 19, 2019.
51. Itzkoff D. Bill Maher apologizes for use of racial slur on 'real time'. https://www.nytimes.com/2017/06/03/arts/television/bill-maher-n-word.html. Published June 3, 2017. Accessed February 19, 2019.
52. Congressional stagnation in the United States. Wikipedia. https://en.wikipedia.org/wiki/Congressional_stagnation_in_the_United_States. Published May 30, 2021. Accessed October 10, 2021.
53. Why delayed gratification in the marshmallow test doesn't equal success. Smithsonian Magazine. https://www.smithsonianmag.com/smart-news/new-research-marshmallow-test-suggests-delayed-gratification-doesnt-equal-success-180969234/. Published June 5, 2018. Accessed October 10, 2021.
54. Pentagon Says Snowden Took Most U.S. Secrets Ever: Rogers. https://www.bloomberg.com/news/articles/2014-01-09/pentagon-finds-snowden-took-1-7-million-files-rogers-says. Published January 4, 2009. Accessed October 14, 2021.
55. Gellman B, Soltani A. NSA infiltrates links to Yahoo, Google Data Centers Worldwide, Snowden documents say. https://www.washingtonpost.com/world/national-security/nsa-infiltrates-links-to-yahoo-google-data-centers-worldwide-snowden-documents-say/2013/10/30/e51d661e-4166-11e3-8b74-d89d714ca4dd_story.html. Published October 30, 2013. Accessed October 10, 2021.

56. Greenwald G, Grim R. Top-secret document reveals NSA spied on porn habits as part of plan to discredit 'radicalizers'. https://www.huffpost.com/entry/nsa-porn-muslims_n_4346128. Published December 7, 2017. Accessed September 22, 2021.
57. Gellman B. Code name 'Verax': Snowden, in exchanges with post reporter, made clear he knew risks. The Washington Post. https://www.washingtonpost.com/world/national-security/code-name-verax-snowden-in-exchanges-with-post-reporter-made-clear-he-knew-risks/2013/06/09/c9a25b54-d14c-11e2-9f1a-1a7cdee20287_story.html. Published June 9, 2013. Accessed September 22, 2021.
58. Phillips K. Trump once demanded Edward Snowden's execution for giving 'serious information' to Russia. The Washington Post. https://www.washingtonpost.com/news/the-fix/wp/2017/05/16/trump-once-demanded-edward-snowdens-execution-for-giving-serious-information-to-russia/. Published April 28, 2019. Accessed September 22, 2021.
59. Bengali S, Dilanian K. Edward Snowden vows more disclosures about U.S. surveillance. Los Angeles Times. https://www.latimes.com/world/la-xpm-2013-jun-17-la-fg-nsa-leak-20130618-story.html. Published June 17, 2013. Accessed September 22, 2021.
60. Satter R. U.S. court: Mass surveillance program exposed by Snowden was illegal. https://www.reuters.com/article/us-usa-nsa-spying/u-s-court-mass-surveillance-program-exposed-by-snowden-was-illegal-idUSKBN25T3CK. Published September 2, 2020. Accessed September 10, 2021.
61. Afghanistan war logs: Massive leak of secret files exposes truth of Occupation. The Guardian. https://www.theguardian.com/world/2010/jul/25/afghanistan-war-logs-military-leaks. Published July 25, 2010. Accessed September 11, 2021.
62. Julian Assange like a hi-tech terrorist, says Joe Biden. The Guardian. https://www.theguardian.com/media/2010/dec/19/assange-high-tech-terrorist-biden. Published December 19, 2010. Accessed September 11, 2021.
63. US embassy cables culprit should be executed, says Mike Huckabee. The Guardian. https://www.theguardian.com/world/2010/dec/01/us-embassy-cables-executed-mike-huckabee. Published December 1, 2010. Accessed September 11, 2021.
64. Greenwald G, Gallagher R. Snowden documents reveal covert surveillance and pressure tactics aimed at WikiLeaks

and its supporters. The Intercept. https://theintercept.com/2014/02/18/snowden-docs-reveal-covert-surveillance-and-pressure-tactics-aimed-at-wikileaks-and-its-supporters/. Published February 18, 2014. Accessed September 10, 2021.

65. Wikileaks: Brazil president Lula Backs Julian Assange. BBC News. https://www.bbc.com/news/world-latin-america-11966193. Published December 10, 2010. Accessed September 11, 2021.

66. When Wikileaks founder Julian Assange met Ecuadorean president Rafael Correa - Telegraph. https://web.archive.org/web/20120621082341/http:/www.telegraph.co.uk/news/worldnews/wikileaks/9344556/When-Wikileaks-founder-Julian-Assange-met-Ecuadorean-president-Rafael-Correa.html. Published June 20, 2012. Accessed September 11, 2021.

67. Russia: Julian Assange deserves a nobel prize. https://www.jpost.com/International/Russia-Julian-Assange-deserves-a-Nobel-Prize. Published December 11, 2010. Accessed September 11, 2021.

68. 'Angry' Julian Assange starts fifth year living in Ecuador's London Embassy. The Guardian. https://www.theguardian.com/media/2016/jun/19/angry-julian-assange-starts-fifth-year-living-in-ecuadors-london-embassy. Published June 19, 2016. Accessed September 11, 2021.

69. Peters M. Leaked Democratic Party emails show members tried to undercut Sanders. NPR. https://www.npr.org/sections/thetwo-way/2016/07/23/487179496/leaked-democratic-party-emails-show-members-tried-to-undercut-sanders. Published July 23, 2016. Accessed September 11, 2021.

70. Assange charged with violating espionage act, faces up to 170 years in jail. South China Morning Post. https://www.scmp.com/news/world/united-states-canada/article/3011588/us-charges-wikileaks-founder-julian-assange. Published May 23, 2019. Accessed September 11, 2021.

71. Herrera J. Why 15,000 migrants ended up in one spot on the U.S.-Mexico Border. POLITICO. https://www.politico.com/news/magazine/2021/09/23/del-rio-desperation-dysfunction-immigration-513978. Published September 23, 2021. Accessed October 14, 2021.

72. Sonmez F. All migrants have been cleared from encampment in Del Rio, Homeland Security secretary says. The Texas Tribune. https://www.texastribune.org/2021/09/24/texas-border-migrants-camp-del-rio-haitians/. Published September 24, 2021. Accessed October 14, 2021.

73. Many Haitian migrants are staying in the U.S. even as expulsion flights rise. NPR. https://www.npr.org/2021/09/23/1040000579/many-haitian-migrants-are-staying-in-the-u-s-even-as-expulsion-flights-rise. Published September 23, 2021. Accessed October 14, 2021.
74. Press briefing by Press secretary Jen Psaki, September 10, 2021. The White House. https://www.whitehouse.gov/briefing-room/press-briefings/2021/09/10/press-briefing-by-press-secretary-jen-psaki-september-10-2021. Published September 10, 2021. Accessed October 14, 2021.
75. Discrimination based on hair texture in the United States. Wikipedia. https://en.wikipedia.org/wiki/Discrimination_based_on_hair_texture_in_the_United_States. Published August 5, 2021. Accessed October 14, 2021.
76. President Donald J. Trump's Tweets of December 19, 2020. https://www.presidency.ucsb.edu/documents/tweets-december-19-2020. Published December 19, 2020. Accessed August 17, 2021.
77. York B. Byron York's daily memo: What were the Capitol Rioters Thinking? Washington Examiner. https://www.washingtonexaminer.com/opinion/byron-yorks-daily-memo-what-were-the-capitol-rioters-thinking. Published February 22, 2021. Accessed August 17, 2021.
78. President Donald J. Trump's Tweets of December 30, 2020. https://www.presidency.ucsb.edu/documents/tweets-december-30-2020. Published December 30, 2020. Accessed August 17, 2021.
79. President Donald J. Trump's Tweets of January 1, 2021. https://www.presidency.ucsb.edu/documents/tweets-january-1-2021. Published January 1, 2021. Accessed August 17, 2021.
80. Wolfe J. Trump wanted troops to protect his supporters at Jan. 6 rally. Reuters. https://www.reuters.com/world/us/congresswoman-says-trump-administration-botched-capitol-riot-preparations-2021-05-12/. Published May 12, 2021. Accessed August 17, 2021.
81. Sonne P. Pentagon restricted commander of D.C. Guard ahead of Capitol Riot. The Washington Post. https://www.washingtonpost.com/national-security/dc-guard-capitol-riots-william-walker-pentagon/2021/01/26/98879f44-5f69-11eb-ac8f-4ae05557196e_story.html. Published January 26, 2021. Accessed August 17, 2021.
82. President Donald J. Trump's Tweets of January 6, 2021. https://www.presidency.ucsb.edu/documents/tweets-january-6-2021.

Published January 6, 2021. Accessed August 17, 2021.

83. Dorman JL. Trump said he 'wouldn't dispute' reports that he called pence 'A pussy' on Jan. 6 for refusing to challenge the 2020 election results. Business Insider. https://www.businessinsider.com/trump-called-pence-pussy-for-certifying-biden-electoral-vote-win-2021-11. Published November 14, 2021. Accessed November 15, 2021.

84. Edmondson C, Broadwater L. Before capitol riot, Republican lawmakers fanned the Flames. The New York Times. https://www.nytimes.com/2021/01/11/us/politics/republicans-capitol-riot.html. Published January 12, 2021. Accessed August 18, 2021.

85. Palma B. Did Rudy Giuliani call for 'trial by Combat' before Trump Mob broke into Capitol? Snopes.com. https://www.snopes.com/fact-check/giuliani-rally-speech/. Published January 6, 2021. Accessed August 18, 2021.

86. Naylor B. Read trump's Jan. 6 speech, a key part of impeachment trial. NPR. https://www.npr.org/2021/02/10/966396848/read-trumps-jan-6-speech-a-key-part-of-impeachment-trial. Published February 10, 2021. Accessed August 18, 2021.

87. Sprunt B, Grisales C. Ousted capitol security officials say they didn't have Intel to plan for riot. NPR. https://www.npr.org/2021/02/23/970259610/ousted-capitol-security-officials-to-testify-on-insurrection-in-1st-public-heari. Published February 23, 2021. Accessed August 18, 2021.

88. Peterson B, Winsor M. Former acting defense secretary testifies he was trying to avoid another Kent State on Jan. 6. ABC News. https://abcnews.go.com/Politics/house-oversight-committee-chair-testify-government-unprepared-capitol/story?id=77639074. Published May 12, 2021. Accessed August 18, 2021.

89. Wolfe J. Four officers who responded to U.S. capitol attack have died by suicide. Reuters. https://www.reuters.com/world/us/officer-who-responded-us-capitol-attack-is-third-die-by-suicide-2021-08-02/. Published August 3, 2021. Accessed August 18, 2021.

90. Hall M, Gould S, Harrington R, et al. 691 people have been charged in the capitol insurrection so far. this searchable table shows them all. Insider. https://www.insider.com/all-the-us-capitol-pro-trump-riot-arrests-charges-names-2021-1. Published October 28, 2021. Accessed October 28, 2021.

91. Cabral S. Capitol riots: Did Trump's words at rally incite violence? BBC News. https://www.bbc.com/news/world-us-canada-55640437. Published February 14, 2021. Accessed August

21, 2021.
92. Postal voting in the United States. Wikipedia. https://en.wikipedia.org/wiki/Postal_voting_in_the_United_States#:~:text=In%20the%202016%20US%20Presidential,mail%20and%20others%20absentee%20votes. Published October 24, 2021. Accessed October 25, 2021.
93. Durkee A. Pennsylvania man charged with voter fraud for casting ballot for Trump under dead mother's name. https://www.forbes.com/sites/alisondurkee/2020/12/21/pennsylvania-man-charged-with-voter-fraud-for-casting-ballot-for-trump-under-dead-mothers-name/?sh=42d47a5459bf. Published December 21, 2020. Accessed August 21, 2021.
94. Schwartz D, Layne N. 'Truth is truth': Trump dealt blow as Republican-led Arizona Audit Reaffirms Biden win. https://www.reuters.com/world/us/arizona-republicans-release-findings-widely-panned-election-audit-2021-09-24/. Published September 27, 2021. Accessed October 10, 2021.
95. Democratic debate: Which enemy are you most proud of? CBS News. https://www.cbsnews.com/news/democratic-debate-which-enemy-are-you-most-proud-of/. Published October 14, 2015. Accessed July 16, 2021.
96. Party identification trends, 1992-2014. https://www.pewresearch.org/politics/2015/04/07/party-identification-trends-1992-2014/. Published August 28, 2020. Accessed July 17, 2021.
97. Obama angers Midwest voters with guns and religion remark. The Guardian. https://www.theguardian.com/world/2008/apr/14/barackobama.uselections2008. Published April 14, 2008. Accessed February 16, 2019.
98. 2010 census population of Michigan. http://censusviewer.com/state/MI/2010. Published 2011. Accessed September 18, 2021.
99. Bureau USC. Michigan's population topped 10 million in 2020. Census.gov. https://www.census.gov/library/stories/state-by-state/michigan-population-change-between-census-decade.html. Published October 8, 2021. Accessed October 15, 2021.
100. Booker B. Former Michigan gov. Rick Snyder charged in Flint Water Crisis. NPR. https://www.npr.org/2021/01/13/956592508/new-charges-in-flint-water-crisis-including-former-michigan-gov-rick-snyder. Published January 14, 2021. Accessed October 15, 2021.
101. Bosman J, Smith M. Gov. Rick Snyder of Michigan apologizes in Flint Water Crisis. The New York Times. https://www.nytimes.com/2016/01/20/us/obama-set-to-meet-with-mayor-

of-flint-about-water-crisis.html. Published January 19, 2016. Accessed October 15, 2021.

102. Snyder R. Former Michigan Governor Rick Snyder: I am a Republican vote for Biden. USA Today. https://www.usatoday.com/story/opinion/2020/09/03/rick-snyder-why-im-voting-joe-biden-even-republican-column/5696508002/. Published September 3, 2020. Accessed October 15, 2021.

103. Kucinich J. The most annoying governor in the country. The Daily Beast. https://www.thedailybeast.com/the-most-annoying-governor-in-the-country. Published April 14, 2017. Accessed October 15, 2021.

104. Shamus KJ. Michigan shatters peak COVID-19 case rate. 1 in 10 cases in US are from the State. https://www.freep.com/story/news/health/2021/11/20/michigan-covid-case-rate-face-mask-advisory-issued/8688930002/. Published November 20, 2021. Accessed November 21, 2021.

105. Payne D. Panic buttons and bulletproof vests: Fearful lawmakers stock up on protection. POLITICO. https://www.politico.com/news/2021/03/18/lawmakers-protection-jan-6-476929. Published March 18, 2021. Accessed October 16, 2021.

106. Smith A. 'That woman from Michigan': Gov. Whitmer stands out in the pandemic. Just ask Trump. NBC News. https://www.nbcnews.com/politics/donald-trump/woman-michigan-gov-whitmer-stands-out-pandemic-just-ask-trump-n1170506. Published April 8, 2020. Accessed October 16, 2021.

107. Mauger C, LeBlanc B. Trump tweets 'LIBERATE' Michigan, two other states with Dem governors. The Detroit News. https://www.detroitnews.com/story/news/politics/2020/04/17/trump-tweets-liberate-michigan-other-states-democratic-governors/5152037002/. Published April 17, 2020. Accessed October 16, 2021.

108. Baldas T. Whitmer kidnap suspects don't want jury to hear comments in video. Detroit Free Press. https://www.freep.com/story/news/local/michigan/2021/07/14/what-gretchen-whitmer-kidnap-suspects-dont-want-jurors-hear/7954135002/. Published July 14, 2021. Accessed October 16, 2021.

109. Romo V. Florida is blocking money from 2 school districts over mask mandates, defying a judge. NPR. https://www.npr.org/sections/back-to-school-live-updates/2021/08/31/1033067718/florida-schools-mask-mandates-desantis. Published September 1, 2021. Accessed October 16, 2021.

110. Hernandez S. Kamala Harris said she wouldn't take a COVID vaccine only recommended by Trump. BuzzFeed News. https://www.buzzfeednews.com/article/salvadorhernandez/kamala-harris-covid-vaccine-vp-debate. Published October 8, 2020. Accessed October 16, 2021.
111. Elflein J. U.S. COVID-19 cases and deaths. Statista. https://www.statista.com/statistics/1101932/coronavirus-covid19-cases-and-deaths-number-us-americans/. Published October 29, 2021. Accessed October 29, 2021.
112. DeYoung K, Miller ME, Kuo L. Biden's submarine accord with Australia Angers both France and China. The Washington Post. https://www.washingtonpost.com/world/asia_pacific/australia-us-subs-relations/2021/09/16/3db2e820-1699-11ec-a019-cb193b28aa73_story.html. Published September 17, 2021. Accessed October 16, 2021.
113. Hickey C, Merrill C, Chang RJ, Sullivan K, Boschma J, O'Key S. Here are the executive actions Biden signed in his first 100 Days. CNN. https://www.cnn.com/interactive/2021/politics/biden-executive-orders/. Published April 30, 2021. Accessed October 16, 2021.
114. Drug overdose deaths in the U.S. top 100,000 annually. National Center for Health Statistics. https://www.cdc.gov/nchs/pressroom/nchs_press_releases/2021/20211117.htm. Published November 17, 2021. Accessed November 21, 2021.
115. Dangor G. Stop giving booster shots so poor countries can have vaccines, who says. Forbes. https://www.forbes.com/sites/graisondangor/2021/08/04/stop-giving-booster-shots-so-poor-countries-can-have-vaccines-who-says/?sh=69f9893a4cb5. Published August 4, 2021. Accessed August 19, 2021.
116. Bourla A. An open letter from Pfizer chairman and CEO Albert Bourla. Pfizer. https://www.pfizer.com/news/hot-topics/an_open_letter_from_pfizer_chairman_and_ceo_albert_bourla. Published September 16, 2021. Accessed September 27, 2021.
117. FDA authorizes booster dose of Pfizer-BioNTech COVID-19 vaccine for certain populations. U.S. Food and Drug Administration. https://www.fda.gov/news-events/press-announcements/fda-authorizes-booster-dose-pfizer-biontech-covid-19-vaccine-certain-populations. Published September 22, 2021. Accessed September 27, 2021.
118. COVID-19 Guidance for Safe Schools. https://www.aap.org/en/pages/2019-novel-coronavirus-covid-19-infections/clinical-guidance/covid-19-planning-considerations-return-to-in-person-education-in-schools/. Published July 2021. Accessed

August 9, 2021.

119. Durkee A. COVID spread was 8% lower in Democrat-led states than GOP because of stricter restrictions, study finds. Forbes. https://www.forbes.com/sites/alisondurkee/2021/10/11/covid-spread-was-8-lower-in-democrat-led-states-than-gop-because-of-stricter-restrictions-study-finds. Published October 11, 2021. Accessed October 24, 2021.

120. Kottasová I. Long COVID is a bigger problem than we thought. CNN. https://www.cnn.com/2021/09/29/world/coronavirus-newsletter-intl-29-09-21/index.html. Published September 29, 2021. Accessed October 17, 2021.

121. Non-Aggression Axiom. Wikipedia. https://en.wikipedia.org/wiki/Non-aggression_principle. Published September 28, 2021. Accessed October 17, 2021.

122. Dzhanova Y. Florida's new Surgeon General refused to mask up during a meeting with a state senator who has cancer. Business Insider. https://www.businessinsider.com/florida-surgeon-general-refused-mask-legislator-cancer-2021-10. Published October 24, 2021. Accessed October 25, 2021.

123. Meta-ethics. Wikipedia. https://en.wikipedia.org/wiki/Meta-ethics. Published September 6, 2021. Accessed September 25, 2021.

124. List of Ethicists. Wikipedia. https://en.wikipedia.org/wiki/List_of_ethicists. Published September 9, 2021. Accessed September 25, 2021.

125. Divine Command Theory. Internet Encyclopedia of Philosophy. https://iep.utm.edu/divine-c/. Accessed September 25, 2021.

126. Religion by Country 2021. World Population Review. https://worldpopulationreview.com/country-rankings/religion-by-country. Accessed September 25, 2021.

127. Constitution of the United States. United States Senate. https://www.senate.gov/civics/constitution_item/constitution.htm. Published July 21, 2021. Accessed September 25, 2021.

128. Non-Cognitivism in Ethics. Internet Encyclopedia of Philosophy. https://iep.utm.edu/non-cogn. Accessed September 25, 2021.

129. Mackie's Error Theory. Internet Encyclopedia of Philosophy. https://iep.utm.edu/moralrea/#SSH1a.ii. Accessed September 25, 2021.

130. Moral Nihilism. Internet Encyclopedia of Philosophy. https://iep.utm.edu/nihilism/. Accessed September 25, 2021.

131. Moral Relativism. Internet Encyclopedia of Philosophy. https://iep.utm.edu/moral-re/. Accessed September 25, 2021.

132. Tikkanen A. Cannibalism: Cultures, Cures, Cuisine, and Calories. Encyclopedia Britannica. https://www.britannica.com/story/cannibalism-cultures-cures-cuisine-and-calories#:~:text=Also%20common%20were%20religious%20rituals,the%20ultimate%20act%20of%20revenge. Accessed September 25, 2021.
133. Pragmatic Ethics. Internet Encyclopedia of Philosophy. https://iep.utm.edu/pragmati/. Accessed September 25, 2021.
134. Non-Aggression Axiom. Internet Encyclopedia of Philosophy. https://iep.utm.edu/libertar. Accessed September 25, 2021.
135. Banyan ME. Tragedy of the Commons. Encyclopedia Britannica. https://www.britannica.com/science/tragedy-of-the-commons. Accessed September 25, 2021.
136. The 1984 national minimum drinking age act. National Institute on Alcohol Abuse and Alcoholism. https://alcoholpolicy.niaaa.nih.gov/the-1984-national-minimum-drinking-age-act. Accessed November 22, 2021.